THE

TRUE-BLUE LAWS

OF

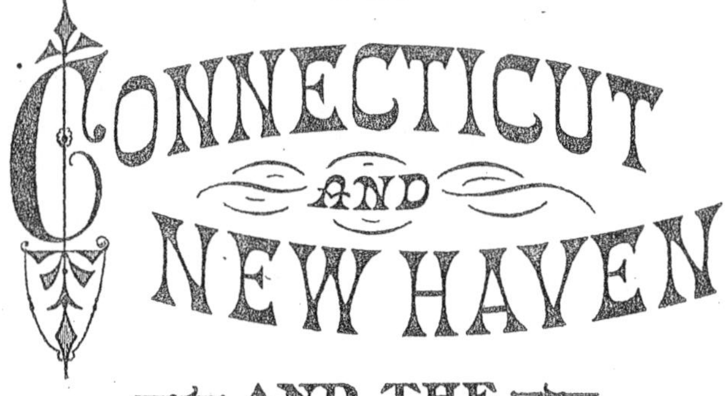

CONNECTICUT AND NEW HAVEN

AND THE

FALSE BLUE LAWS

FORGED BY PETERS

EDITED BY

J. HAMMOND TRUMBULL

HARTFORD

1876

THE

TRUE-BLUE LAWS

OF

CONNECTICUT AND NEW HAVEN

AND THE

FALSE BLUE-LAWS

INVENTED BY THE REV. SAMUEL PETERS

TO WHICH ARE ADDED

SPECIMENS OF THE LAWS AND JUDICIAL PROCEEDINGS OF OTHER COLONIES AND SOME BLUE-LAWS OF ENGLAND IN THE REIGN OF JAMES I.

EDITED BY

J. HAMMOND TRUMBULL

HARTFORD CONN.

AMERICAN PUBLISHING COMPANY.

1876

CONTENTS.

PREFACE.

The publishers assure me that a new edition of the "Blue Laws" is wanted, and at their request I have undertaken to prepare one. I have regarded this as, in some sort, missionary work. There are regions, in which schools and printing-presses have for years been at work, where Peters's "History of Connecticut" is still read *as* history. There are hundreds who still believe—and thousands who profess to believe—that to kiss one's child on the Sabbath-day, to make minced pies, and to play on any instrument of music except the drum, trumpet, and jews'-harp, were made criminal offences by the ancient laws of New Haven. There are honest inquirers, not a few, who write, week after week, to the newspapers, for information about these 'Blue-Laws,' and to ask where authentic copies of them can be found. It has seemed worth while to bring together, in one volume of convenient size, the truth and the falsehood about the early legislation of Connecticut and New Haven colonies. Those who like to read the famous code which Peters gave to "the independent dominion of New Haven," may find it here, in unadulterated mendacity. They may find also some *genuine* curiosities of legislation and jurisprudence, taken from the records of Connecticut —and other American colonies; and, for comparison with these, a few specimens of the laws which were in force in England, in the reign of James the First.

I have aimed to give this volume some permanent value to

another class of readers. It comprises accurate copies (in modernized orthography) of the first constitutions and the first codes, criminal and civil, of Connecticut and New Haven. In these colonial governments, "deriving their authority from the voluntary association and agreement of the people, we have," said Chief Justice Swift, "the most singular, and the fairest example of the operation of that natural principle which impels mankind to unite in society: here the social compact was made and entered into, in the most explicit manner: here is the origin of a government upon natural principles." The Connecticut constitution of 1638–9 is the foundation of the republican institutions of the colony and state. It may claim, on still higher considerations, the attention of students of political science and of general history,—as "the first properly American constitution—a work in which the framers were permitted to give body and shape, for the first time, to the genuine republican idea, that dwelt as an actuating force, or inmost sense, in all the New England colonies."

J. H. T.

HARTFORD, Nov. 1st, 1876.

INTRODUCTION.

"TRUE BLUE WILL NEVER STAIN" says an old proverb, and Bailey's Dictionary gives this explanation of it: "As a true blue colour or dye never fades or changes its colour, so a man of fixed principles and resolutions, firmly grounded upon the reasonableness and justice of such principles, will not be easily drawn aside to depart from them, or be guilty of any evil or mean action." The epithet *True blue* had nearly the same meaning as that by which a democrat of the old school is occasionally commended as "dyed in the wool." Blue was the symbol of constancy and fidelity. In Chaucer's Court of Love, the

—"folke that knele in *blew*
They weare the colour, ay and ever shal,
In signe they ever were and ever wil be true,
Withouten change."

Fixed principles were out of fashion after the Restoration. Nothing could be more unpopular at the court of Charles the Second than constancy in virtue and adherence to convictions of duty. "True blue" became a term of reproach, reserved for puritans and schismatics. It served to point Butler's satire, in the description of Sir Hudibras:

"For his religon, it was fit
To match his learning and his wit;
'Twas Presbyterian *true blue.*"

To be "blue" was to be "puritanic," precise in the observance of legal and religious obligations, rigid, gloomy, over-strict,—in a word, to be in morals and manners the very opposite of a courtier, wit, or gallant of the time.

The colonists of New England were, with very few exceptions, "true blue," and their legislation everywhere caught a reflection of the color. They accepted the word of God as a sufficient rule of conduct. The freemen of Massachusetts resolved to model their Body of Liberties from the code of Moses; and the early laws of Connecticut and New Haven were in great part copied from those of Massachusetts. The first planters of New Haven resolved "that, as in matters that concern the gathering and ordering of a church, so likewise in all public offices which concern civil order, as choice of magistrates and officers, making and repealing of laws, dividing allotments of inheritance, and all things of like nature, we would all of us be ordered by those rules which the scripture holds forth to us." "There is," observes Dr. Palfrey (History of N. England, ii. 27), "no higher, and no other just conception of human law, than was theirs, when they recognized it as an embodiment of the will—in other words, of the law—of God. . . The mistake which had more or less clouded the mind of the Puritan New-Englander was in his regarding the law of Moses as a declaration of the law of God *for all times* and *places*. But he did not embrace this error in its full extent." In New Haven, such only of "the judicial laws of God, delivered by Moses," as are "a fence to the moral law, being neither typical nor ceremonial, nor having any reference to Canaan," were made a rule to the courts in their proceedings against offenders.* No one of the colonies adopted the whole code of Moses, even in respect to capital offences. A recent editor of the "Blue Laws of Connecticut and New Haven" has commented on the "quaintness, bluntness, particularity, and antiquated excess of penalty, which have gained for them the equivocal epithet by which they have been generally designated for several generations."† Quaint and blunt enough, certainly, some of these laws appear in the light of the nineteenth century. They are often perhaps *too* particular and precise in their application of "rules of righteousness" to the conduct of individuals. But he who believes that the early legislation of New England was distinguished, in its time, by the severity of its penalties, knows little of the history of criminal law in Great Britain or America. "In determining what kind of men our fathers were, we are to compare their laws, not with ours, but with the laws which they renounced."‡ *Thirty-one* offences were

*New Haven Colony Records, I. 130. (1644.)

†The Blue Laws of Connecticut; edited by Samuel M. Smucker, LL.D. (Philadelphia, 1861), Preface, p. 3.

‡Dr. Bacon's Historical Discourses, p. 32.

punished by death, in England, at the beginning of the reign of James the First. The list grew larger from year to year, until in 1819 it had reached the number of *two hundred and twenty-three*, of which *one hundred and seventy-six* were without benefit of clergy. Massachusetts by her first code, in 1641, and Connecticut in 1642,* imposed the penalty of death on *twelve* offences only. New Haven added two or three to the number of "capital laws," but with such reservations as to leave the exaction of the supreme penalty to the discretion of the courts.

In the reform of penal legislation New England was at least a century in advance of the mother country. If any one doubts this, let him look into the State Trials or the old Reports.

Two years before the sailing of the Mayflower, "one Wrennum" was prosecuted, in the Star Chamber, on the charge of having "divers times *petitioned the King* against Sir Francis Bacon, the Lord Chancellor, pretending that the said Lord Bacon had done him great injustice," and moreover, for having dedicated to King James a book in which the Chancellor was "traduced and scandalized." On his conviction, the attorney-general cited a precedent in the same court, in the second year of the same reign, "where one Ford, for an offence in like manner against "the late Chancellor, was censured, that he should be "*perpetually imprisoned*, and pay a *fine* of £1000, and "that he *should ride, with his face to the tail*, from the "Fleet to Westminster, with his fault written upon his "head, and that he should *acknowledge his offence in all the courts in Westminster*, and that he should *stand a reasonable time upon the pillory*, and that *one of his ears should be cut off*, and from thence should be carried to prison again, and in like manner should go to Cheapside, and should have his *other ear cut off*, &c." And the Court proceeded to sentence Wrennum "according to the said precedent."†

The case of William Prynne, a learned barrister, is more familiar to American readers. His *real* offence

* Four years later, two additional offences were made capital, by both colonies.

† Popham's Reports.

was in publishing anti-prelatical tracts and opposing the innovations in religious worship introduced by Archbishop Laud. He was prosecuted in 1633, in the Star Chamber, for having written a book (Histriomastix, or a Scourge for Stage-Players") in which he had "railed not only against stage-plays," but, as was alleged, "against hunting, public festivals, christmas-keeping, bonfires and may-poles," etc. He was sentenced to lose both his ears in the pillory, to degradation from the bar, a fine of £3000, and imprisonment for life. Three years afterwards, he gave new offence to Laud, by publishing a pamphlet against the hierarchy. He was again prosecuted, and was sentenced to lose *what remained of his ears*, to pay a fine of £5000, to be *branded on both his cheeks* with the letters S L (for 'Seditious Libeller'), and to remain in prison for life. The severity of this sentence was equalled by the savage rigor of its execution.

With such precedents, is it strange that the colonists of New England chose to frame a new code on the model of the Mosaic, rather than trust themselves to the tender mercies of English law?

The law of England which condemned a prisoner who "stood mute"—or refused to plead—to be slowly pressed to death by weights placed upon his chest (the *peine fort et dure*), was not repealed till 1772. Several instances of the infliction of this horrible penalty after 1700, are recorded; one, so late as 1741.

Until 1790, every woman convicted of counterfeiting gold or silver coin of the realm, was sentenced to be drawn on a hurdle to the place of execution and there "*to be burned with fire* till she was dead." This, says Blackstone,* was "the usual punishment for all sorts of treasons committed by those of the female sex." After 1700, the practice became more humane than the law authorized, and usually the offender was strangled before being burned: "there being *very few* instances, and those accidental or by negligence, of any person's being emboweled or burned, till previously deprived of sensation by strangling."† By such an *accident*, a woman was actually burned alive at Tyburn in 1726,

* 4 Blackstone's Commentaries, 204. † *Ibid*, 377.

for killing her husband (a crime that English law made "petty treason"). Twenty thousand people gathered to see a woman burned, in 1773.* Another suffered the same penalty in 1777; and another, for making counterfeit shillings, in 1786.

In the reign of Henry VIII, poisoners were, by act of parliament, condemned to be *boiled to death.* This act was repealed in the following reign, but not before several offenders had suffered its penalty. In Germany, even in the 17th century, this horrible punishment was inflicted on coiners and counterfeiters. Taylor, the Water Poet, describes an execution he witnessed in Hamburg, in 1616. The judgment pronounced against a coiner of false money was that he should "be boiled to death in oil; not thrown into the vessel at once, but with a pulley or rope to be hanged under the armpits, and then let down into the oil *by degrees*; first the feet, and next the legs, and so to boil his flesh from his bones alive."

When Connecticut and New Haven were framing their first codes, larceny above the value of twelve pence was a capital crime in England—as it had been since the time of Henry I. In some cases the thief might claim "benefit of clergy" for the first offence, but the second was punished by death. From many descriptions of larceny, the law expressly took away the benefit of clergy: to steal a horse, or a *hawk*, or woollen cloth from the weaver, was a hanging matter. So it was, to kill a deer in the king's forest, or to export sheep from the kingdom. "Outlandish persons calling themselves *Egyptians*" (i. e. gipsies) who remained more than one month in England, and all persons who consorted with them, were declared felons, without benefit of clergy. Thirteen gipsies were executed, under sentence of court, at one term, in Suffolk, for no greater crime than vagabondage. The brutal severity of the laws against vagrants and idlers, in the sixteenth and seventeenth century almost surpasses belief. In the reign of Edward the Sixth, it was enacted, that "if any man or woman able to work should refuse to labor, and remain idle for three days, he or she should be branded on the breast with the letter V, and adjudged the slave, for two years, of any

* Elizabeth Herring. See the "Annual Register," 1773, p. 131.

one who should inform against such idler:" if the slave ran away, he or she when recaptured was to be branded on the cheek with the letter S, and to become a *slave for life*; and running away a second time, was to be punished with death. It was not much better in the reign of James the First, when a law—which continued in force till the time of Queen Anne—provided that any mendicant or vagrant whom a justices' court should adjudge "incorrigible and dangerous, should be branded on the left shoulder with a hot iron of the breadth of a shilling having a Roman R upon it, and if after such judgment they were found begging and wandering, they were to be adjudged felons and to suffer death, without benefit of clergy."

Before criticising too sharply the penal codes of New England in the first half of the seventeenth century, it may be well to look at the picture a recent English historian has drawn, of England in the middle of the eighteenth, and at the beginning of the reign of George the Third. "Our criminal law," says Phillimore,—"at that time the inexorable scourge of the lower orders, cart-loads of whom were carried off every month to execution—administered in that day too frequently by corrupt and ignorant judges, generally, as any one who turns to the reports of the period will see, by narrow-minded and inferior men, was—for the cruelty, multitude, and inutility of the punishments it inflicted, no less than for the caprice and brutality with which it was abused by the lower officers of justice, and the bottomless magazine of absurdity in the technical forms, rules, and language to which the lawyers clung with interested tenacity—in all probability the worst, for its effects upon the temper and morals of the community, in civilized Europe. . . . . It is difficult to find, in the history of the most despotic countries in the darkest ages, proofs of more stupid and revolting injustice. . . The reader of the state trials. . . might almost imagine that he is reading the narrative of Gregory of Tours, or the history of some tribe in the infancy of civilization."*

The planters of New England were Englishmen, not exempt from English prejudices in favor of English

* Phillimore's History of England during the Reign of Geogre III. pp. 47, 48, 50.

institutions, laws, and usages. They were Englishmen of the sixteenth century, not social scientists and law-reformers of the nineteenth. They lived half a dozen generations too early for the discovery that sanguinary and excessive punishments multiply offences. They had not been taught to question the wisdom or the humanity of English criminal law. They were as unconscious of its barbarism, as were the parliaments which had enacted or the courts which dispensed it. That somewhat of this barbarism appears in their own beginnings of legislation and in their methods of punishment is not to be wondered at.

Nor should it seem more strange, that their laws manifest intolerance of dissent in matters of religion. Most of them were born and nurtured in the Church of England, and that church certainly had been at no pains to teach, by precept or example, the excellence of toleration. Catholic or Protestant, Calvinistic or Arminian, under Henry the Eighth or Mary the Bloody, Elizabeth or James, the English Church held fast at least one article of faith—the obligation of the State to repress heresy, to punish apostacy, to enforce conformity, and to give effect to ecclesiastical censures by penal laws—by fines, imprisonment, confiscation, banishment, or death. "All religious communities"—says Sir James Mackintosh, with reference to the Church of England after the Reformation,—"were at that time alike intolerant; and there was, perhaps, no man in Europe who dared to think that the State neither possessed, nor could delegate—nor could recognize as inherent in another body—any authority over religious opinions."

The Act of Supremacy of 1559 declared the queen to be "supreme governor of the realm . . . . as well in spiritual and ecclesiastical things or causes, as in temporal;" and the Act of Uniformity, the same year, forbade the use of other forms of prayer than those provided in the Book of Common Prayer, under penalty of loss of goods and chattels for the first offence, a year's imprisonment for the second, and imprisonment for life for the third. James the First, shortly after his accession, made known his determination to "have one doctrine and one discipline, one religion in substance and in ceremony," and he gave his sanction to the canons adopted by the Convocation of 1604, by which excommunication—"a precursory judgment of the latter day," as Lord Bacon called it,—was added to the other penalties for nonconformity. "To exercise the right of private judgment, so far as to quit the Church of Rome, which had governed Christendom for centuries, was the duty of every Christian; but to exercise it so far as to differ with the Articles put out not one hundred years before, by a Church that did not pretend to be infallible and teachers that laid no claim to inspiration, was a crime to be punished, in some instances by the stake, in all others by confiscation, by the lash and shears of the hangman, and by the pestilential dungeon, within the walls of which was death."*

The colonists of New England—call them fanatics, bigots, persecutors, or what you will—did no more than repeat, in their new home, a few of the lessons they had been taught in the mother country and by the mother church. They believed it to be the duty of civil magistrates, to maintain the order and discipline of the churches and "the liberty and purity of the gospel." The General Court of Massachusetts took counsel, now and then, with "the neighboring Elders"—just as Parliament gave ear to Convocation. The Plymouth pilgrims who had lived in Holland under the ministry of John Robinson had gained some notion of religious liberty and the right of private judgment. So had Thomas Hooker, the father of Connecticut, and some of those who came with him. But in England of the reign of Elizabeth or James—under the primacy of Whitgift, Bancroft, or Laud—how should a nonconformist learn the meaning of *toleration*—except as he may have heard it denounced as the sin of Gallio?

The writ for burning a heretic (*de hæretico comburendo*) on the judgment of an ecclesiastical tribunal, was not abolished in England till late in the reign of Charles the Second. Elizabeth caused two Dutch baptists to be burned at Smithfield, in 1575, and two Socinians, sentenced by the church as "obstinate, contumacious

* Phillimore's Reign of George III., p. 27.

and incorrigible heretics," were sent to the stake in 1612, by James the First. Two Brownists were hung, in 1583, for circulating a tract in which the queen's supremacy in the church was denied; John Udal, a nonconforming minister, died in prison, under sentence of death, in 1593, for having written a book against the bishops; and the same year, for a similar offence, Greenwood and Penry, ministers, and Barrow, a lawyer, suffered death; several of the Brownists died in prison, and hundreds were driven into exile. As for Puritans—"I will make them conform, or I will harry them out of the land, or else do worse," said King James; and, by help of the High Commission and the Star Chamber, he more than kept his word.

With what fervid zeal "the sweet peace of the church" was in those days guarded against dissent, we get a notion from a passage in one of the letters of honest and pious James Howell, in 1635: "I rather pitty than hate Turk or Infidell," he wrote, "for they are of the same metall, and bear the same stamp as I do, tho' the inscriptions differ: If I hate any, 'tis those *Schismatics* that puzzle the sweet peace of our Church; so that *I could be content to see an* Anabaptist *go to hell on a* Brownist's *back.*"

When New Haven adopted her Code, in 1656, the law of England imposed a fine of 100 marks, for speaking in derogation of the Book of Common Prayer, and for the third offence the penalty was imprisonment for life. Baptists were disqualified to make wills or to receive legacies, and were exposed to corporal punishment; to deny the lawfulness of infant baptism, or to affirm that such baptism was void, subjected the offender to imprisonment; absence from the parish church, a single Sunday, incurred a fine of one shilling only, but absence for a month together was fined £20—which was about twenty-fold the penalty attached to the same offence by the laws of Connecticut and New Haven.

In the reign of Charles the Second—after New Haven was included in the Connecticut charter—the Act of Elizabeth for the "suppression of conventicles" was revived, and with increased severity: "recusants" were punished by banishment, and in case of return, by death, and all meetings of five or more nonconformists, under color or pretence of religious worship, were forbidden under the same penalties. In 1670, this law was re-enacted, with a further provision which imposed a heavy fine on every person *present* at any religious exercise not in accordance with the liturgy of the Church of England (Acts of 16 and 22 Charles II.)

It would be easy to fill a volume with "blue laws" enacted by the parliaments of Elizabeth, James the First, and Charles the First. The instances that have been given are enough to show whence came whatever is harsh or repulsive in the early laws and judicial proceedings of New England and by what lessons the puritan colonists were taught intolerance.

To each of the Capital Laws enacted by Massachusetts was appended a reference to the text or texts of scripture that authorize the penalty of death. The other colonies copied these laws and references, without much alteration. Everyone who has anything to say about the "Blue Laws" alludes to *this* eccentricity of puritan legistation, as showing the judaizing tendency of the religion of New England. To modern eyes, the citation of scriptural authorities, in a penal code, certainly does look odd. The Bible is about the last book to which lawyers or legislatures now-a-days are expected to look for precedents. But Nathaniel Ward, who drafted the Massachusetts Body of Liberties, had been "a student and practiser in the courts of the common law" in England, before he became a minister, and he may have taken an idea from Coke's *Institutes.* When commenting on the infernal penalty attached to high treason by the law of England, Coke was careful to point out the scriptural warrant for each revolting particular of the execution. For drawing to the place of punishment, he cites 1 Kings, 2. 28, the case of Joab; for hanging, that of Bigthan and Teresh, Esther 2. 23; for *emboweling*, that of *Judas*, Acts, 1. 18; for piercing the body "while he was yet alive," that of Absalom, 2 Sam., 18. 14; for beheading, that of Sheba, 2 Sam., 20. 22; for quartering and hanging up, that of Rechab and Baanah, 2 Sam., 4. 11, 12; finally, for corruption of blood and forfeiture of estate, David's imprecation against his enemies, in Psalm 109, 9—13!* And in the last century, Sir William Blackstone, treating

* 3 Institutes, 211.

of those unnatural crimes which are the subject of the 6th and 7th capital laws of the Connecticut code, observes that their punishment is "by the voice of nature and of reason, and the express command of God, determined to be capital,"—and for this he cites in a note * the same texts (Levit. 20. 13, 15) which were cited by Connecticut and New Haven. So, too, when writing of *witchcraft* and its penalty, he refers, as the law-makers of New England in the preceding century had referred, to "the express law of God" in "Exodus, 22. 18."

Something may be said, here, about this law against witchcraft, which to many readers has seemed more deeply tinged with "blue" than any other in the criminal codes of the puritans. "It was not to be expected of the colonists of New England that they should be first to see through a delusion which befooled the whole civilized world, and the gravest and most knowing persons in it. Men are not omniscient, nor is it common, any more than just, to blame them for not being so." † The colonists of New England—in Connecticut and New Haven, as well as in Massachusetts,—"like all other Christian people at that time,—at least, with extremely rare individual exceptions,—believed in the reality of a hideous crime called *witchcraft.*" ‡ Herein, if in nothing else, they remained in conformity with the Church of England. To go back to the reign of Elizabeth, we find good Bishop Jewel writing, in 1559, to his friend Peter Martyr: "The number of witches and sorceresses has everywhere become enormous." The same year, when preaching before the Queen, he called attention to the fact "that this kind of people, within these last few years are marvellously increased" in England: and humbly petitioned, in behalf of her majesty's poor subjects, "that the laws touching such malefactors may be put in due execution." Accordingly, at the next session of parliament a bill was passed declaring enchantment and witchcraft to be felony. § In the visitation of parishes, the commissioners were enjoined to inquire respecting such as used charms, sorcery, witchcraft, "and any like craft, invented by the devil."

* 4 Commentaries, 216.

† Palfrey, History of New England, IV. 127. ‡ Ibid., 96.

§ Jewel's Works (Parker Society), pt. 2, p. 1028; and Strype's Annals, I. i. 88.

A good many witches were convicted in Elizabeth's reign. Three were hanged at Warbois in Huntingdonshire, in 1593, and their property—forfeited by conviction of felony—was used to provide for the delivery of an annual sermon on witchcraft, by some Cambridge doctor or bachelor of divinity. This sermon was preached yearly till 1718, and perhaps later.* It seems to have borne some fruits, for zeal against witchcraft was kept burning in that neighborhood, after it had cooled in other parts of England. In 1716, a woman and her daughter, *nine years old*, were hanged in Huntingdon for selling their souls to the devil, and raising a storm by pulling off their stockings!

The act of 1562 was superseded, in the first year of James the First's reign, by another, more severe, making witchcraft punishable with death, and without benefit of clergy.

The king, who had acquired in Scotland a taste for witch-hunting, did not suffer this law to become a dead letter. He was as zealous for the suppression of witchcraft and sorcery as for the enforcement of conformity. He had devised new tortures † to extract confessions from the accused; and he had published a learned and convincing treatise on the Doctrine of Devils, which all loyal subjects and aspiring courtiers took care to read and admire. That the witchcraft delusion soon became epidemic throughout England, was a natural consequence. Seven or eight years before the sailing of the

* Hutchinson's Hist. Essay on Witchcraft, p. 130.

† Before leaving Scotland, James assisted in the execution of several 'warlocks' and witches. One of them, on his second examination, retracted the confession forced from him by the horrible torture of the iron boot, on his first: "whereupon the King's Majestie, perceiving his stubborn wilfulnesse," suggested a remedy. The finger-nails of the accused "were riven and pulled with an instrument called a *turkas* [a smith's pincers]: and under every nail there was thrust in two needles even up to the heads." Still refusing to confess, "he was then *with all convenient speed*, by commandment, conveyed again to the torment of the boots, where he continued a long time, and abode so many blows in them that his legs were crushed and beaten together as small as might be, and the bones and flesh so bruised, that the blood and marrow spouted forth in great abundance, whereby they were made unserviceable for ever." He had little use for them—for the confession being somehow obtained, he was condemned, strangled, and burnt.—Pitcairn's Criminal Trials, i. 213, and after.

Mayflower, twelve persons were condemned at one time, in Lancaster, and as many more the next year. Two were hanged at Lincoln, in 1618. The wonder is that the Puritans did not bring the mania with them to New England at their first coming. It did not appear here till nearly 1650, and then only in sporadic cases. In Great Britain, it prevailed, with occasional intermissions, for neary a century. The last *execution* under the act of James the First was in 1722, when an old woman was burned at the stake, in the north of Scotland, but the law was not repealed till 1735: and so late as 1759, an old woman, accused of bewitching her neighbor's spinning-wheel, was tried by a self-appointed jury, and stripped to her shift to be weighed, in the church, against the parish Bible. Fortunately she *out*weighed it, and was acquitted by the populace. *

The delusion was at its height in England at the time when Connecticut was framing her criminal code. Seventeen persons had been convicted of witchcraft in Lancashire in 1634, sixteen were condemned at Yarmouth in 1644, fifteen at Chelmsford (Thomas Hooker's old home) in Essex, in 1645; nearly sixty in Suffolk, and as many in Huntingdonshire, in 1645 and 1646. "During the whole of James's reign, amid the civil wars of his successor, the sway of the Long Parliament, the usurpation of Cromwell, and the reign of Charles II., there was no abatement of the persecution." †

The Church manifested as little doubt of the reality of the crime or of the sufficiency of the evidence on which the accused were convicted, as did the courts, the jurors, and the mass of the people of England. The act of 1562 seems to have been passed, as was before mentioned, at the instance of Bishop Jewel. Twelve bishops were in the committee by which the act of James I.—which Coke and Bacon assisted to prepare—was discussed in the House of Lords. Dr. Francis (afterwards Bishop) Hutchinson intimates ‡ that the divines who made the authorized version of the Bible introduced in it "some phrases that favor the vulgar notions" of witchcraft, familiar spirits, etc., at the particular desire of King James, out of "the

* Annual Register, 1759, p. 73.

† Mackay's Memoirs of Popular Delusions, ii. 141.

‡ Hutchinson's Historical Essay on Witchcraft, p. 225.

great reverence they had to the King's judgment." The learned and eminent Dr. Henry More (who was a prebendary of Gloucester, and declined a bishopric) was a firm believer in witchcraft and the power of raising evil spirits. The third book of his "Antidote to Atheism," published after the restoration of Charles the Second, abounds in marvels, some of which are unsurpassed, as tests of credulity, by any in Mather's Magnalia. Bishop Hall, in his treatise on "The Invisible World," proclaimed his belief in "the assumed shapes of Evil Spirits." Dr. Thomas Fuller, in his "Holy and Profane State," maintains that "there are witches in the present" as in the past, and that some of them "indent downright with the devil." Sir Thomas Brown, who wrote on "Vulgar Errors," did not reckon the belief in witchcraft as one of them. "For my part," he said,* "I have ever believed, *and do now know*, that there are witches": and when two women were prosecuted for this crime, in 1664, his testimony had no small influence in procuring their conviction. It was on this trial that Sir Matthew Hale, in his charge to the jury, told them, "he did not in the least doubt there were witches; first, because the Scriptures affirmed it; secondly, because the wisdom of all nations, particularly our own, had provided laws against witchcraft, which implied their belief of such a crime." No book published after the restoration of Charles the Second was more influential in reviving the waning belief in witchcraft, none supplied the magistrates at Salem with so many authoritative precedents, on none did the Mathers draw more largely for "wonders of the invisible world," than the "Sadducismus Triumphatus" of the Rev. Joseph Glanvil—a fellow of the Royal Society, one of the chaplains of Charles II., rector of the Abbey Church at Bath, and subsequently a prebendary of Worcester.

At one of the last witch-trials in England—that of Jane Wenham, in Hertfordshire, in 1711, before Sir John Powell (afterwards Chief Justice),—two clergymen of the Church of England were witnesses against the accused, and testified to the efficacy of the Book of Common Prayer, in exorcism of the bewitched; and a third, the Rev. Francis Bragge, displayed great zeal in the prosecution and published "a defence of the pro-

* Religio Medici, § 30.

ceedings, wherein the possibility and reality of Witchcraft are demonstrated," &c. The accused was found guilty, upon the evidence. "Do you mean," asked Judge Powell, "that you find her guilty upon the *indictment* for conversing with the Devil in the shape of a cat?" "We find her guilty of *that*," replied the foreman; and the poor creature was sentenced to death: but, on the recommendation of the Judge, she received a pardon. Mr. Bragge averred that she was sustained by the dissenters, and that she had received contributions while in prison from their party. "We are willing to part with her," he added, "and wish the Fanaticks much joy of their new convert:" but he deplored "the proneness of the age to Sadducism and Infidelity." *

These instances, which might be multiplied a hundredfold, are mentioned, not as proofs that the Church of England was mainly responsible for the witchcraft delusion and the thousands of lives sacrificed to it in Great Britain, but to counteract the impression which a certain class of writers have been at some pains to produce—that the delusion was confined chiefly to puritans and dissenters, and was to be regarded as in some sort a result of "schism." The truth is, that it pervaded the whole Christian church. The law-makers and the ministers of New England were under its influences just as—and no more than—were the law-makers and the ministers of Old England. The learned and excellent divines and staunch churchmen whose names I have mentioned above, were not, in this matter, in advance of their age. "We clergymen," said Bishop Hutchinson, in 1717, "are not thought to have kept our order altogether free from blame in this matter. . . . Yet, in the main, I believe our Church and its clergy have as little to answer for in this respect as any." † As much may be said, and with equal truth, for the churches of New England; and emphatically, for Connecticut.

"The infatuation never extended to the less gloomy people of Rhode Island," says the historian of that

* Preface to *Witchcraft Further Display'd*, 1712.

† *Hist. Essay concerning Witchcraft*: in Dedication.

colony: "the offence appears on the statute book * but no prosecutions were ever had under it. . . . More important matters to them than the bedevilment of their neighbors engrossed their whole attention."† Distracted by faction—barely able to maintain the semblance of civil order—there was reason enough why Rhode Island should not look beyond her borders for "bedevilment." When New Haven was framing her code of law, the general court at Providence was striving to keep the peace between its members by passing an Act to punish by fine or whipping "any man who should strike another person *in the Court.*"‡ "Torn and rent by divisions," it was some compensation for her troubles, that her magistrates—whether through lack of disposition or of authority to enforce the laws—instituted no prosecutions for witchcraft, and gave themselves or the colony no trouble on account of "familiarity with the devil."

Just when or by whom the acts and proceedings of New Haven colony were first stigmatized as *Blue Laws*, cannot now be ascertained. The presumption, however, is strong that the name had its origin in New York, and that it gained currency in Connecticut, among episcopalian and other dissenters from the established church, between 1720 and 1750.

Several causes contributed to bring Connecticut into disfavor with her western neighbors. In the first place, she had defeated every project for the abrogation of her charter and for annexing her to the province of New York under a governor commissioned by the crown. Andros and Dongan had believed that it would be "impossible for the government of New York to subsist without the addition of Connecticut." Fletcher, and Cornbury, and Hunter, all turned longing eyes to the little colony on the east. They saw not much promise for the future in the condition of affairs at home. They sneered at the set ways of

* In the Laws of 1647: "Witchcraft is forbidden by this present Assembly to be used in this Colonie; and the Penaltie imposed by the *Authoritie that we are subject to* [i. e. the law of England] is Felonie of Death. 1 Jac. 12."—*R. I. Col. Records*, i. 166.

† Arnold's *History of Rhode Island*, i, 525.

‡ R. Island Colonial Records, i. 321.

puritanism and its intolerance of dissent, but they were not insensible to the advantages New England had gained by maintaining a higher standard of morals and a more general regard for at least the externals of religion. Governor Dongan, when questioned by the Board of Trade, in 1687, as to the "religious persuasions" of the people of New York, replied: "New York has, first, a chaplain belonging to the Fort, of the Church of England; secondly, a Dutch Calvinist; thirdly, a French Calvinist; fourthly, a Dutch Lutheran. Here be not many of the Church of England, few Roman Catholics, abundance of Quakers' preachers men, and women especially, singing Quakers, ranting Quakers, Sabbatarians, Anti-sabbatarians, some Anabaptists, some Independents, some Jews; in short, of all sorts of opinions there are some, *and the most part of none at all*."* Colonel Heathcote—a member of the Provincial Council, and for three years mayor of New York,—in a letter to the Society for the Propagation of the Gospel, written in 1704, says,† that at his first coming to the Province in 1692: "I found it the most rude and heathenish country I ever saw in my whole life, which called themselves Christians, there being not so much as the least marks or footsteps of religion of any sort." Matters had not much improved in 1711, when Lewis Morris, chief-justice of the province, wrote to the same Society: "Nine parts in ten of *ours* will add no great credit to whatsoever church they are of; nor can it well be expected otherwise: for as New England—excepting some families—was the scum of the old, so *the greatest part of the English in this Province was the scum of the New*, who brought as many opinions almost as persons, but *neither religion or virtue*, and have acquired a very little since."‡ Mr. Muirson, the Society's missionary in 1708, § was saddened at the hopelessness of Christianizing the Indians of New York, so long as the English "give them such a bad example, and fill their mouths with such objections against our blessed religion:" and the "dissenters, both in this and in the neighboring colony" [Connecticut], say, "that many of the members of the Church

* Doc. History of New York, i. 116.
† Humphrey's *Historical Account*, p. 33.
‡ Doc. Hist. of N. York, iii. 152. § *Ibid.* 566.

of England are irregular in their lives, and therefore they ought not, and will not join it." *

That New England—and especially that portion of New England which was best known to New York—should not be regarded with much favor in such a community as is here described, is not surprising. To the lawless all laws are 'blue,' to the vicious all moral restraints are 'puritanic,' to the men who "are of no religion at all," any profession of religious obligation is hypocrisy or superstition.

There were other considerations which, at the period referred to, provoked hostility to Connecticut laws and institutions, and there were special reasons why this hostility was, after a while, particularly directed toward New Haven.

In 1701—the year in which Yale College was incorporated "for upholding and propagating of the Christian protestant religion, by a succession of learned and orthodox men"—the Society for the Propagation of the Gospel in Foreign Parts was organized in England, and immediately began its work for the establishment of the episcopal church in the colonies. In New York and other provinces dependent on the crown, the Society's missionaries found no great hindrance to their work. In Connecticut, they were less cordially welcomed. "They tell our people," wrote the Rev. George Muirson, to the Society, in 1708, "that they will not suffer the house of God to be defiled with idolatrous worship and superstitious ceremonies. They are so bold that they spare not openly to speak reproachfully and with great contempt of our church." Good Mr. Beach—the Society's missionary at Newtown—complained that this contempt for "the Church" was manifested even by the *Indians* of Connecticut. When he made an attempt to instruct those who lived about Newtown, "after a short time" (he writes), "I found that I laboured in vain, and they refused to hear *anything about religion* from me, and, to shew how much they defied the thoughts of the Church of England, they would call me *Churchman! Churchman!* out of contempt—which they had learned from the neighbouring Dissenters." Connecticut had an estab-

* Beach's Second Address (Boston, 1751), p. 70.

lished church of her own, and was somewhat jealous of its privileges. Col. Heathcote, in a report made to the Society, in 1705, says: "For Connecticut, I am and have been pretty conversant, and always was as much in their good graces as any man:" as to "the best and most probable way of doing good among them—there is nothing more certain than that *it is the most difficult task the Society have to wade through. . . .* They have abundance of *odd kinds of Laws* to prevent any dissenting from their church," etc.* For such "odd kinds of laws," *blue* was a convenient epithet; and not for these only, but for whatever else in colonial laws and proceedings looked over-strict, or queer, or 'puritanic.'

Early in the episcopal controversy in New England, the religion of the "dissenters" was ridiculed as "true blue." John Checkley, of Boston, was prosecuted and fined, in 1724, for publishing, under the title of "A Discourse concerning Episcopacy," a virulent attack on the churches of Massachusetts, which the court held to be "a false and scandalous libel." In 1738, the book was reprinted for Checkley, in London, with the addition of his Plea to the court and his sentence; and, on a single page, was given "A Specimen of a True Dissenting Catechism, upon Right TRUE-BLUE Dissenting Principles," followed by the lines,

> "They're so perverse and opposite
> As if they worship'd God for Spite.'"

This couplet, taken from Butler's description of the religion of Hudibras (which was "presbyterian *true-blue*") shows where Checkley found the epithet.† His book, it appears, continued to be very "industriously handed about," among the episcopalians in western

* Doc. History of New York, iii. 80.

† Rev. Sam. Peters, also, made this couplet serviceable. Describing "the grand meeting-house" in Norwich, Conn., of which "the steeple stands at the east end," he said: "The following couplet was written by a traveller, on the steeple:

> 'They're so perverse and opposite,
> As if they *built* to God in spite."

Hist. of Connecticut, p. 140.

Connecticut, twenty years after its publication,* and doubtless helped to give the epithet currency.

Colonel Caleb Heathcote, before mentioned, who was a member of the Society for the Propagation of the Gospel and directed its work in New York and the neighboring colonies, lived at Westchester, on the western border of Connecticut. It was from this quarter, and with his introduction, that the first missionaries of the Society were brought into the Colony. "In those days" (as Mr. Wm. L. Kingsley remarks),† "when all traveling was attended with every kind of difficulty, New Haven—which was the nearest town of importance and the one with which the English at New York had most to do—was to them practically 'New England.' It was the part of New England about which they knew the most, and that part of it which they pictured to themselves whenever 'New England' was spoken of." Another circumstance contributed to draw attention to New Haven, as the strong-hold of 'puritanism' and dissent. "*A thing which they call a college*, wherein a commencement was made some three or four months ago"—as Col. Heathcote informed the Society, in November, 1705,‡ —was permanently established at New Haven, in 1716. [Six years after, when the Rev. Timothy Cutler, was won to episcopacy, the fact that he was "President of Yale College in New England, a station of credit and profit,"§ added a laurel to the triumph.] The Rev. Dr. Samuel Johnson, a missionary of the Society, formerly a tutor in Yale, felt it necessary to apologize to his employers for sending his son to New Haven: "It is indeed a great mortification to me and to him," wrote Mr. Johnson, "that I am obliged to send him to a dissenting college, or deny him any public education at all, and rather than deny any collegiate education, I confess I do not deny him *going to meeting, when he can't help it.*" ‖ It is a comfort to know that the young man

* Rev. Dr. Noah Welles, in Dedication of a Sermon preached at Stamford, April 10, 1763, page iii., note.

† In a valuable paper on the "Blue Laws," in *The New Englander*, for April, 1871.

‡ Doc. History of New York, iii., 80.

§ Humphreys, Historical Account, 333.

‖ Hawkins, Hist. Notices of the Missions of the Church of England.

was not quite ruined. William Samuel Johnson is not the least among the magnates of Yale.

There was another reason—and it is perhaps the principal one—for visiting upon New Haven the authorship of all the "odd kinds of laws" which New York found objectionable. In the colony of New Haven, before the union with Connecticut, the privileges of voting and of holding civil office were, by the "fundamental agreement," restricted to church-members. This peculiarity of her constitution was enough to give color to the assertion that her legislation was, pre-eminently, *blue*. That her old record-book contained a code of "blue laws" which were discreditable to puritanism and which testified to the danger of schism—became, among certain classes, an assured belief. To this imaginary code wit and malice made large additions, sometimes by pure invention, sometimes by borrowing absurd or arbitrary laws from the records of other colonies. And so the myth grew—till the last vestige of truth was lost in fable.

The earliest mention of the "New Haven Blue Laws" that I remember to have seen in print, is in a satirical pamphlet published in 1762, entitled: "The Real Advantages which Ministers and People may enjoy, especially in the Colonies, by conforming to the Church of England," etc. The anonymous author (probably the Rev. Noah Welles, D. D. of Stamford, a zealous opponent of episcopacy,) addressing a young friend who had some thoughts of conforming, tells him that "it is a principal advantage of the Church of England, that the religion which is generally practised by her members is *perfectly agreeable to polite gentlemen*; whereas no gentleman can belong to other persuasions without meeting with a great deal of uneasiness from their *doctrines*, but more especially from their *discipline*" (p. 6):

"You have doubtless often observed, that the dissenters in New England have such a *discipline* among them as is very shocking to many fine gentlemen, and ladies too. If a gentleman drinks a little freely, or happens to love a pretty girl somewhat too warmly, nothing will content these rigid bigots, but they must stand on the *stool of repentance*, or in the *broad-alley*, and make a *long whining confession*. Now you know that this rigorous discipline is chiefly levelled and contrived to *pester* and afflict polite gentlemen, to whom women and wine are far from being disagreeable, now and then. Indeed I have heard that some of them begin to be ashamed of their *blue laws at New Haven*, yet they still retain so many penances, confessions, and satisfactions, as are extremely disagreeable to every fashionable gentleman" (p. 29).

From the manner in which this allusion is introduced it is evident that reproach of New Haven for her "blue laws" was already a familiar weapon of religious controversy. A few years later—in 1767—William Smith, Chief-Justice of New York, had the curiosity to inspect "the first records of the colony of New Haven, *vulgarly called the Blue Laws.*" In the continuation of his History of New York, he gives (p. 93) the result of his examination:

"A note ought not to be supressed concerning these records, to correct a voice of misplaced ridicule. Few there are, who speak of the *Blue Laws*, (a title, of the origin of which the author was ignorant,) who do not imagine they form a code of rules for future conduct, drawn np by an enthusiastic, precise set of religionists; and if the inventions of wits, humorists, and buffoons were to be credited, they must consist of many volumes. The author had the curiosity to resort to them, when the Commissaries met at New Haven, for adjusting a partition line between New York and the Massachusetts, in 1767; and a parchment-covered book of demi-royal paper was handed to him for the laws asked for, as the only volume in the office passing under this odd title. [It is not likely that there was, at this time, a copy of the printed "Laws for Government," of 1656, in the office at New Haven, or that its contents were known to those who talked of "Blue laws."] It contains the memorials of the first establishment of the colony, which consisted of persons who had wandered beyond the limits of the old charter of the Massachusetts Bay, and who, as yet unauthorized by the crown to set up any civil government in due form of law, resolved to conduct themselves by the Bible. As a necessary consequence, the judges they chose took up an authority similar to that which every religious man exercises over his own children and domestics. Hence their attention to the morals of the people. in instances with which the civil magistrate can never intermeddle under a regular well-policied institution; because, to preserve liberty, they are cognizable only by parental authority. . . . . So far is the common idea of the blue laws being a collection of rules from being true, that they are only records of convictions, consonant, in the judgment of the magistrates, to the word of God, and dictates of reason."

Chief-Justice Smith, was educated at Yale College. So was his father, Judge William Smith, who for many years enjoyed the distinction of being one of the *two* men (Judge James Delancey was the other) in the province of New York who had received a liberal education. The "Blue Law" story probably came to the Chief-Justice by inheritance, and—like his fellow citizens of New York, generally,—he never questioned its truth, till his visit to New Haven twenty-two years after his graduation.

Occasional allusions to the "Blue Laws" are found in

newspapers and pamphlets printed before the Revolution, but no *specimens* of the laws so stigmatised seem to have been published before 1781, when "a sketch of some of them" was given to the world by the

REV. SAMUEL PETERS,

in "A General History of Connecticut, from its First Settlement under George Fenwick, Esq.," etc.: "By a Gentleman of the Province:" printed in London, "for the Author."

Five or six years before this "History" was fabricated, its author was the subject of a one-line sketch in *McFingal*;

"Our fag-end man, poor Parson Peters,"

As the sole authority for the only "New Haven Blue Laws" that are now popularly known by the name, he and his book are entitled here to a larger notice.

The late Professor J. L. Kingsley, in the notes to his Historical Discourse at New Haven (1838), was at the pains of pointing out "a few of the errors"—as he charitably named them—of "the work which, more than any other, has given currency to various misrepresentations respecting the New Haven colony:" and in this connection, he quoted a remark made by the the Rev. Dr. Trumbull, the historian, who was a townsman of Peters and had known him from childhood,—that, "of all men with whom he had ever been acquainted, Dr. Peters, he had thought, from his first knowledge of him, the least to be depended upon as to any matter of fact; especially in story-telling." The best excuse that can be made for him is, that he was a victim of *pseudomania*; that his abhorrence of truth was in fact a disease, and that he was not morally responsible for its outbreaks. He could not keep even his name clear of falsification. It passes into history with doubtful initials and fictitious titles. He wrote himself, sometimes "Samuel Peters," sometimes "Samuel Andrew (or, Samuel A.) Peters." He appended to his name the letters "LL. D."—but no one can guess how he came by them. Some books of reference have made him D. D.; others (including the latest American biographical dictionary) have conferred on him *both* the doctorates. His life begins with fable—in fact, the fable is pre-natal, for he claimed descent from a brother of Hugh Peters, who (if proof of a negative can ever be trusted) had no existence. His autobiography—which he was fond of writing—is everywhere as untruthful as are his contributions to history. In one place he describes himself as

"The Rev. Samuel Peters, an episcopal clergyman, who by his generosity and zeal for the Church of England, and loyalty to the House of Hanover, has rendered himself famous both in New and Old England, and in some degree made an atonement for the fanaticism and treasons of his uncle Hugh, and of his ancestor on his mother's side, Major-General Thomas Harrison, both hanged at Charing-Cross in the last century."—*History of Connecticut*, 172.

In a "History of Jonathan Trumbull, the Rebel Governor," etc., evidently from the pen of Peters, in a London "Political Magazine," for January, 1781, he introduces himself as

—"the Rev. Mr. Peters, a church clergyman, of an ancient and opulent family in the Colony, and one of those they stiled their *Noblesse*, being a descendant" etc. . . . "and his wife was a descendant of Dr. John Owen." [As a matter of *fact*, he married the great-granddaughter of a John Owen who was living in Windsor, Conn., before 1650,—the cotemporary and only eight years the junior of Dr. John Owen.] . . . . "Mr Peters had been brought up to the law, and was extremely popular in the country; but . . . renouncing the independent faith, he received holy ordination from the Lord Bishop of London." . . . .

"In proportion to a man's goodness, is he persecuted. Mr. Peters's stile of life in Connecticut was generous and exemplary, and his fortune considerable. It is most likely he would have arrived to the Government of the Colony, had he not forsaken the Republican system of his ancestors, and become an admirer of the English constitution and a convert to the Church of England."

To descend to prose: Mr. Peters was born in Hebron in 1735, graduated at Yale College in 1757, went to England for episcopal ordination, and returned in 1760, to take charge of the little episcopal church in his native town, where he continued to reside till the beginning of the revolutionary contest. In 1774, his obstinate and aggressive toryism rendered him very obnoxious to his neighbors and finally provoked the resentment of the Sons of Liberty. A party of two or three hundred men paid him a visit, threatened him (so he averred) with tar and feathers, handled him somewhat roughly when they detected him in falsehood, and drew from him a promise that he would not again meddle in public affairs. After a few weeks, he gave new offence, and was again called to account. This time, he was made to subscribe, "without equivocation or mental reservation," a pledge to "support the measures taken to obtain redress of our grievances," etc. He was not much hurt, in person or property, but was badly frightened, and apprehensive of worse to come. He fled from Hebron to Boston, breathing out threatenings and slaughter against his tormentors. "For my telling the Church people not to take up arms, etc., it being high treason, etc.,"—he wrote from his place of refuge, to his friend, the Rev. Dr. Auchmuty, of New York,—"the Sons of Liberty have destroyed my windows, rent my clothes, even my gown, etc., crying out, down with the Church, the rags of Popery, etc.; their rebellion is obvious—treason is common—and robbery is their daily diversion: the Lord deliver us from anarchy." He found his only comfort in the anticipation that, if his plans of vengeance should succeed, Connecticut might be blotted out: "the bounds of New York may directly extend to Connecticut river, Boston meet them, New Hampshire take the Province of Maine, and Rhode Island be swallowed up as Dathan." In October, 1774, he sailed for England, where he remained until 1805. He obtained a small pension from the crown, and some compensation for the property he professed to have lost in Connecticut: and it was perhaps in the hope of eking out a livelihood, as well as of gratifying his resentment, that he employed his pen in abuse of the colony which gave him birth, and the religion of his fathers. He did not, says Mr. Duykinck, "carry his point of dismembering Connecticut, but he punished the natives almost as effectually by writing a book—his History of the State. It was published anonymously, but it was as plainly Peters's as if every page had been subscribed by him, like the extorted declarations." *

His work seems to have been in no sense a success. He had presumed too far both on the credulity of English readers and on their ill-will to America. With less inveterate aversion to truth, he might have imparted plausibility to fiction; with less exuberance of malice, he might have tickled the English ear with the absurdities and misdeeds of the "rebels," and have passed for a humorist. As it was, the *Monthly Review* doubtless expressed the general sentiment:

"We find it destitute of every claim to the rare quality [of impartiality]; and observe in it so many marks of party spleen and idle

* Cyclopædia of American Literature, i. 191.

credulity, that we do not hesitate to pronounce it altogether unworthy of the public attention."

"Extravagant and incredible," "ludicrous and apocryphal," are the epithets by which the historian of Episcopacy in Connecticut (the Rev. Dr. Beardsley) has characterized the statements of Peters's book. It would have fallen forever into the oblivion it merits, had it not been that its malignant fabrications have supplied so many respectable and reverend authors with facilities for breaking the ninth commandment without incurring personal responsibility.

The book was first published in 1781. The next year, it received a new *title-page*, which described it as a "second edition." Whether this was done to stimulate the sale, or merely to improve a blank space in the title, by the insertion of one more falsehood, is not clear.

"Its narrations," says Duykinck, in his notice of the author, "are independent of time, place, and probability. A sober critic would go mad over an attempt to correct its misstatements." What could sober criticism do, for instance, with the account of Bellows Falls, where "the water is consolidated by pressure, by swiftness, between the pinching, sturdy rocks, to *such a degree of induration that no iron crow can be forced into it*," and the stream is "harder than marble" (p. 127),—or, with the bridge over the Quinebaug, at Norwich, "under which ships pass with all their sails standing"(p. 139),—or with "the infamous villainy of [the Rev. Thomas] Hooker, who *spread death upon the leaves of his Bible* and struck Connecticote (a great Sachem) mad with disease" (134),—or with the Rev. Mr. Vesey's exorcism of the devils who came to attend an Indian powwaw at Stratford, and the resulting introduction of episcopacy into Connecticut (215—217),—or with the statement, that the people of Massachusetts "sent Mr. John Winthrop privately to Hartford, to promote a petition to Charles II. for a charter, as a security against the ambition of New Haven" (74),—or with the assertion that Yale College was "originally a school established *by the Rev. Thomas Peters* at Saybrook" (199),—or with the story of the alarming incursions of the Windham frogs, or the descriptions of those remarkable quadrupeds "the whappernocker" and "the cuba,"—or with the conviction and punishment of an episcopal clergyman in 1750, for breaking the Sabbath by walking too fast from church and combing a lock of his wig on Sunday (p. 305),—or, in fine, with any half-dozen consecutive sentences in this wonderful "History." Its lies, like Falstaff's, are "gross as a mountain, open, palpable." Indeed, some of the apologists for Peters have insisted that he never intended his book to he believed. Yet—through this slough of mendacity, a Lord Bishop of Oxford (Wilberforce) could wade, to cull specimens of the "Blue Code of Connecticut" which "made it criminal in a mother to kiss her infant on the Sabbath-day," and "which strictly forbids making mince-pies," etc., etc.,*—and the Reverend Henry Caswall, "D. D. of Trinity College, Connecticut, Prebendary of Sarum," etc., could repeat in his work on "The American Church and the American Union," (on the authority of this History of Connecticut, "*as quoted by the Bishop of Oxford*,") the story of "the fundamental principles of the New Haven settlement," and "the most remarkable of the laws passed by the New Haven dominion",—and the Reverend Isaac Taylor, vicar of Holy Trinity, Twickenham, can transfer to the pages of his "Words and Places" (4th edition, 1873, p. 11,) these same blue laws, "mince-pies, trumpet, drum, Jews'-harp," and all, as "a curious picture of life in this Puritan Utopia," and can retain through several editions of a popular book a statement which he had, to say the least, good reason to suspect to be untrue —that these laws are "given by Hutchinson,"—and the Reverend J. S. M Anderson, Chaplain to the Queen, etc., etc., in a "History of the Church of England in the Colonies," can quote, and cite as authority (vol ii. pp. 353, 354) this "General History of Connecticut" of 1781. With such teachings is it strange that the average Englishman believes the story of the 'Blue Laws' as implicitly as he believes the Thirty-nine Articles—and with much less mental reservation.

Judge Haliburton of Nova Scotia, the author of "Sam Slick" and several other quasi-historical works, in a note to one of them—"Rule and Misrule of the English

* History of the Prot. Episcopal Church in America (2d edition), p. 76. In a note, Bishop Wilberforce cited as his authority Peters's "History of Connecticut, 1781," and—"Capt. Marryat's Diary, Blue Code. A copy of which, through the kindness of the last named gentleman, lies before me." He might have added, that Peters lied before Capt. Marryat.

in America"—remarked that "the *Connecticut* Laws, which were framed and executed by people vastly inferior in ability and education to those of Massachusetts, are conspicuous for their harshness as well as their absurdity;" and in proof of this, quotes four of Peters's fabulous *New Haven* Blue Laws,—"No man shall run on the Sabbath," etc: "No one shall read Common Prayer, make mince pies," etc.

So lately as 1867, Mr. "M. Mc N. Walsh, A. M., LL.B., of the New York Bar," published a handy-book entitled "The Lawyer in the School Room,"—in which appears Peters's whole code, as veritable laws of New Haven colony.

Worse yet: Prof. Schele De Vere, of the University of Virginia, in his recent volume of "Americanisms" (N. York, 1872, p. 273), endorses the Blue-Law story of Peters, as "confirmed beyond doubt." Connecticut, he says, "is still often mentioned as the *Blue State*, unquestionably from its being [as, unquestionably, it was not] the original stronghold of the Presbyterians." Prof. De Vere admits that "the authenticity of the famous laws of New Haven . . . . known as the Blue Laws" has been "often denied, and Dr. Peters's *well-known book on the subject* has been declared a libel;" but "they are *confirmed beyond any doubt* by"—what? —"by the reprint of the 'Abstract of Laws of New England" [which were laws *proposed* for *Massachusetts*, by John Cotton, but were never in force in that colony or any other,] in Governor Hutchinson's 'Collection of Papers,' London, 1655 [that is, Boston, 1769], where the identical provisions [but not one of those given by Peters which are vulgarly denominated "blue laws"] may be found."

When divines, jurists, and learned professors concur in maintaining that fiction is fact, we cannot wonder that so many of the laity are under the "delusion, that they should believe a lie." Every now and then, the well-worn specimens of "New Haven Blue Laws" go the rounds of the newspaper press—and certain classes of readers swallow them with as much avidity and confidence as they swallow the quack nostrums advertised in the next column. "Thousands," said Professor Kingsley, "have believed implicitly in the existence of the 'blue laws,' who could scarcely be said to have any other article of faith." With such, disproof avails no more than contradiction. He who is predetermined to believe, *will* believe. Inshallah!

In the bitterness of political strife, between 1800 and the triumph of "Democracy and Toleration" in Connecticut in 1817, the "Blue Laws" were much talked of by the opponents of "steady habits" and "the standing order." During the war of 1812-1814, the "Blue Lights" story came into being, and supplied another taunt at the federalists. In 1817, a poem was published in New York, entitled: "Blue Lights, or The Convention. In four Cantos. By Jonathan M. Scott, Esq." Of course, the author introduces some allusions to the Blue Laws. He tells how the law-students in Yale College are taught to

"Explain old codes, and wisely shew
The good effects of statutes Blue,
Beneath whose stern control, the swain
Might never swear nor drink in vain;
Whose rule the nuptial kiss restrains
On Sabbath day, in legal chains;
And should some youth, in daring brunt,
Answer with oath the dire affront,
Enrich'd by pettifogging toil,
The parish battens on the spoil;
And should the rash offender fail
To pay the fine or find his bail,
In cloven stick his tongue must rest,
'Till ev'ning shades embrown the west."—(p. 31.)

In a note, the writer says, that, "as this excellent code of laws has never, we believe, been committed to the press, he has, with infinite pains, obtained a few extracts from it, principally for the benefit of our western brethren": and proceeds to give "some specimens of the wisdom of the New Haven lawgivers"—conceived in the spirit of Peters, but without the pretence of writing "history." For example:

"1. Whosoever kisseth his wife on the Sabbath day, shall be fined in the sum of three shillings and four pence, or in default thereof shall receive at the post, forty stripes save one."

"4. Whosoever shall be convicted of profane swearing, shall have the oath of which he was convicted, written on his hat, with chalk, for the space of one week; and for the second offence, shall stand with his tongue in a split stick until the going down of the sun."

"5. All cracking of nuts, eating of apples, and such like unbecoming amusements, are strictly forbidden, during the time of divine service, as being highly repugnant to ecclesiastical discipline," etc.

Peters's finished "sketch" of the "Blue Laws" will be given in another part of this volume. But the *True* Blue legislation of Connecticut and New Haven must have precedence of the false; and we begin with—

1. THE CONNECTICUT CONSTITUTION OF 1638-39,

or the "fundamental orders" by which "the inhabitants and residents of Windsor, Hartford, and Wethersfield," became "associated and conjoined to be as one Public State or Commonwealth,"—not a confederacy of petty sovereignties, but a union under a government of the people's choice, exercising "the supreme power of the commonwealth," and maintaining *liberty*, under *law*. It has been justly characterized as "THE FIRST PROPERLY AMERICAN CONSTITUTION—a work in which the framers were permitted to give body and shape, for the first time, to the genuine republican idea, that dwelt as an actuating force, or inmost sense, in all the New England colonies." *

A sketch of the Rev. Thomas Hooker's sermon preached before the General Court in May, 1638, and an extract from his letter to Governor Winthrop of Massachusetts, giving his views of the nature of civil government and his conviction that "a general council, chosen by all, to transact businesses which concern all" is "most safe for the relief of the whole,"—are prefixed to the copy of the first Constitution.

2. THE CAPITAL LAWS, ESTABLISHED, 1642.

These, as was before stated, are copied, with little alteration, from the capital laws of Massachusetts.

3. THE FIRST CONNECTICUT CODE.

This code, adopted by the General Court, May, 1650, was compiled, probably, by Roger Ludlow, who, in April, 1646, was desired "to take some pains in drawing forth a Body of Laws for the government of this Commonwealth, and present them to the next General Court." The work was not completed in May, 1647, and it was then ordered, that when the Body of Laws should be perfected,

* Dr. Bushnell's Historical Estimate ("Work and Play," p. 177).

as the Court had desired, Mr. Ludlow "should, besides the paying the hire of a man, be further considered for his pains." Nothing more, concerning the progress and completion of the work, appears on the records, until February, 1651, when the Court ordered compensation to the Secretary for "his great pains in drawing out and transcribing the Country Orders, concluded and established in May last."—*Colonial Records*, I. 138, 154, 216.

The code comprises all laws of general concernment enacted by the General Court, and remaining in force in May, 1650, with large additions, most of which were taken from the laws of Massachusetts.

4. Orders of the Connecticut Court, 1636-1662. Under this head are comprised some orders which were repealed before the adoption of the code of 1650, and some which were made between 1650 and the re-establishment under the Charter, in 1662; with a few judgments rendered and sentences pronounced by the General and Particular Courts.

The Particular Court, or Court of Magistrates, was constituted (under the 10th Fundamental Order of the Constitution) of the Governor and at least four other magistrates: after February, 1645, of the Governor or Deputy Governor and three other magistrates.—*Colonial Records*, I. 71, 119.

5. The Fundamental Agreement of the Planters of New Haven.

This agreement—the Constitution of New Haven colony—was adopted by "all the free planters," June 14th, 1639, and continued in force until the Union of the two colonies in 1665.

It differs from the Connecticut constitution, radically, by restricting to church-members the management of public affairs and the right of suffrage. Mr. Hooker maintained that "the foundation of authority is laid, *firstly*, in the free consent of the *people*." Mr. Davenport believed that in "a new plantation, where all, or the most considerable part of the free planters, profess their purpose and desire of securing to themselves and their posterity the pure and peaceable enjoyment of Christ's ordinances," "such planters are bound, in laying the foundations of Church and Civil State, to take order that all the free burgesses be such as are in fellowship of the

Church or Churches which are or may be gathered according to Christ,"—and "that this course will most conduce to the common welfare of all." *

"If you call their adoption of this principle fanaticism, it is to be remembered," says Dr. Bacon, "that the same fanaticism runs through the history of England. How long has any man in England been permitted to hold office under the crown, without being *a communicant* in the Church of England?"

6. The New Haven Code of Laws. 1655.

"The laws in this code were passed at various times, and perhaps collected and digested about 1648 or 1649, though revised and in some degree altered in 1655, upon the perusal by Governor Eaton of the "new book of laws in the Massachusetts Colony," and the "small book of laws newly come from England, which is said to be Mr. Cotton's." †

"The laws which, at the Court's desire have been drawn up by the governor," Theophilus Eaton, were "read and seriously weighed by the Court, and by vote concluded, and ordered to be sent to England to be printed," at the October Court, 1655. ‡

In June, 1656, Gov. Eaton "informed the Court that there is sent over now, in Mr. Garret's ship, 500 law books, which Mr. Hopkins hath gotten printed," etc. §

A copy of this volume of the New Haven Laws, "printed by M. S. for Livewell Chapman," London, 1656, is in the Library of the American Antiquarian Society at Worcester, Mass. Until lately, this copy was regarded as perhaps unique, and in 1834 a transcript of it was made, at the request of the General Assembly of Connecticut, to be preserved in the office of the Secretary of State. Since then, two copies of the original edition

* "A Discourse about Civil Government in a New Plantation whose design is Religion," written (as Dr. Bacon has demonstrated) by Davenport. though attributed, by its publisher, to John Cotton. For an exposition of the New Haven constitution, and a defence of the colonists from the stereotyped charges of "fanaticism and bigotry," see Dr. Bacon's admirable *Historical Discourses*, pp. 25-32. Extracts from the "Discourse about Civil Government" are given in his Appendix, pp. 289-292.

† C. J. Hoadly, in Preface to New Haven Colonial Records, vol. i.

‡ New Haven Records, ii. 154. § *Ibid.* 186.

have been discovered (one of which is somewhat imperfect), and both are now in the library of the late Mr. George Brinley, of Hartford.

This code was first reprinted (from the manuscript copy in the Secretary's Office) in 1838, in a volume entitled: "The Blue Laws of New Haven Colony, usually called Blue Laws of Connecticut," etc. "Compiled by an Antiquarian." (Hartford, 12mo.) The Compiler was the Hon. R. R. Hinman, then Secretary of State. It was reprinted again—and with absolute accuracy—by Mr. Hoadly, at the end of his second volume of New Haven Colonial Records, in 1858.

7. Laws and Judgments of the New Haven General Court, before 1655.

What Hutchinson has said of early judicial proceedings in Massachusetts is equally true for New Haven: "Whilst they were without a code or body of laws, and the colony had but just come to its birth, their sentences seem to be adapted to the circumstances of a large family of children and servants." A remark of Chief Justice Smith, to the same effect, has been quoted (on page 30). The judges, he says, "took up an authority similar to that which every religious man exercises over his own children and domestics." By the unanimous agreement of the planters, the General Court was entrusted with the power not only of "declaring and establishing, for the plantations, the laws of God," and of "making and repealing orders for smaller matters, not particularly determined in Scripture,"—but, generally, "with all care and diligence from time to time to provide for the maintenance of the purity of religion and suppress the contrary," etc.

"Their judicial proceedings," says Hutchinson (i. 83), varied in very few circumstances from the Massachusetts; one, indeed, was a material one, that they had no *jury*, neither in civil nor criminal cases. All matters of fact, as well as law, were determined by the court."

From specimens of the *true blue* laws and judgments of New Haven, we pass to

8. The "Blue Law" Forgeries of Peters.

His first reference to New Haven "Blue Laws" is as follows:

"The lawgivers soon discovered that the precepts in the Old and

New Testaments were insufficient to support them in their arbitrary and bloody undertakings: they, therefore, gave themselves up to *their own inventions* in making others, wherein, in some instances, they betrayed such an extreme degree of wanton cruelty and oppression, that even the rigid fanatics of Boston and the mad zealots of Hartford, put to the blush, christened them the *Blue Laws;* and the former held a day of thanksgiving, because God, in his good providence, had stationed Eaton and Davenport so far from them" (Peters's "History," p. 43).

After giving a "sketch of some of these laws" (which will be found in this volume), he remarks that

"They consist of a vast multitude, and were very properly termed *Blue Laws,* i. e. *bloody Laws;* for they were all sanctified with excommunication, confiscation, fines, banishment, whippings, cutting off the ears, burning the tongue, and death. . . . And did not *similar laws still* [that is, in 1782] *prevail over New England as the common law of the country,* I would have left them in silence," etc. (pp. 69, 70).

Writers who have copied the "blue law" fiction seem to have overlooked the very important statement which is here italicized. That the provision that "every male should have his hair cut round according to a cap" (or "the hard shell of a pumpkin") and the law forbidding the making of mince-pies were in force not only in New Haven colony, but that they or "similar laws" still prevailed over *New England,* in the last quarter of the eighteenth century—is a fact which the Bishop of Oxford and the Rev. Isaac Taylor would have done well to note.

The definition of 'blue' by 'bloody' was probably original with Peters. It is amusing to see how unsuspiciously it has been adopted by believers in the "Blue Laws." When we tell a friend that he is "looking *blue,*" we do not usually intend to convey the impression that his aspect is remarkably *sanguine*—or *sanguinary.*

9. EARLY LAWS AND JUDGMENTS OF OTHER COLONIES.

For comparison, in "quaintness, bluntness, particularity, and antiquated excess of penalty," with the laws of Connecticut and New Haven, some specimens of laws enacted in several other American colonies—particularly New York, and Virginia,—are grouped under the several heads: Crimes and Punishments; Laws against Dissenters, Quakers, Papists, and Disturbers of the Church; and Sumptuary Laws, regulating dress, diet, and expenditure, with some other curiosities of legislation.

Peters's Blue Laws have often been reprinted, and several compilations, more or less complete, of the early laws of Connecticut and New Haven have been published under the name of "Blue Laws." Some of these may be named here, beginning with

A General History of Connecticut. . . . By a Gentleman of the Province. *London*, 1781. 8vo.

The same work, with a new title-page (and a "P. S." of three lines on the last page of the text, mentioning the death of the Rev. Nathaniel Hooker of Hartford), called "Second Edition." *London*, 1782.

The same: "To which is added, A Supplement verifying many important statements made by the author. Illustrated with eight engravings." *New Haven*, Published by D. Clark and Co., 1829. 12 mo.

This reprint has an additional preface of 6 pages, and a Supplement (of Notes) of 87 pp. (319—405). The editor has hitherto escaped detection, or, if suspected, has not been absolutely convicted.

The Code of 1650: being a compilation of the Laws and Orders of the General Court of Connecticut: also, the Constitution, or civil Compact, entered into and adopted by the towns of Windsor, Hartford, and Wethersfield, in 1638–9. To which is added, Some Extracts from the Laws and Judicial Proceedings of New Haven Colony, commonly called BLUE LAWS. *Hartford*, Published by Silas Andrus, 1822. (12 mo, pp. 120.)

Some copies had, by way of frontispiece, a coarse wood-cut representing the arrest of a tobacco-taker, by a constable.

The Code of 1650 was first printed in this volume—and with creditable accuracy. Peters's "Blue Laws" are not included in the compilation. Like other publications of Mr. Andrus, this book was a favorite with the book-peddlers, by whose agency several editions of it were scattered through the country.

The same: *Hartford*, Silas Andrus, 1825. 12mo, pp. 119. *Woodcut.*

The same: with a new title-page only. *Hartford*, S. Andrus & Son, n. d. 12mo, pp. 119.

The Blue Laws of New Haven Colony, usually called the Blue Laws of Connecticut; Quaker Laws of Massachusetts; Blue Laws of New York [and other colonies] . . . . Compiled by an Antiquarian. *Hartford*, 1838. 12mo. pp. 336.

The compiler was Royal R. Hinman, who was Secretary of Connecticut, 1835—1842. The New Haven Code of 1655 was for the first time reprinted, in this volume, from a manuscript copy (in the Secretary's Office) of the London edition of 1656. Peters's "Blue Laws" are found on pages 121—124.

The Blue Laws of Connecticut. [The Code of 1650, and Laws and Orders of 1638—39.] *Cincinnati*, 1850. 12mo.

The Blue Laws of Connecticut: a Collection of the earliest statutes and judicial proceedings of that Colony; being an exhibition of the rigorous morals and legislation of the Puritans. Edited, with an

Introduction, by Samuel M. Smucker, LL. D. *Philadelphia*, 1861. 12mo.

This editor, like some of his predecessors, mistakes the *Connecticut* code of 1650 for "the celebrated code at present stigmatized as the 'Blue Laws.'" The fabulous code of *New Haven* colony was so 'stigmatized' by Peters and those who believed or professed to believe his story; but the name was not given, till the present generation, to the genuine *Connecticut* code of 1650, or to any laws enacted by Connecticut.

Every now and then, some English or Scotch writer parades the choicest specimens of Peters's collection as genuine "curiosities of Puritan legislation," or as "affording a curious picture of life in this Puritan Utopia." Only a few years ago, a paper on the "Blue Laws" was published in *Blackwood's Magazine* (for April, 1870), in which the old story was repeated, that

"In the Blue Laws of New Haven, which were not, however, drawn up or codified by the State of Connecticut [why should they have been ?], it was ordered that no one should 'travel, cook victuals, make beds, sweep house, cut hair, or shave on the Sabbath-Day; that no woman should kiss her child on the Sabbath or Fasting-day, that no one should keep Christmas or Saint days; and that every male should have his hair cut round, according to a cap?" "Such were the Blue Laws," etc., etc.

This article contains, in its dozen pages, more misstatements than even Peters managed to condense in the same compass. The writer tells us that "the laws codified by Roger Ludlow [i. e. the Connecticut laws of 1650] were the famous 'Blue Laws;'" that "the phrase was suggested by the old English phrase of 'the blues,' and 'blue-devils' [which, as every English scholar knows, are *not* old English phrases] and the common vulgarism 'to look blue;'" that "this code remained in operation until 1686, when Sir Edward Andros suspended the charter of the Colony, as well as the Puritanic laws" [Sir *Edmund* Andros assumed the government of Connecticut in 1687, and did *not* suspend the "puritanic laws," though he promulgated some new laws; but the whole body of Connecticut laws, including the code of 1650, had been revised, amended, re-codified, and published, in 1673, long before Andros's coming]; that *shortly after the completion* of his task of codification, "the worthy Justice Ludlow was publicly called 'Justass Ludlow,' by one Captain Stone," and "for this offence the Captain was fined £100," etc. [Captain Stone's offence was committed and punished in *Massachusetts*, two years before Connecticut was settled, and about seventeen years before the Connecticut laws were codified]; and the "one significant paragraph by Roger Ludlow," which is quoted is, in fact, the declaration of rights prefixed to the Massachusetts "Body of Liberties" of 1640, and adopted by Connecticut, nearly word for word, in 1650.* It was this article, perhaps, which suggested the remarks made by the late Rev. Dr. John Todd, in a conversation with an intelligent Scotch traveller who subsequently published his impressions of "The Americans at Home." †

"Speaking of the old Puritan strictness, and of the so-called Blue Laws of Connecticut, the Doctor said: 'I have been amused to see that some of your writers imagine that there really *were* such laws in New England. The whole thing is an absurd fiction. . . . It was not wonderful, perhaps, that people so ignorant about us as the English *were* should have been hoaxed into the belief that there had really been laws in Connecticut making it penal for a man to kiss his wife on Sundays, and all that nonsense; but to find some of *your living writers* still falling into an error so preposterous, is very melancholy. What would you think of an American, writing about England, and quoting 'Jack and the Bean Stalk' as an authentic historical work?"

"These Blue Laws," says the writer in Blackwood's, "were of five kinds—general, theological, municipal, commercial, and personal." A somewhat similar classification might be made, of the writers who believe—or profess to believe—the Blue-Law story. Perhaps the "theological" believers are the most numerous. English churchmen, particularly, find it difficult *not* to believe in the fabricated code which has so conveniently been appropriated *in pios usus*, or that laws forbidding the making of mince-pies and playing on any musical instrument, "except the drum, trumpet, and jews' harp," were not the natural and necessary fruits of schism. There seems to be, in some minds, an honest doubt, whether the prohibition in the ninth

---

* This article was put to a better use than it deserved, by Mr. Wm. L. Kingsley—who made it the target of "A Long-range Shot," in *The New Englander*, for April, 1871 (vol. xxx., pp. 284–304).

† By David Macrae. 2 vols. Edinburgh, 1870. The passage was quoted by Mr. J. A. Picton, in "Notes and Queries," January, 1871.

commandment really extends to witness borne against New England puritanism.

Several communications on the Blue Laws appeared in "Notes and Queries," in 1871. In the number for March 4th (4th Series, vii. 191) the Rev. J. A. Picton, after searching all the authorities within his reach, presented the result of his inquiries. The work on which he was obliged mainly to rely was the little volume published by Silas Andrus, in 1825, as a chap book—with its rude frontispiece, representing the arrest of a tobacco-taker; but he had also examined—what that compilation did not include—the genuine New Haven Code of 1655. Of course, he found, neither in this, nor in the Connecticut Code of 1650, "the slightest traces of the absurdities usually attached to the idea of the *Blue Laws*." Mr. Picton went further, and "having seen what the Connecticut and New Haven Codes are *not*," was at the pains of "stating what they really *are*"—with an intelligent appreciation that it is really refreshing to meet with in an English periodical. He is mistaken as to the identification of church and state—even in New Haven Colony, where only church-members were entrusted with the privileges of freemen—certainly, in Connecticut; and he seemingly exaggerates the severity of these codes—as compared with the laws of England, at the same period—by his reference to "the ruthless sacrifice of human life," which they exacted.

"They are," writes Mr. Picton, "very valuable illustrations of the tone and temper of mind of the stern pioneers who went out to people the wilderness, and whose customs, manners, and civil and religious opinions have been *the normal type after which the great American commonwealth has been modeled.* The founders of New England were resolute God-fearing men of the Roundhead stamp. In the foundation of their institutions, the following principles lie at the base:—

1. Perfect equality and mutual responsibility amongst all the members of the commonwealth.

2. The identity of Church and State, with the necessary corollary that all laws should be founded on the Word of God.

3. The obligation of the civil magistrate to enforce ecclesiastical discipline.

4. That the law should take cognizance of immorality as well as of crime.

These principles were logically and relentlessly carried out into practice: sometimes making one shudder at the ruthless sacrifice of human life, and at other times raising a smile at the ludicrous minuteness with which the law intermeddled with private affairs.

(1.) The Enactments of the Code breathe the true spirit of *freedom and equal rights*, the system of manhood-suffrage and annual elections containing the germ of the future institutions of the United States. Several of these laws *are far in advance of their age*, such as voting by written papers, freedom of debtors from arrest except in case of fraud, etc.

(2.) The Word of God was held to be supreme in all cases not otherwise provided for by the law, and all enactments were supposed to be founded thereon. Unfortunately it was the Mosaic Code rather than the Gospel, which was resorted to. . . . . .

(3 & 4.) The ecclesiastical discipline enforced by the magistrate descended to the ordinary intercourse of private life, in the most minute particulars.

On this point, Mr. Picton cited from the New Haven Records, May, 1660, the proceedings in the case of two young persons, "the charge being that, after some chaffing, Jacob had taken away Sarah's gloves." We have no objection to joining him in a laugh over this or other illustrations of the strictness with which, in "the day of small things," the rule of righteousness was applied to the conduct of individuals. Indeed, some pains has been taken, in making selections for this volume, to *amuse* good-natured readers,—as well as to remove unfounded prejudices and correct popular misconceptions. Connecticut can well afford to let her records go to the world. "There is no State in the Union," wrote Mr. Bancroft, "and I know not any in the world, in whose early history, if I were a citizen, I could find more of which to be proud, and less that I should wish to blot." "Nearly two centuries have elapsed,"—the same historian has said elsewhere,—"the world has been wiser by various experience, political institutions have become the theme on which the most powerful and cultivated minds have been employed, dynasties of kings have been dethroned, recalled, dethroned again, and so many constitutions have been framed or reformed, stifled or subverted, that memory may despair of a completed catalogue; but the people of Connecticut have found no reason to deviate from the government established by their fathers." The state came to be known as "the land of steady habits," and was proud of the name. It was her boast that her sons were "antiquâ virtute ac fide"—which, according to Ainsworth, is the Latin equivalent of "TRUE BLUE WILL NEVER STAIN." ("Di boni!" said Terence's Demea,—

> "Næ illiusmodi jam nobis magna civium
> Pĕnuria 'st, homo antiqua virtute ac fide:
> Haud cito mali quid ortum ex hoc sit publice.")

And to the charge that "the advancement of political science, generated by our Revolution, had neither changed her constitution nor affected her *steady habits*,"—one of her poets replied, in 1804:

> "Straight on her course she firmly steers,
> Nor jibes, nor tacks, nor scuds, nor veers,
> Not the whole force they all can yield,
> Can drive her vet'rans from the field,
> The same pure, patriotic fires
> Which warm'd the bosoms of their Sires,
> That generous, that effulgent flame,
> Which glow'd in WINTHROP'S deathless name,
> Unsullied through their bosoms runs,
> Inspires and animates her sons."

The Constitution of 1638–9,—"the first one written out, as a complete frame of civil order, in the new world, embodies," said Dr. Bushnell, in his noble Speech for Connecticut, "all the essential features of the constitutions of our States, and of the Republic itself, as they exist at the present day. It is the free representative plan, which now distinguishes our country in the eyes of the world." Mr. Calhoun declared in the Senate of the United States, that it was owing mainly to two States,—Connecticut and New Jersey,—that we have, as a nation, "the best government instead of the worst and most intolerant on earth. Who are the men of the States to whom we are indebted for this admirable government? I will name them," he said,—"their names ought to be engraved on brass and live forever. They were Chief-Justice ELLSWORTH, ROGER SHERMAN, and Judge PATTERSON of New Jersey. . . . To the coolness and sagacity of these three men, aided by a few others, not so prominent, we owe the present Constitution."

LIBERTY UNDER LAW.

"I fully assent to those staple principles which you set down ; to wit, that the people should choose some from amongst them,—that they should refer matter of counsel to their counsellors, matter of judicature to their judges ; only, the question here grows, what rule the judge must have to judge by? secondly, who those counsellors must be?

" That in the matter which is referred to the judge, the sentence should lie in his breast or be left to his discretion, according to which he should go, I am afraid it is a course which wants both safety and warrant. I must confess, I ever looked at it as a way which leads directly to tyranny and so to confusion, and must plainly profess, if it was in my liberty, I should choose neither to live nor leave my posterity under such a government. *Sit liber judex*, as the lawyers speak. 17 Deut., 10, 11, 'Thou shalt observe to do according to all that they inform, according to the *sentence of the Law.*' Thou shalt seek the Law at his mouth: not ask what his discretion allows, but what the Law requires. And therefore the Apostles, when the rulers and high priest passed sentence against their preaching, as prejudicial to the State, the Apostle Peter made it not dainty to profess and practice contrary to their charge, because their sentence was contrary to law, though they might have pretended discretion and depth of wisdom and policy in their charge.

"And we know in other countries, had not the law overruled the lusts of men and the crooked ends of judges, many times, both places and people had been, in reason, past all relief, in many cases of difficulty. You will know what the heathen man said, by the candle-light of common sense ; 'The law is not subject to passion, nor to be taken aside with self-seeking ends, and therefore ought to have chief rule over rulers themselves.'

"Its's also a truth, that counsel should be sought from counsellors ; but the question yet is, who those should be? Reserving small matters, which fall in occasionally in common course, to a lower counsel, in matters of greater consequence, which concern the common good, a general counsel, chosen by all, to transact businesses which concern all, I conceive, under favor, most suitable to rule and most safe for relief of the whole. This was the practice of the Jewish church, directed by God, Deut., 17: 10, 11 ; 2 Chron., 19 ; and the approved experience of the best ordered States give in evidence this way.

Solomon's one wise man, and the one wise woman in Abel that delivered the city, shows the excellency of wisdom and counsel where it is, but doth not conclude that one or few should be counsellors, since 'in the multitude of counsellors there is safety.'"—*Rev. Thomas Hooker's Letter to Gov. Winthrop of Massachusetts*, 1638.

THE PEOPLE'S PRIVILEGE OF ELECTION; ABSTRACT OF MR. HOOKER'S DISCOURSE BEFORE THE GENERAL COURT AT HARTFORD, MAY 31, 1638.

Deut. I. 13. "Take you wise men, and understanding, and known among your tribes, and I will make them rulers over you." (Captains over thousands, and captains over hundreds—over fifties—over tens etc.)

Doctrine. I. That the choice of public magistrates belongs unto the people, by God's own allowance.

II. The privilege of election, which belongs to the people, therefore must not be exercised according to their humours, but according to the blessed will and law of God.

III. They who have power to appoint officers and magistrates, it is in their power, also, to set the bounds and limitations of the power and place unto which they call them.

Reasons. 1. Because the foundation of authority is laid, firstly, in the free consent of the people.

2. Because, by a free choice, the hearts of the people will be more inclined to the love of the persons chosen and more ready to yield obedience.

3. Because of that duty and engagement of the people.

Uses. The lesson taught is threefold :—

1st, There is matter of thankful acknowledgment—in the appreciation of God's faithfulness toward us, and the permission of these measures that God doth command and vouchsafe.

2dly, Of reproof—to dash the conceits of all those that shall oppose it.

3dly, Of exhortation—to persuade us, as God hath given us Liberty, to *take* it.

And lastly,—as God hath spared our lives, and given us them in liberty, so to seek the guidance of God, and to choose *in* God and *for* God.

I.

FIRST CONSTITUTION OF CONNECTICUT.

FUNDAMENTAL LAWS, ADOPTED BY THE INHABITANTS OF THE THREE RIVER TOWNS, 1638-9.

FORASMUCH as it hath pleased the Almighty God by the wise disposition of his divine providence so to order and dispose of things that we the inhabitants and residents of Windsor, Harteford, and Wethersfield are now cohabiting and dwelling in and upon the River of Conectecotte and the lands thereunto adjoining; and well knowing where a people are gathered together the word of God requires that to maintain the peace and union of such a people there should be an orderly and decent Government established according to God, to order and dispose of the affairs of the people at all seasons as occasion shall require; do therefore associate and conjoin ourselves to be as one Public State or Commonwealth; and do, for ourselves and our Successors, and such as shall be adjoined to us at any time hereafter, enter into combination and confederation together, to maintain and preserve the liberty and purity of the gospel of our Lord Jesus which we now profess, as also the discipline of the Churches, which according to the truth of the said gospel is now practiced amongst us; as also in our Civil Affairs to be guided and governed according to such laws, rules, orders, and decrees, as shall be made ordered and decreed, as followeth:—

1. It is Ordered, sentenced, and decreed, that there shall be yearly two General Assemblies or Courts, the one the second Thursday in April, the other the second Thursday in September following; the first shall be called the Court of Election, wherein shall be yearly chosen from time to time so many magistrates and other public officers as shall be found requisite: whereof one to be chosen Governor for the year ensuing and until another be chosen, and no other magistrate to be chosen for more than one year; provided always there be six chosen besides the Governor; which being chosen and sworn according to an oath recorded for that purpose, shall have power to administer justice according to the laws here established, and for want thereof according to the rule of the word of God; which choice shall be made by all that are admitted freemen and have taken the Oath of Fidelity, and do cohabit within this jurisdiction, (having been admitted inhabitants by the major part of the town wherein they live,*) or the major part of such as shall be then present.

2. It is Ordered, sentenced, and decreed, that the election of the aforesaid magistrate shall be on this manner: every person present and qualified for choice shall bring in (to the persons deputed to receive them) one single paper, with the name of him written in it whom he desires to have Governor, and he that hath the greatest number of papers shall be Governor for that year. And the rest of the magistrates or public officers to be chosen in this manner: The secretary for

* This clause has been interlined, in a different handwriting and at a more recent period.

the time being shall first read the names of all that are to be put to choice and then shall severally nominate them distinctly, and every one that would have the person nominated to be chosen shall bring in one single paper written upon, and he that would not have him chosen shall bring in a blank; and every one that hath more written papers than blanks shall be a magistrate for that year; which papers shall be received and told by one or more that shall be then chosen by the court and sworn to be faithful therein; but in case there should not be six chosen as aforesaid, besides the Governor, out of those which are nominated, then he or they which have the most written papers shall be a magistrate or magistrates for the ensuing year, to make up the foresaid number.

3. It is Ordered, sentenced, and decreed, that the secretary shall not nominate any person, nor shall any person be chosen newly into the magistracy, which was not propounded in some General Court before, to be nominated the next election; and to that end it shall be lawful for each of the towns aforesaid by their deputies to nominate any two whom they conceive fit to be put to election; and the court may add so many more as they judge requisite.

4. It is Ordered, sentenced, and decreed, that no person be chosen Governor above once in two years, and that the Governor be always a member of some approved congregation, and formerly of the magistracy within this jurisdiction; and all the magistrates, freemen of this commonwealth: and that no magistrate or other public officer shall execute any part of his or their office before they are severally sworn, which shall be done in the face of the court if they be pre-

sent, and in case of absence by some deputed for that purpose.

5. It is Ordered, sentenced, and decreed, that to the aforesaid Court of election the several towns shall send their deputies, and when the elections are ended they may proceed in any public service as at other courts. Also the other General Court in September shall be for making of laws, and any other public occasion which concerns the good of the commonwealth.

6. It is Ordered, sentenced, and decreed, that the Governor shall, either by himself or by the secretary, send out summons to the constables of every town for the calling of these two standing courts, one month at least before their several times: And also if the Governor and the greatest part of the magistrates see cause upon any special occasion to call a General Court, they may give order to the secretary so to do within fourteen days warning: and if urgent necessity so require, upon a shorter notice, giving sufficient grounds for it to the deputies when they meet, or else be questioned for the same; And if the Governor and major part of magistrates shall either neglect or refuse to call the two general standing courts or either of them, as also at other times when the occasions of the commonwealth require, the freemen thereof, or the major part of them, shall petition to them so to do: if then it be either denied or neglected, the said freemen or the major part of them shall have power to give order to the constables of the several towns to do the same, and so may meet together, and choose to themselves a moderator, and may proceed to do any act of power which any other General Court may.

7. It is Ordered, sentenced, and decreed, that after there are warrants given out for any of the said General Courts, the constable or constables of each town shall forthwith give notice distinctly to the inhabitants of the same, in some public assembly or by going or sending from house to house, that at a place and time by him or them limited and set, they meet and assemble themselves together to elect and choose certain deputies to be at the General Court then following, to agitate the affairs of the commonwealth; which said deputies shall be chosen by all that are admitted inhabitants in the several towns and have taken the oath of fidelity;* provided that none be chosen a deputy for any General Court which is not a freeman of this commonwealth.

The foresaid deputies shall be chosen in manner following: every person that is present and qualified as before expressed, shall bring the names of such, written in several papers, as they desire to have chosen for that employment, and these three or four, more or less, being the number agreed on to be chosen for that time, that have the greatest number of papers written for them, shall be deputies for that court; whose names shall be endorsed on the back side of the warrant and returned into the court, with the constable or constables' hand unto the same.

8. It is Ordered, sentenced, and decreed, that Windsor, Hartford, and Wethersfield shall have power, each

---

* "Whereas in the Fundamental Order it is said 'that such who have taken the oath of fidelity and are admitted inhabitants' shall be allowed as qualified for choosing of deputies, the Court declares their judgment, that such only shall be counted admitted inhabitants, who are admitted by a general vote of the major part of the town that receiveth them."—Voted, Nov. 10, 1643.

town, to send four of their freedmen as their deputies to every General Court; and whatsoever other towns shall be hereafter added to this jurisdiction, they shall send so many deputies as the court shall judge meet, a reasonable proportion to the number of freemen that are in the said towns being to be attended therein; which deputies shall have the power of the whole town to give their votes and allowance to all such laws and orders as may be for the public good, and unto which the said towns are to be bound.

9. It is Ordered and decreed, that the deputies thus chosen shall have power and liberty to appoint a time and a place of meeting together before any General Court, to advise and consult of all such things as may concern the good of the public, as also to examine their own elections, whether according to the order, and if they or the greatest part of them find any election to be illegal they may seclude such for present from their meeting, and return the same and their reasons to the court; and if it prove true, the court may fine the party or parties so intruding and the town, if they see cause, and give out a warrant to go to a new election in a legal way, either in part or in whole. Also the said deputies shall have power to fine any that shall be disorderly at their meetings, or for not coming in due time or place according to appointment; and they may return the said fines into the court if it be refused to be paid, and the treasurer to take notice of it, and to estreat or levy the same as he doth other fines.

10. It is Ordered, sentenced, and decreed, that every General Court, except such as through neglect of the Governor aud the greatest part of magistrates the

freemen themselves do call, shall consist of the Governor, or some one chosen to moderate the court, and four other magistrates at least, with the major part of the deputies of the several towns legally chosen; and in case the freemen or major part of them, through neglect or refusal of the Governor and major part of the magistrates, shall call a court, it shall consist of the major part of freemen that are present or their deputies, with a moderator chosen by them: In which said General Courts shall consist the supreme power of the Commonwealth, and they only shall have power to make laws or repeal them, to grant levies, to admit of freemen, dispose of lands undisposed of, to several towns or persons, and also shall have power to call either court or magistrate or any other person whatsoever into question for any misdemeanor, and may for just causes displace, or deal otherwise, according to the nature of the offence; and also may deal in any other matter that concerns the good of this commonwealth, except election of magistrates, which shall be done by the whole body of freemen.

In which Court the Governor or Moderator shall have power to order the court,to give liberty of speech, and silence unseasonable and disorderly speakings, to put all things to vote, and in case the vote be equal to have the casting voice. But none of these courts shall be adjourned or dissolved without the consent of the major part of the court.

11. It is ordered, sentenced, and decreed, that when any General Court upon the occasions of the commonwealth have agreed upon any sum or sums of money to be levied upon the several towns within this Jurisdiction, that a committee be chosen to set out and appoint what shall be the proportion of every town to

pay of the said levy; provided the committees be made up of an equal number out of each town.

14th January, 1638-39, the 11 Orders above said are voted.

THE OATH OF THE GOVERNOR, FOR THE PRESENT.

I, N. W. being now chosen to be Governor within this Jurisdiction for the year ensuing, and until a new be chosen, do swear by the great and dreadful name of the everliving God, to promote the public good and peace of the same, according to the best of my skill; as also will maintain all lawful privileges of this commonwealth; as also that all wholesome laws that are or shall be made by lawful authority here established, be duly executed; and will further the execution of justice according to the rule of God's word; so help me God, in the name of the Lord Jesus Christ.

THE OATH OF A MAGISTRATE, FOR THE PRESENT.

I, N. W. being chosen a Magistrate within this Jurisdiction for the year ensuing, do swear by the great and dreadful name of the everliving God, to promote the public good and peace of the same, according to the best of my skill, and that I will maintain all the lawful privileges thereof according to my understanding, as also assist in the execution of all such wholesome laws as are made or shall be made by lawful authority here established, and will further the execution of Justice for the time aforesaid, according to the righteous rule of God's word; so help me God, etc.

THE OATH OF A CONSTABLE.

I, A. B., of W, do swear by the great and dreadful

name of the everliving God, that for the year ensuing, and until a new be chosen, I will faithfully execute the office and place of a Constable, for and within the said plantation of W. and the limits thereof, and that I will endeavour to preserve the public peace of the said place, and Commonwealth, and will do my best endeavour to see all watches and wards executed, and to obey and execute all lawful commands or warrants that come from any Magistrate or Magistrates or Court; so help me God, in the Lord Jesus Christ.

II.

CAPITAL LAWS.

Capital Laws established by the General Court, the first of December, 1642.*

1. If any man after legal conviction shall have or worship any other God but the Lord God, he shall be put to death. Deut. 13. 6, and 17. 2: Ex. 22. 20.

2. If any man or woman be a witch (that is, hath or consulteth with a familiar spirit,) they shall be put to death. Ex. 22. 18: Lev. 20. 27: Deut. 18. 10, 11.

3. If any person shall blaspheme the name of God,

*All these are copied from the capital laws of Massachusetts, established (with her Body of Liberties), Dec. 1641,—except the 9th (against rape of a married or betrothed woman) which was enacted by Massachusetts, in June, 1642. One of the Massachusetts laws, punishing *manslaughter* with death, was not adopted by Connecticut, and only the first clause of the Massachusetts law against *conspiracy, rebellion, etc.*, was taken.

the Father, Son or Holy Ghost, with direct, express, presumptuous, or highhanded blasphemy, or shall curse God in the like manner, he shall be put to death. Lev. 24. 15, 16.

4. If any person shall commit any wilful murder, which is manslaughter committed upon malice, hatred, or cruelty, not in a man's necessary and just defence, nor by mere casualty against his will, he shall be put to death. Ex. 21. 12, 13, 14. Numb. 35. 30, 31.

5. If any person shall slay another through guile, either by poisonings or other such devilish practice, he shall be put to death. Ex. 21. 14.

6. If any man or woman shall lie with any beast or brute creature, by carnal copulation, they shall surely be put to death, and the beast shall be slain and buried. Lev. 20. 15, 16.

7. If any man lie with mankind as he lieth with a woman, both of them have committed abomination, they both shall surely be put to death. Lev. 20. 13.

8. If any person committeth adultery with a married or espoused wife, the adulterer and the adulteress shall surely be put to death. Lev. 20. 10, and 18. 20: Deut. 22. 23, 24.

9. If any man shall forcibly and without consent ravish any maid or woman that is lawfully married or contracted, he shall be put to death. Deut. 22. 25.

10. If any man stealeth a man or mankind, he shall be put to death. Ex. 21. 16.

11. If any man rise up by false witness, wittingly and of purpose to take away any man's life, he shall be put to death. Deut. 19. 16, 18, 19.

12. If any man shall conspire or attempt any invasion, insurrection or rebellion against the commonwealth, he shall be put to death.

III.

THE FIRST CODE OF LAWS,

ESTABLISHED BY THE GENERAL COURT OF CONNECTICUT, MAY, 1650.*

Forasmuch † as the free fruition of such liberties, immunities, and privileges, as humanity, civility, and Christianity call for, as due to every man in his place and proportion, without impeachment and infringement, hath ever been and ever will be the tranquillity and stability of churches and commonwealths, and the denial or deprival thereof, the disturbance if not ruin of both:—

It is therefore ordered by this court and authority thereof, that no man's life shall be taken away, no man's honor or good name shall be stained, no man's person shall be arrested, restrained, banished, dismembered, nor any way punished, no man shall be deprived of his wife or children, no man's goods or estate shall be taken away from him, nor any ways endamaged, under color of law or countenance of authority, unless it be by the virtue or equity of some express law of the country warranting the same, established by a

---

* See the introduction, page 38.

† The preamble and the paragraph which follows are copied from the Massachusetts Body of Liberties (or from the Massachusetts Book of Laws printed in 1648).

General Court and sufficiently published, or, in case of the defect of a law in any particular case, by the word of God.

ABILITY.

It is ordered by this court, that all persons of the age of twenty-one years and of right understanding, whether excommunicated, condemned, or other, shall have full power and liberty to make their wills and testaments, and other lawful alienations of their lands and estates and may be plaintiffs in a civil case.

ACTIONS.

It is further ordered and decreed, that in all actions brought to any court, the plaintiff shall have liberty to withdraw his action, or to be nonsuited, before the jury have given in their verdict, in which case he shall always pay full costs and charges to the defendant, and may afterward renew his suit at another court, the former nonsuit being first recorded.

AGE.

It is ordered by this court and the authority thereof, that the age for passing away of lands or such kind of hereditaments, or for giving of votes, verdicts, or sentences in any civil courts or causes, shall be twenty and one years, but in case of choosing of guardians, fourteen years.

ARRESTS.

It is ordered and decreed by this court and authority thereof, that no person shall be arrested or imprisoned for any debt or fine, if law can find any competent means of satisfaction otherwise from his estate; and if not, his person may be arrested and imprisoned, where he shall be kept at his own charge, not the plaintiff's, till satisfaction be made, unless the court that had cognizance of the cause or some superior court shall otherwise determine; provided nevertheless, that no man's person shall be kept in prison for debt, but when there appears some estate which he will not produce, to which end any court or commissioners authorized by the general court may administer an oath to the party or any others suspected to be privy in concealing his estate; and if no estate appear, he shall satisfy the debt by service, if the creditor require it, but shall not be sold to any but of the English nation.

ATTACHMENTS.

It is ordered, sentenced, and decreed, that the ordinary summons or process for the present within this jurisdiction and until other provision made to the contrary, be a warrant fairly written, under some magistrate or magistrates' hand or hands, mentioning the time and place of appearance, and if the said party or parties do not appear according to the said warrant or summons, upon affidavit first made of the serving of the said person or persons, the court shall grant an attachment against the person or persons delinquent to arrest or apprehend the said person or persons for his or their wilful contempt; and in case no sufficient security or bail be tendered, to imprison the party or parties, returnable the next court that is capable to take cognizance of the said business in question; and upon return of the said attachment, the said court to do therein as according to the laws and orders of this jurisdiction; and in that case also the party delinquent to bear his own charge.

It is also ordered, that attachments to seize upon any man's lands or estate be only granted for, or against, such goods as are foreigners' and do not dwell or inhabit within this jurisdiction; or in any case upon credible information it appear that any inhabitant that is indebted, or engaged, go about to convey away his estate to defraud his creditors, or to convey away his person out of this jurisdiction, so as the process of this jurisdiction may not be served upon his person; in that or any other just causes there may be attachment or attachments granted upon the limitations expressed; provided that in all cases of attachments, all or any of the creditors have liberty to declare upon the said attachment, if he come in at the return of the said attachment; provided also, that if any attachment laid upon any man's estate, upon a pretence of a great sum, and if it be not proved to be due in some near proportion to the sum challenged and mentioned in the attachment, then the security given shall be liable to such damages as are sustained thereby.

It is further ordered and decreed by this court, that whosoever takes out an attachment against any man's person, goods, chattels, lands or hereditaments, sufficient security and caution shall be given by him to prosecute his action in Court and to answer the defendant such costs as shall be awarded him by the court; and in all attachments of goods or lands, legal notice shall be given unto the party or left in writing at his house or place of usual abode if he live within this jurisdiction, otherwise his suit shall not proceed. And it is further ordered and declared, that every man shall have liberty to replevy his cattle or goods impounded, distrained, seized or extended, (unless it be upon execution after judgment and in payment of fines,) provided in like manner he put in good security to prosecute his replevy and to satisfy such damage, demands or dues as his adversary shall recover against him in law.

BALLAST.

It is ordered by this court and authority thereof, that no ballast shall be taken from any shore in any town within this jurisdiction, by any person whatsoever, without allowance under the hands of those men that are to order the affairs in each town, upon the penalty of six pence for every shovel full so taken, unless such stones as they had laid there before. It is also ordered by the authority aforesaid, that no ship nor other vessel shall cast out any ballast in the channel or other place inconvenient, in any harbor within this jurisdiction; upon the penalty of ten pounds.

BARRATRY.

It is ordered, decreed, and by this court declared, that if any man be proved and adjudged a common barrater, vexing others with unjust, frequent and needless suits, it shall be in the power of courts both to reject his cause and to punish him for his barratry.

BILLS.

It is ordered by the authority of this court, that any debt or debts due upon bill or other specialty assigned to another, shall be as good a debt and estate to the assignee as it was to the assigner, at the time of its assignation, and that it shall be lawful for the said assignee to sue for and recover the said debt due upon bill and so assigned, as fully as the original creditor might have done; provided the said assignment be made upon the backside of the bill or specialty; not excluding any just or clear interest any man may have in any bills or specialties made over to them by letters of attorney or otherwise.

BOUNDS OF TOWNS AND PARTICULAR LANDS.

Forasmuch as the bounds of towns and of the lands of particular persons are carefully to be maintained, and not without great danger to be removed by any; which notwithstanding by deficiency and decay of marks may at unawares be done, whereby great jealousies of persons, trouble in towns and incumbrances in courts do often arise, which by due care and means might be prevented:

It is therefore ordered by this court and authority thereof, that every town shall set out their bounds within twelve months after the publishing hereof, and after their bounds are granted; and that when their bounds are once set out, once in the year three or more persons in the town, appointed by the selectmen, shall appoint with the adjacent towns to go the bounds betwixt their said towns and renew their marks, which marks shall be a great heap of stones or a trench of six foot long and two foot broad, the most ancient town (which for the river is determined by the court to be Wethersfield,*) to give notice of the

* This early decision, by the General Court, of the question of priority of settlement of the River towns, seems to have been overlooked by writers on our colonial history. The clause within the

time and place of meeting for this perambnlation, which time shall be in the first or second month, upon pain of five pounds for every town that shall neglect the same; provided, that the three men appointed for perambulation shall go in their several quarters, by order of the selectmen and at the charge of the several towns. And it is further ordered, that if any particular proprietor of lands lying in common with others shall refuse to go, by himself or his assign, the bounds betwixt his land and other men's, once a year, in the first or second month, being requested thereunto upon one week's warning, he shall forfeit for every day so neglecting, ten shillings, half to the party moving thereto, the other half to the town. And the owners of all impropriated grounds shall bound every particular parcel thereof with sufficient mear stones, and shall preserve and keep them so upon the former penalty.

BURGLARY AND THEFT.

Forasmuch as many persons of late years have been and are apt to be injurious to the goods and lives of others, notwithstanding all care and means to prevent and punish the same:

It is therefore ordered by this court and authority thereof, that if any person shall commit burglary, by breaking up any dwelling house, or shall rob any person in the field or highways, such a person so offending shall for the first offence be branded on the

---

parenthesis is, in the original record, interlined. As, however, it is in the handwriting of Capt. Cullick, who ceased to be Secretary in 1658, the interlineation must have been made within a few years after the adoption of the code. The clause is retained in the first printed revision of the Laws, of 1672-3, and in that of 1702; but is omitted in subsequent revisions.

forehead with the letter (B): If he shall offend in the same kind the second time, he shall be branded as before, and also be severely whipped; and if he shall fall into the same offence the third time, he shall be put to death as being incorrigible. And if any person shall commit such burglary or rob in the fields or house on the Lord's day, besides the former punishments, he shall for the first offence have one of his ears cut off; and for the second offence in the same kind, he shall lose his other ear in the same manner; and if he fall into the same offence the third time, he shall be put to death.

2. Secondly, for the prevention of pilfering and theft, it is ordered by this court and authority thereof, that if any person, whether children, servants or others, shall be taken or known to rob any orchards or garden, that shall hurt or steal away any grafts or fruit trees, fruits, linen, woolen, or any other goods left out in orchards, gardens, backsides, or other place in house or fields, or shall steal any wood or or other goods from the waterside, from men's doors or yards, he shall forfeit treble damage to the owners thereof, and such severe punishment as the court shall think meet.

And forasmuch as many times it so falls out that small thefts and other offences of a criminal nature are committed, both by English and Indians, in towns remote from any prison or other fit place to which such malefactors may be committed till the next court; It is therefore hereby ordered, that any magistrate, upon complaint made to him, may hear and upon due proof determine any such small offences of the aforesaid nature, according to the laws here established, and give warrant to the constable of that town where the offender lives to levy the same, provided the damage or fine exceed not forty shillings; provided also it shall be lawful for either party to appeal to the next court to be holden in that jurisdiction, giving sufficient caution to prosecute the same to effect at the said court. And every magistrate shall make return yearly to the court of the jurisdiction wherein he liveth, of what cases he hath so ended. And also the constable, of all such fines as they have received; and where the offender hath nothing to satisfy, such magistrate may punish by stocks or whipping, as the cause shall deserve.

It is also ordered that all servants or workmen embezzling the goods of their masters, or such as set them on work, shall make restitution, and be liable to all laws and penalties as other men.

CAPITAL LAWS.

[Of the Capital Laws, fourteen in number, the first twelve agree, word for word, with those adopted in Dec. 1642, printed on pages 59, 60. It has not been thought necessary to repeat them here. The others follow :—]

13. If any child or children about sixteen years old and of sufficient understanding, shall curse or smite their natural father or mother, he or they shall be put to death, unless it can be sufficiently testified that the parents have been very unchristianly negligent in the education of such children, or so provoke them by extreme and cruel correction, that they have been forced thereunto to preserve themselves from death or maiming. Exod. 21. 17; Lev. 20. [9]; Exod. 21. 15.

14. If a man have a stubborn and rebellious son of

sufficient years and understanding, viz: sixteen years of age, which will not obey the voice of his father or the voice of his mother, and that when they have chastened him will not hearken unto them, then may his father and mother, being his natural parents, lay hold on him and bring him to the magistrates assembled in court, and testify unto them that their son is stubborn and rebellious and will not obey their voice and chastisement, but lives in sundry notorious crimes, such a son shall be put to death. Deut. 21. 20, 21.

It is also ordered by this court and authority thereof that whatsoever child or servant, within these liberties, shall be convicted of any stubborn or rebellious carriage against their parents or governors, which is a forerunner of the aforementioned evils, the governor or any two magistrates have liberty and power from this court to commit such person or persons to the house of correction, and there to remain under hard labor and severe punishment so long as the court or the major part of the magistrates shall judge meet.*

And whereas frequent experience gives in sad evidence of several other ways of uncleanness and lascivious carriages practiced among us, whereunto, in regard of the variety of circumstances, particular and express laws and orders cannot suddenly be suited; this court cannot but look upon evils in that kind as very pernicious and destructive to the welfare of the common weal, and do judge that severe and sharp punishment should be inflicted upon such delinquents, and as they do approve of what hath been already done

*Enacted Dec. 1649 (Col. Rec., I. 78) with this preamble:—"Forasmuch as incorrigibleness is also adjudged to be a sin of death, but no law yet amongst us established for the execution thereof: For the preventing that great evil, It is ordered, &c."

by the particular court, as agreeing with the general power formerly granted, so they do hereby confirm the same power to the particular court, who may proceed either by fine, committing to the house of correction or other corporal punishment, according to their discretion, desiring such seasonable, exemplary executions may be done upon offenders in that kind, that others may hear and fear.

CASK AND COOPER.

It is ordered by this court and authority thereof, that all cask used for tar or other commodities to be put to sale, shall be assized as follows, viz: every cask commonly called barrels or half hogsheads shall contain twenty-eight gallons wine measure, and other vessels proportionable; and, that fit persons shall be appointed from time to time, in all places needful, to gauge all such vessels or casks and such as shall be found of due assize shall be marked with the gauger's mark and no other, who shall have for his pains four pence for every tun, and so proportionably.

And it is also ordered, that every cooper shall have a distinct brandmark on his own cask, upon pain of forfeiture of twenty shillings in either case, and so proportionably for lesser vessels.

CATTLE, CORNFIELDS, FENCES.

Forasmuch as complaints have been made of a very evil practice of some disordered persons in the country, who use to take other men's horses, sometimes upon the commons, sometimes out of their own grounds, common fields, and inclosures, and ride them at their pleasure, without a leave or privity of their owners:—

It is therefore ordered and enacted by the authority of this Court, that whosoever shall take any other man's horse, mare, or drawing beast, out of his inclosure, upon any common, out of any common field or elsewhere, except such be taken damage faisant and disposed of according to law, without leave of the owners, and shall ride or use the same, he shall pay to the parties wronged treble damages, or if the complainant shall desire it, then to pay only ten shillings; and such as have not to make satisfaction shall be punished by whipping, imprisonment, or otherwise, as by law shall be adjudged, and any one magistrate may hear and determine the same.

It is also further ordered, that where lands lie common, unfenced, if one shall improve his lands by fencing in several, and another shall not, he who shall so improve shall secure his land against other men's cattle, and shall not compel such as join upon him to make any fence with him, except he shall also improve in several, as the other doth; and where one man shall improve before his neighbor, and so make the whole fence, if after his said neighbor shall improve also, he shall then satisfy for half the other's fence against him, according to the present value, and shall maintain the same. And if either of them shall after lay open his said fields (which none shall doe without three months' warning,) he shall have liberty to buy the dividend fence, paying according to the present valuation to be set by two men, chosen by either party one. The like order shall be [*attended*] where any man shall improve land against any town common, provided this order shall not extend to house lots not exceeding ten acres: but if in such, one shall improve, his neighbor shall be compellable to make and maintain one half of the fence between them, whether he improve or not.

Provided also, that no man shall be liable to satisfy for damage done in any ground not sufficiently fenced, except it shall be for damage done by swine under a year old, or unruly cattle which will not be restrained by ordinary fences, or where any man shall put his cattle, or otherwise voluntarily trespass, upon his neighbor's ground. And if the party damnified find the cattle damage faisant, he may impound or otherwise dispose of them. *6th October*, 1652. *The Court declares and explains, this order doth not reach the lands on ye east side of the Great River.*

CATTLE TO BE MARKED.

For the preventing of differences that may arise in the owning of cattle that be lost or stray away,

It is ordered by this Court, that the owners of any cattle within this jurisdiction shall ear-mark or brand all their cattle and swine that are above half a year old, (except horses,) and that they cause their several marks to be registered in the town book, and whatsoever cattle shall be found unmarked after the first of July next shall forfeit five shillings a head, whereof two shillings sixpence to him that discovers it, and the other to the country.

COMMON FIELDS.

Whereas the condition of these several plantations in these beginnings wherein we are, is such that necessity constrains to improve much of the ground belonging to the several towns, in a common way, and it is observed that the public and general good, (which ought to be attended in all such improvements as are most proper to them, and may best advance the same,) receives much prejudice through want of a prudent ordering and disposing of those several common lands so as may best effect the same ;—

It is ordered by this Court and authority thereof, that each town shall choose from among themselves five able and discreet men, who by this order have power given them, and are required, to take the common lands belonging to each of the several towns respectively into serious and sad consideration, and after a through digesting of their own thoughts, set down under their hands in what way the said lands may, in their judgments, be best improved for the common good. And whatsoever is so decreed and determined by the said five men in each town, or any three of them, concerning the way of improvement of any such lands, shall be attended by all such persons that have any propriety or interest in any such lands so judged [by the said committee].

And whereas also, much damage hath risen not only from the unruliness of some kind of cattle but also from the weakness and insufficiency of many fences, whence much variance and difference hath followed, which if not prevented for the future may be very prejudicial to the public peace ;—

It is likewise therefore ordered, that the said five men so chosen or at least three of them shall set down what fences shall be made in any common grounds, and after they are made to cause the same to be viewed, and to set such fines as they judge meet upon any as shall neglect or not duly attend their order therein ; and where fences are made and judged sufficient by them, whatsoever damage is done by hogs or any other cattle, shall be paid by the owners of the said cattle. And the several towns shall have liberty once every year to alter any three of the former five, and to make choice of others in their room. It being provided, that any particular man or men shall have liberty to inclose any of their particular grounds and improve them according to their own discretion, by mutual agreement, notwithstanding this order.* This service is committed to the townsmen, as appears by an order of court, 5th of February, 1650, on the other side of this book.†

CAVEATS ENTERED.

Whereas it appears that divers to defeat and defraud their creditors may secretly and underhand make bargains and contract of their lands, lots, and accommodations, by means whereof, when the creditor thinks he hath a means in due order of law to declare against the said lands, lots, and accommodations, and so recover satisfaction for his debt, he is wholly deluded and frustrated, which is contrary to a righteous rule that every man should pay his debt with his estate, be it in what it will be, either real or personal, this court taking it into consideration, do order sentence and decree, That if any creditor for the future do suspect any debtor, that he may prove nonsolvent in his personal estate, he may repair to the register or recorder of the plantation where the lands, lots, or accommodations lies, and enter a caveat against the lands, lots, and accommodations of the said debtor,

---

* Enacted Feb. 14th. 1643-4 ; with an amendment authorizing the appointment of *five* men in place of *seven*, Feb. 5th, 1644-5.

† Conn. Col. Rec., i. 214.

and shall give to the said register or recorder four pence for the entry thereof: And the said creditor or creditors shall take out summons against the said debtor and, in due form of law, the next particular court either for the whole colony or for the particular plantation where the said lands, lots, or accommodations lies, or the next court ensuing, declare against the said debtor's lands, lots, or accommodations. And so if the creditor recover, he may enter a judgment upon the said lots, lands, and accommodations, and take out an extent against the said land, directed to a known officer, who may take two honest and sufficient men of the neighbors, to apprise the said lands, lots, and accommodations, either to be sold outright if the debt so require, or set a reasonable rent upon the same until the debt be paid, and deliver the possession thereof either to the creditor or creditors, his or their assign or assigns, or any other; and what sale or sales, lease or leases, the said officer makes, being orderly recorded, according to former order of recording of lands, shall be as legal and binding to all intents and purposes as though the debtor himself had done the same; provided that if the said debtor can then presently procure a chapman or tenant that can give to the creditor or creditors satisfaction to his or their content, he shall have the first refusing thereof. Also it is declared, that he which first enters caveats as abovesaid, and his debt being due at his entering the said caveat, shall be first paid; and so every creditor as he enters his caveat and his debt becomes due shall be orderly satisfied, unless it appear at the next court, the debtor's lands, lots, and accommodations prove insufficient to pay all his creditors, then every man to have a suitable proportion to his debt out of the same, and yet notwithstanding every man to receive his part according to the entry of his caveat. Yet this is not to seclude any creditor to recover other satisfaction, either upon the person or estate of the debtor according to law and custom of the colony. As also it is further decreed, that what sale or bargain soever the debtor shall make concerning the said lots, lands, and accommodations, after the entering of the said caveat, shall be void, as to defraud the said creditors.

It is also further explained and declared, that if the said debtor be known to be a non-solvent man before the first caveat entered against the said lots, lands, and accommodations, and the same appear at the next particular court, then the court shall have power to call in all the creditors in a short time, and set an equal and indifferent way how the creditors shall be paid out of the said lots, lands, and accommodations; otherwise, if the said debtor prove insolvent after the first caveat entered, then this order to be duly observed, according to the premises and true intent and meaning thereof.

It is also further declared and explained, that the said recorder or register of the said caveats, shall, the next particular court as aforesaid, return the said caveats that are with him; at which time and court the enterers of the said caveats shall be called forth to prosecute the same the next particular court following; and if the enterers of the said caveats fail to prosecute according to this order, the register or recorder of the said caveat or caveats shall put a vacat upon the said caveat or caveats which shall be invalid or or void to charge the said lots, lands, and accommodations aforesaid.

DISORDER IN COURT.

It is ordered by this court that whosoever doth disorderly speak privately during the sitting of the court, with his neighbor, or two or three together, shall presently pay twelve pence, if the court so think meet.

SECRETS IN COURT.

It is ordered and decreed, that whatsoever member of the General Court shall reveal any secret which the court enjoins to be kept secret, or shall make known to any person what any one member of the court speaks concerning any person or businesses that may come into agitation in the court, shall forfeit for every such fault ten pounds, and be otherwise dealt withal at the discretion of the court. And the secretary is to read this order at the beginning of every General Court.

CHILDREN.

Forasmuch as the good education of children is of singular behoof and benefit to any commonwealth, and whereas many parents and masters are too indulgent and negligent of their duty in that kind:

It is therefore ordered by this court and authority thereof, that the selectmen of every town, in the several precincts and quarters where they dwell, shall have a vigilant eye over their brethren and neighbors, to see first, that none of them shall suffer so much barbarism in any of their families as not to endeavor to teach by themselves or others their children and apprentices so much learning as may enable them perfectly to read the English tongue, and knowledge of the capital laws, upon penalty of twenty shillings for each neglect therein; also, that all masters of families do once a week at least, catechise their children and servants in the grounds and principles of religion; and if any be unable to do so much, that then at the least they procure such children and apprentices to learn some short orthodox catechism, without book, that they may be able to answer to the questions that shall be propounded to them out of such catechisms by their parents or masters or any of the selectmen, when they shall call them to a trial of what they have learned in this kind.

And further, that all parents and masters do breed and bring up their children and apprentices in some some honest lawful calling, labor, or employment, either in husbandry, or some other trade profitable for themselves and the commonwealth, if they will not nor cannot train them up in learning to fit them for higher employments. And if any of the selectmen, after admonition by them given to such masters of families, shall find them still negligent of their duty in the particulars aforementioned, whereby children and servants become rude, stubborn, and unruly, the said selectmen, with the help of two magistrates, shall take such children or apprentices from them and place them with some masters for years, boys till they come to twenty-one and girls to eighteen years of age complete, which will more strictly look unto, and force them to submit unto government, according to the rules of this order, if by fair means and former instructions they will not be drawn unto it.

CONSTABLES.

It is further ordered by the authority aforesaid, that any person tendered to any constable of this jurisdiction by any constable or other officer belonging to any foreign jurisdiction in this country, or by warrant from any such authority, such shall presently be received and conveyed forthwith from constable to constable, till they shall be brought unto the place to which they are sent, or before some magistrate of this jurisdiction, who shall dispose of them as the justice of the cause shall require; and that all hue and cries shall be duly received and diligently pursued to full effect.

It is ordered by the authority of this court, that every constable within our jurisdiction shall henceforth have full power to make, sign and put forth pursuits, or hue and cries, after murderers, malefactors, peacebreakers, thieves, robbers, burglarers and other capital offenders, where no magistrate is near hand. Also to apprehend without warrant such as are overtaken with drink, swearing, Sabbath breaking, slighting of the ordinances, lying, vagrant persons, night walkers, or any other that shall offend in any of these, provided they be taken in the manner, either by sight of the constable or by present information from others: as also to make search for all such persons either on the Sabbath day or other, when there shall be occasion, in all houses licensed to sell either beer or wine, or in any other suspected or disordered places, and those to apprehend and keep in safe custody, till opportunity serves to bring them before one of the next magistrates for further examination; provided that when any constable is employed by any of the magistrates for apprehending of any person, he shall not do it without warrant in writing; and if any person shall refuse to assist any constable in the execution of his office in any of the things aforementioned, being by him required thereto, they shall pay for neglect thereof ten shillings to the use of the country, to be levied by warrant from any magistrate before whom any such offender shall be brought; and if it appear by good testimony that any shall wilfully, obstinately, or contemptuously refuse or neglect to assist any constable, as is before expressed, he shall pay to the use of the country forty shillings; and if any magistrate or constable, or any other upon urgent occasions shall refuse to do their best endeavor in raising and prosecuting hue and cries, by foot, and if need be by horse, after such as have committed capital crimes, they shall forfeit to the use aforesaid for every such offence, forty shillings.

And it is also ordered, that the constables in each town shall be chosen from year to year before the first of March, and sworn to that office, the next court following, or by some magistrate or magistrates.

CONVEYANCES FRAUDULENT.

It is ordered by this court and authority thereof, that all covenous or fraudulent alienations or conveyances of land, tenements or any hereditaments, shall be of no validity to defeat any man from due debts or legacies, or from any just title, claim or possession of that which is so fraudulently conveyed, and that no conveyance, deed or promise whatsoever shall be of validity, if it be gotten by illegal violence, imprisonment, threatening, or any kind of forcible compulsion called duress.

CRUELTY.

It is ordered by this court and authority thereof, that no man shall exercise any tyranny or cruelty towards any brute creatures which are usually kept for the use of man.

DAMAGES PRETENDED.

It is ordered by this court, that no man in any suit or action against another shall falsely pretend great damages or debts, to vex his adversary; and if it shall appear any doth so, the court shall have the power to set a reasonable fine on his head.

DEATH UNTIMELY.

It is ordered by this court and authority thereof, that whensoever any person shall come to any very sudden, untimely, or unnatural death, some magistrate or the constable of that town shall forthwith summon a jury of six or twelve discreet men to inquire of the cause and manner of their death, who shall present a true verdict thereof unto some near magistrate upon their oath.

DELINQUENTS.

It is ordered, that all persons hereafter committed upon delinquency, shall bear the charges the country shall be at in the prosecution of them; and shall pay to the master of the prison or house of correction, two shillings six pence, before he be freed therefrom. Vide *Execution upon Delinquents.*

ECCLESIASTICAL.

Forasmuch as the open contempt of God's word, and messengers thereof, is the desolating sin of civil states and churches, and that the preaching of the word by those whom God doth send is the chief ordinary means ordained by God for the converting, edifying, and saving the souls of the elect, through the presence and power of the Holy Ghost thereunto promised; and that the ministry of the word is set up by God in his churches for those holy ends, and according to the respect or contempt of the same and of those whom God hath set apart for his own work and employment, the weal or woe of all Christian states is much furthered and promoted;—

It is therefore ordered and decreed, that if any Christian (so called) within this jurisdiction shall contemptuously behave himself towards the word preached or the messenger thereof called to dispense the same in any congregation, when he faithfully execute his service and office therein according to the will and word of God, either by interrupting him in his preaching, or by charging him falsely with an error which he hath not taught in the open face of the church, or like a son of Korah cast upon his true doctrine or himself any reproach, to the dishonor of the Lord Jesus who hath sent him, and to the disparagement of that his holy ordinance, and making God's ways contemptible or ridiculous, that every such person or persons (whatsoever censure the church may pass,) shall for the first scandal, be convented and reproved openly by the magistrate, at some lecture, and bound to their good behavior: and if a second time they break forth into the like contemptuous carriages, they shall either pay five pounds to the public treasure, or stand two hours openly upon a block or stool four foot high, upon a lecture day, with a paper fixed on his breast written with capital letters, AN OPEN AND OBSTINATE CONTEMNER OF GOD'S HOLY ORDINANCES, that others may fear and be ashamed of breaking out into the like wickedness.*

* Copied (with the preamble) from the Massachusetts law of Nov. 1646, with the substitution of "AN OPEN AND OBSTINATE CONTEMNER" &c., for "A WANTON GOSPELLER." (Mass. Rec., ii. 179.)

It is ordered and decreed by this court and authority thereof, that wheresoever the ministry of the word is established according to the order of the Gospel, throughout this jurisdiction, every person shall duly resort and attend thereunto respectively upon the Lord's day and upon such public fast days and days of Thanksgiving as are to be generally kept by the appointment of authority. And if any person within this jurisdiction shall without just and necessary cause withdraw himself from hearing the public ministry of the word, after due means of conviction used, he shall forfeit for his absence from every such public meeeting, five shillings: all such offences to be heard and determined by any one magistrate or more, from time to time.

Forasmuch as the peace and prosperity of churches and members thereof, as well as civil rights and liberties, are carefuly to be maintained,—It is ordered by this court and decreed, that the civil authority here established hath power and liberty to see the peace, ordinances and rules of Christ be observed in every church according to his word; as also to deal with any church member in a way of civil justice, notwithstanding any church relation, office, or interest, so it be done in a civil and not in an ecclesiastical way: nor shall any church censure degrade or depose any man from any civil dignity, office, or authority he shall have in the commonwealth.

ESCHEATS.

It is ordered by this court and authority thereof, that where no heir or owner of houses, lands, tenements, goods or chattels can be found, they shall be seized to the public treasury till such heirs or owners shall make due claim thereunto, unto whom they shall be restored upon just and reasonable terms.

EXECUTIONS.

Whereas by reason of the great scarcity of money, execution being taken of several persons' goods that have been sold at very cheap rates, to the extreme damage of the debtor;

It is therefore ordered, that whatsoever execution shall be granted upon any debts made after the publishing of this order, the creditor shall make choice of one party, the debtor of a second, and the court of a third, who shall prize the goods so taken upon execution aforesaid, and deliver them to the creditor.

EXECUTION UPON DELINQUENTS.

It is ordered, that the Governor or any other magistrate in this jurisdiction shall have liberty and power to call forth any person that has been publicly corrected for any misbehavior, to do execution upon any person or persons, by whipping or otherwise, and that at any time hereafter as occasion doth require; and in case of defect or want of such, any other person, as he or they shall think meet.

FENCES.

For the preventing of differences that may arise in making or setting down of fences as well in meadows as upland,—

It is ordered, that in the setting of posts and rails or hedges in the meadow and homelots, there shall be a liberty for either party of twelve inches from the divident line, for breaking of the ground to set the posts on [*or*] for the laying on the hedge; but the stakes and posts are to be set in the divident line; and in upland there is allowed a liberty of four foot for a ditch from the divident line for either of the bordering parties where the proportion of fences belong unto them.*

FINES.

It is ordered by this court, that the estreats for the levying of fines shall go forth once every year, both in the towns on the River and by the seaside, and that some officer in each place shall be appointed to levy and receive the same, and the accounts to be given in by the several plantations of their general charge, at the court in September, for the perfecting of the accounts betwixt them. Mr. Ludlow is desired to grant out warrants for the fines by the seaside.

FIRE.

It is ordered by this court and the authority thereof, that whosoever shall kindle any fire, in woods [or] grounds lying in common or inclosed, so as the same shall run into such common grounds or inclosures, before the tenth of the first month,† or after the last of the second month, or on the last day of the week, or on the Lord's day, shall pay all damages, and half so much for a fine; or if not able to pay, then to be corporally punished, by a warrant from one magistrate or more, as the offence shall deserve, not exceeding twenty stripes for one offence; provided, that any man may kindle fire upon his own ground at any time, so as no damage come thereby, either to the country or to any

* Enacted, June 3d, 1644. The accidental substitution of *on* for *or*, made in transcribing this order from the original record, was followed in the printed revision of 1673.

† The first month was March. The new year began, March 25th.

particular person. And whosoever shall wittingly and willingly burn or destroy any frame, timber hewn, sawn, or riven, heaps of wood, charcoal, corn, hay, straw, hemp, flax, pitch or tar, he shall pay double damages.

FORGERY.

It is ordered by this court and authority thereof, that if any person shall forge any debt * or conveyance, testament, bond, bill, release, acquittance, letter of attorney, or any writing to prevent equity and justice, he shall stand in the pillory three several lecture days, and render double damages to the party wronged, and also be disabled to give any evidence or verdict to any court or magistrate.

FORNICATION.

It is ordered by this court and authority thereof, that if any man shall commit fornication with any single woman, they shall be punished either by enjoining to marriage, or fine, or corporal punishment, or all or any of these, as the court or magistrates shall appoint, most agreeable to the word of God.

GAMING.

Upon complaint of great disorder by the use of the game called Shuffle-board, in houses of common entertainment, whereby much precious time is spent unfruitfully, and much waste of wine and beer occasioned,—

It is therefore ordered and enacted by the authority of this court, that no person shall henceforth use the

* "*Debt*" for "*deed.*" See Massachusetts Act of 1648 (ii. 181), from which this is copied.

said game of shuffle-board, in any such house, nor in any other house used as common for such purpose, upon pain for every keeper of such house to forfeit for every such offence twenty shillings; and for every person playing at the said game in any such house to forfeit for every such offence, five shillings. The like penalty shall be for playing in any place at any unlawful game.

GUARDS AT MEETING.

It is ordered by this court, that there shall be a guard of twenty men, every Sabbath and lecture day, complete in their arms, in each several town upon the river; and at Seabrooke and Farmington, eight apiece; each town upon the seaside in this jurisdiction, ten; and as the number of men increase in the towns, their guards are to increase.

And it is further ordered, that each man in the guards aforesaid shall be allowed half a pound of powder yearly, by their several towns.

HIGHWAYS.

Whereas the maintaining of highways in a fit posture for passage according to the several occasions that occur, is not only necessary for the comfort and safety of man and beast, but tends to the profit and advantage of any people in the issue,—

It is thought fit and ordered, that each town within this jurisdiction shall every year choose one or two of their inhabitants as surveyors, to take care of, and oversee the mending and repairing of the highways within their several towns respectively, who have hereby power allowed them to call out the several carts or persons fit for labor in each town, two days at least in each year, and so many more as in his or their judgments shall be found necessary for the attaining of the aforementioned end, to be directed in their work by the said surveyor or surveyors, and it is left to his or their liberties either to require the labor of the several persons in any family, or of a team and one person, where such are, as he finds most advantageous to the public occasions, he or they giving at least three days' notice or warning beforehand of such employment; and if any refuse or neglect to attend the service in any manner aforesaid, he shall forfeit for every day's neglect of a man's work, two shillings sixpence, and of a team, six shillings, which said fines shall be employed by the surveyors to hire others to work in the said ways; And the surveyors shall, within four days after the several days appointed for work, deliver in to some magistrate a true presentment of all such as have been defective, with their several neglects, who are immediately to grant a distress to the marshal or constable, for the levying of the incurred forfeiture, by them to be delivered to the surveyors for the use aforesaid. And if the surveyor neglect to perform the service hereby committed to him, either in not calling out all the inhabitants in their several proportions as before, or shall not return the names of those that are deficient, he shall incur the same penalty as those whom he so passes by are liable to by virtue of this order, which shall be employed to the use aforesaid, and to be levied also by distress upon information and proof before any one magistrate.

IDLENESS.

It is ordered by this court and authority thereof, that no person, householder or other, shall spend his time idly or unprofitably, under pain of such punishment as the court shall think meet to inflict: and for this end, It is ordered, that the constable of every place shall use special care and diligence to take knowledge of offenders in this kind, especially of common coasters, unprofitable fowlers, and tobacco takers, and present the same unto any magistrate, who shall have power to hear and determine the case or transfer it to the next court.

INDIANS.

It is ordered and decreed, that where any company of Indians do sit down near any English plantations, that they shall declare who is their sachem or chief, and that the said chief or sachem shall pay to the said English such trespasses as shall be committed by any Indian in the said plantation adjoining, either by spoiling or killing any cattle or swine, either with traps, dogs, or arrows: and they are not to plead that it was done by strangers, unless they can produce the party and deliver him or his goods into the custody of the English: and they shall pay the double damage if it were done voluntarily. The like engagement this court also makes to them in case of wrong or injury done to them by the English, which shall be paid by the party by whom it was done, if he can be made to appear, or otherwise by the town in whose limits such facts are committed.

Forasmuch as our lenity and gentleness towards Indians hath made them grow bold and insolent, to enter into Englishmen's houses, and unadvisedly handle swords and pieces and other instruments, many times to the hazard of limbs or lives of English or Indians, and also oft steal divers goods out of such houses where they resort; for the preventing whereof, It is ordered, that whatsoever Indian shall hereafter meddle with or handle any Englishman's weapons, of any sort, either in their houses or in the fields, they shall forfeit for every such default half a fathom of wampum; and if any hurt or injury shall thereupon follow to any person's life or limb, (though accidental,) they shall pay life for life, limb for limb, wound for wound, and shall pay for the healing such wounds and other damages. And for anything they steal, they shall pay double, and suffer such further punishment as the magistrates shall adjudge them. The constable of any town may attach and arrest any Indian that shall transgress in any such kind beforementioned; and bring them before some magistrate, who may execute the penalty of this order upon offenders in any kind except life or limb; and any person that doth see such defaults may prosecute, and shall have half the forfeiture.

It is ordered by this court and authority thereof, that no man within this jurisdiction shall, directly or indirectly, amend, repair, or cause to be amended or repaired, any gun, small or great, belonging to any Indian, nor shall endeavor the same; nor shall sell nor give to any Indian, directly or indirectly, any such gun, nor any gunpowder, or shot, or lead, or shot mould, or any military weapon or weapons, armor, or arrow heads; nor sell, nor barter, nor give, any dog or dogs, small or great; upon pain of ten pounds fine for every offence, at least, in any one of the aforementioned particulars; and the court shall have power to increase the fine, or to impose corporal punishment where a fine cannot be had, at their discretion.

And it is also ordered, that no person nor persons shall trade with them at or about their wigwams, but in their vessels or pinnaces, or at their own houses, under penalty of twenty shillings for each default.

Whereas, it doth appear that notwithstanding the former laws made against selling guns and powder to Indians, they are yet supplied by indirect means, it is therefore ordered and declared, that if any person after publishing of this order shall sell, barter or transport any guns, powder, bullets or lead, to any person inhabiting out of this jurisdiction, without license of this court or from some two magistrates, he shall forfeit for every gun ten pounds, for every pound of gunpowder five pounds, for every pound of bullets or lead forty shillings, and so proportionably for any greater or lesser quantity; provided notwithstanding, that it is left to the judgment of the court, that where any offence is committed against the said order, either to aggravate or lessen the penalty, according as the nature of the offence shall require.

Whereas divers persons depart from amongst us, and take up their abode with the Indians, in a profane course of life; for the preventing whereof,

It is ordered that whatsoever person or persons that now inhabiteth, or shall inhabit within this jurisdiction, and shall depart from us and settle or join with the Indians, that they shall suffer three years' imprisonment at least, in the house of correction, and undergo such further censure, by fine or corporal punishment, as the particular court shall judge meet to inflict in such cases.

Whereas the French, Dutch, and other foreign nations do ordinarily trade guns, powder, shot, etc. with the Indians, to our great prejudice, and the strengthening and animating of the Indians against us, as by daily experience we find; and whereas the aforesaid French, Dutch, etc. do prohibit all trade with the Indians within their respective jurisdictions under penalty of confiscation;

It is therefore hereby ordered by this court and authority thereof, that after due publication hereof, it shall not be lawful for any Frenchmen, Dutchmen, or person of any other foreign nation, or any English living amongst them or under the government of them, or any of them, to trade with any Indian or Indians within the limits of this jurisdiction, either directly or indirectly, by themselves or others, under penalty of confiscation of all such goods and vessels as shall be found so trading, or the due value thereof, upon just proof made of any goods or any vessels so trading or traded: and it shall be lawful for any person or persons inhabiting within this jurisdiction, to make seizure of any such goods or vessels trading with the Indians as by this law is prohibited, the one half whereof shall be to the proper use and benefit of the party seizing, and the other to the public.*

This court, judging it necessary that some means should be used to convey the light and knowledge of God and of his word to the Indians and Natives amongst us, do order that one of the teaching Elders of the churches in this jurisdiction, with the help of Thomas Stanton, shall be desired, twice at least in every year, to go amongst the neighboring Indians and endeavour to make known to them the counsels of the Lord, and thereby to draw and stir them up to direct and order all their ways and conversations according to the rule of his word: and Mr. Governor

*Passed, Sept. 18th, 1649, upon the recommendation of the Commissioners of the U. Colonies of New England. Col. Rec., i. 197.

and Mr. Deputy and the other magistrates are desired to take care to seo the thing attended, and with their own presence, so far as may be convenient, encourage the same.

This court having duly weighed the joint determination and argument of the Commissioners of the United English Colonies at New Haven, in Anno 1646, in reference to the Indians, and judging it to be both according to rules of prudence and righteousness, do fully assent thereunto, and order that it be recorded amongst the acts of this court, and attended in future practice as occasions may present and require. The said conclusion is as followeth:—

The Commissioners seriously considering the many wilful wrongs and hostile practices of the Indians against the English, together with their entertaining, protecting, and rescuing of offenders, as late our experience sheweth, (which if suffered, the peace of the Colonies cannot be secured,) it is therefore concluded, that in such cases the magistrates of any of the jurisdictions may, at the charge of the plaintiff, send some convenient strength of English, and according to the nature and value of the offence and damage, seize and bring away any of that plantation of Indians that shall entertain, protect, or rescue the offender, though it should be in another jurisdiction, when through distance of place, commission or direction cannot be had, after notice and due warning given them, as actors, or at least accessory to the injury and damage done to the English: only women and children to be sparingly seized, unless known to be some way guilty. And because it will be chargeable keeping Indians in prison, and if they should escape they are like to prove more insolent and dangerous after, it was thought fit that upon such seizure, the delinquent or satisfaction be again demanded of the Sagamore or plantation of Indians guilty or accessory as before; and if it be denied, that then the magistrates of the jurisdiction deliver up the Indian seized to the party or parties endamaged, either to serve or to be shipped out and exchanged for negroes, as the case will justly bear. And though the Commissioners foresee that such severe though just proceeding may provoke the Indians to an unjust seizing of some of ours, yet they could not at present find no better means to preserve the peace of the colonies, all the aforementioned outrages and insolences tending to an open war: only they thought fit that before any such seizure be made in any plantation of Indians, the ensuing declaration be published, and a copy given to the particular Sagamores:—

The Commissioners for the United Colonies, considering how peace with righteousness may be preserved betwixt all the English and the several plantations of the Indians, thought fit to declare and publish, as they will do no injury to them, so if any Indian or Indians, of what plantation soever, do any wilful damage to any of the English Colonies, upon proof, they will in a peaceable way require just satisfaction, according to the nature of the offence and damage. But if any Sagamore or plantation of Indians, after notice and due warnings, entertain, hide, protect, keep, convey away or further the escape of any such offender or offenders, the English will require satisfaction of such Indian and Sagamore, or Indian plantation; and if they deny it, they will right themselves as they may upon such as so maintain them that do wrong, keeping peace and all terms of amity and agreement with all other Indians.

INNKEEPERS.

Forasmuch as there is a necessary use of houses of common entertainment in every commonwealth, and of such as retail wine, beer and victuals, yet because there are so many abuses of that lawful liberty, both by persons entertaining and persons entertained, there is also need of strict laws and rules to regulate such an employment;

It is therefore ordered by this court and authority thereof, that no person or persons licensed for common entertainment shall suffer any to be drunken or drink excessively, viz: above half a pint of wine for one person at one time, or to continue tippling above the space of half an hour, or at unseasonable times, or after nine of the clock at night, in or about any of their houses, on penalty of five shillings for every such offence. And every person found drunken, viz: so that he be thereby bereaved or disabled in the use of his understanding, appearing in his speech or gesture, in any of the said houses or elsewhere, shall forfeit ten shillings; and for excessive drinking, three shillings four pence; and for continuing above half an hour tippling, two shillings six pence; and for tippling at unseasonable times or after nine a clock at night, five shillings, for every offence in these particulars, being lawfully convicted thereof; and for want of payment, such shall be imprisoned until they pay, or be set in the stocks, one hour or more, in some open place, as the weather will permit, not exceeding three hours at one time: provided notwithstanding, such licensed persons may entertain seafaring men or land travellers in the night-season when they come first on shore, or from their journey, for their necessary refreshment, or when they prepare for their voyage or journey the next day early, if there be no disorder amongst them; and also strangers and other persons in an orderly way may continue in such houses of common entertainment during meal times or upon lawful business, what time their occasions shall require.*

And it is also ordered that if any person offend in drunkenness, excessive or long drinking, the second time, they shall pay double fines: and if they fall into the same offence the third time, they shall pay treble fines: and if the parties be not able to pay their fines, then he that is found drunk shall be punished by whipping to the number of ten stripes, and he that offends by excessive or long drinking, shall be put into the stocks for three hours, when the weather may not hazard his life or limbs; and if they offend the fourth time they shall be imprisoned until they put in two sufficient sureties for their good behavior.

And it is further ordered, that the several towns upon the River within this jurisdiction, shall provide amongst themselves in each town, one sufficient inhabitant to keep an Ordinary, for provision and lodging in some comfortable manner, that passengers or strangers may know where to resort. And such inhabitants as by the several towns shall be chosen for the said service shall be presented to two magistrates, that they may be judged meet for that employment. And this to be effected by the several towns within one

* Some of the provisions of this section were included, in substance, in an Order of May 25th, 1647. Compare Mass. law of Nov. 1646 (ii. 172). The English statute of 4 James I. (chap. 5, § 4.) imposed a penalty on every person continuing drinking or tippling in inns, victualling-houses or ale-houses.

month, under the penalty of forty shillings a month for each month that either town shall neglect the same.*

And it is also further ordered, that every innkeeper or victualler shall provide for entertainment of strangers' horses, viz: one or more inclosures for summer, and hay or provender for winter, with convenient stable room and attendance, under penalty of two shillings sixpence for every day's default and double damage to the party thereby wronged, except it be by inevitable accident.

Lastly, it is ordered by the authority aforesaid, that all constables may and shall, from time to time, duly makes search throughout the limits of their towns, upon Lord's days and Lecture days, in times of exercise, and also at other times so oft as they shall see cause, for all offences and offenders against this law in any the particulars thereof: and if upon due information or complaint of any of their inhabitants or other credible persons, whether taverner, victualler, tabler, or other, they shall refuse to make search as aforesaid, or shall not to their power perform all other things belonging to their place or office of constableship, then upon complaint and due proof before any one magistrate, within three months after such refusal or neglect, they shall be fined for every such offence ten shillings, to be levied by the marshal as in other cases, by warrant from such magistrate before whom they are convicted, or warrant from the treasurer upon notice from such magistrate.

It is ordered by this court and authority thereof, that no innkeeper, victualler, wine-drawer, or other,

* Ordered, June 3d, 1644. Col. Rec., i. 103.

shall deliver any wine, nor suffer any to be delivered out of his house, to any which come for it, unless they bring a note under the hand of some one master of some family and allowed inhabitant of that town; neither shall any of them sell or draw any hot water to any but in case of necessity, and in such moderation for quantity as they may have good grounds to conceive it may not be abused; and shall be ready to give an account of their doings herein, when they are called thereto, under censure of the court in case of delinquency.

INDICTMENTS.

If any person shall be indicted of any capital crime (who is not then in durance,) and shall refuse to render his person to some magistrate within one month after three proclamations publicly made in the town where he usually abides, there being a month betwixt proclamation and proclamation, his lands and goods shall be seized to the use of the common treasury, till he make his lawful appearance, and such withdrawing of himself shall stand instead of one witness to prove his crime, unless he can make it appear to the court that he was necessarily hindered.

JURIES AND JURORS.

It is ordered by the authority of this court, that in all cases which are entered under forty shillings, the suit shall be left to be tried by the court of magistrates as they shall judge most agreeable to equity and righteousness. And in all cases that are tried by juries, it is left to the magistrates to impanel a jury of six or twelve, as they shall judge the nature of the case shall require; and if four of six, or eight of twelve, agree, the verdict shall be deemed to all intents and

and purposes sufficient and full; upon which judgment may be entered and execution granted, as if they had all concurred; but if it fall out that there be not such a concurrence as is before mentioned, the jurors shall return the case to the court with their reasons, and a special verdict is to be drawn thereupon, and the vote of the greater number of magistrates shall carry the same; and the judgment to be entered and other proceedings as in case of a verdict by a jury.

And it is further ordered, that the court of magistrates shall have liberty (if they do not find in their judgments, the jury to have attended the evidence given in, and true issue of the case, in their verdict,) to cause them to return to a second consideration thereof; and if they still persist in their former opinion, to the dissatisfaction of the court, it shall be in the power of the court to impanel another jury, and commit the consideration of the case to them. And it is also left in the power of the court to vary and alter the damages given in by any jury, as they shall judge most equal and righteous, provided, that what alteration shall at any time be made in that kind, be done in open court, before plaintiff and defendant, or affidavit made that they have been required to be present, and that alteration which is made be done either the same court, or provision madé to secure the verdict of the jury until the case be fully issued. And whereas many persons, after their several causes in court have been tried and issued, have slipped away or otherwise neglected, if not refused, to pay the charges of the court, according to order; for preventing thereof for the future, It is ordered, that whosoever shall have any action or suit in court, after the publishing hereof, shall, as soon as his cause is issued pay the whole charges of the court, that concerns either jury or secretary, before he departs the same. And the like also shall be done by all those whose actions are not taken up, and withdrawn before the sitting of the court wherein they were to be tried; or otherwise, for neglect or non-performance of either, be committed to prison, there to remain till he or they have satisfied the same.

GRAND JURY.

It is ordered and decreed, that there shall be a grand jury of twelve or fourteen able men warned to appear every court yearly, in September, or as many and oft as the governor or court shall think meet, to make presentment of the breaches of any laws or orders or any other misdemeanors they shall know of in this jurisdiction.*

LANDS; FREE LANDS.

It is ordered, and by this court declared, that our lands and heritages shall be free from all fines and licenses upon alienations, and from all harriots, wardships, liveries, primer seisins, year, day, and waste, escheats and forfeitures upon the death of parents or ancestors, be they natural, unnatural, casual or judicial, and that for ever.†

LEVIES.

Forasmuch as the marshals and other officers have complained to this court that they are oftentimes in great doubt how to demean themselves in the execution of their offices;

It is ordered by the authority of this court, that in case of fines and assessments to be levied, and upon

* July 5th, 1643. Col. Rec., i. 91.

† Massachusetts Body of Liberties, § 10.

execution in civil actions, the officer shall demand the same of the party or at his house and place of usual abode; and upon refusal or non-payment, he shall have power (calling the constable, if he see cause for his assistance) to break open the door of any house, chest, or place where he shall have notice that any goods liable to such levy or execution shall be; and if he be to take the person, he may do the like, if upon demand he shall refuse to render himself; and whatsoever charges the officer shall necessarily be put unto, upon any such occasion, he shall have power to levy the same as he doth the debt, fine, or execution; and if the officer shall levy any such goods upon execution as cannot be conveyed to the place where the party dwells for whom such execution shall be levied, without considerable charge, he shall levy the said charge, also with the execution. The like order shall be observed in levying of fines; provided, it shall not be lawful for such officer to levy any man's necessary bedding, apparel, tools, or arms, neither implements of household which are for the necessary upholding of his life; but in such cases he shall levy his land or person, according to law; and in no case shall the officer be put to seek out any man's estate further than his place of abode; but if the party will not discover his goods or land, the officer may take his person. And it is also ordered and declared, that if any officer shall do injury to any, by color of his office, in these or any other cases, he shall be liable upon complaint of the party wronged, by action or information, to make full restitution. *See* MARSHAL.

LYING.

Whereas truth in words as well as in actions is

required of all men, especially of Christians who are the professed servants of the God of Truth; and whereas all lying is contrary to truth, and some sorts of lies are not only sinful (as all lies are), but also pernicious to the public weal and injurious to particular persons;

It is therefore ordered by this court and authority thereof, that every person of the age of discretion, which is accounted fourteen years, who shall wittingly and willingly make or publish any lie which may be pernicious to the public weal, or tending to the damage or injury of any particular person, [or with intent] to deceive and abuse the people with false news or reports, and the same duly proved in any court or before any one magistrate, who hath hereby power granted to hear and determine all offences against this law, such persons shall be fined for the first offence ten shillings, or if the party be unable to pay the same, then to be set in the stocks, so long as the said court or magistrate shall appoint, in some open place, not exceeding three hours; for the second offence in that kind, whereof any shall be legally convicted, the sum of twenty shillings, or be whipped upon the naked body not exceeding twenty stripes; and for the third offence that way, forty shillings, or if the party be unable to pay, then to be whipped with more stripes not exceeding thirty, And if yet any shall offend in like kind and be legally convicted thereof, such person, male or female, shall be fined ten shillings at a time more than formerly, or if the party so offending be unable to pay, then to be whipped with five or six stripes more than formerly, not exceeding forty at any time. And for all such as being under age of discretion, that shall offend in lying, contrary to this order, their parents or masters shall give them due correction, and that in the presence of some officer, if any magistrate shall so appoint. Provided also, that no person shall be barred of his just action of slander or otherwise, by any proceeding upon this order.*

MASTERS, SERVANTS, SOJOURNERS.

It is ordered by this court and authority thereof, that no master of a family shall give entertainment or habitation to any young man to sojourn in his family, but by the allowance of the inhabitants of the town where he dwells, under the penalty of twenty shillings per week. And it is also ordered, that no young man that is neither married nor hath any servant, nor is a public officer, shall keep house of himself without the consent of the town for and under pain or penalty of twenty shillings a week.†

It is also ordered by the authority aforesaid, that no servant, either man or maid, shall either give, sell or truck, any commodity whatsoever, without license from their master, during the time of their service, under pain of fine or corporal punishment at the discretion of the court, as the offence shall deserve. And that all workmen shall work the whole day, allowing convenient time for food and rest.

It is also ordered, that when any servants shall run from their masters, or any other inhabitants shall privately go away with suspicion of ill intentions, it shall be lawful for the next magistrate, or the con-

---

* Copied (with the preamble) from the Massachusetts law of 1645. (Mass. Rec., ii. 104.)

† Feb. 21st 1637. Col. Records, i. 8. The words 'for and,' in the line before the last, were probably substituted for 'first had,' by an error of the compiler, or recorder, of the code of 1650.

stable and two of the chiefest inhabitants, where no magistrate is, to press men and boats or pinnaces, at the public charge, to pursue such persons by sea or land, and bring them back by force of arms.

And whereas many stubborn, refractory and discontented servants and apprentices, withdraw themselves from their masters' services to improve their time to their own advantage; for the preventing whereof, It is ordered, that whatsoever servant or apprentice shall hereafter offend in that kind, before their covenants or term of service are expired, shall serve their said masters, as they shall be apprehended or retained, the treble term or threefold time of their absence in such kind.*

MANSLAUGHTER.

It is ordered by this court and authority thereof, that if any person in the just and necessary defence of his life, or the life of any other, shall kill any person attempting to rob or murder in the field or highway, or to break into any dwelling house, if he conceive he cannot with safety of his own person otherwise take the felon or assailant, or bring him to trial, he shall be holden blameless.†

MAGISTRATES.

This court being sensible of the great disorder growing in this commonwealth, through the contempts cast upon the civil authority, which willing to prevent, doth order and decree :—

That whosoever shall henceforth openly or willingly defame any court of justice, or the sentences and pro-

* June, 1644. Col. Rec., i. 105.

† Mass. Records, ii. 212 (1647).

ceedings of the same, or any of the magistrates or judges of any such court, in respect of any act or sentence therein passed, and being thereof lawfully convicted in any general court, or court of magistrates, shall be punished for the same by fine, imprisonment, disfranchisement or banishment, as the quality and measure of the offence shall deserve.

MARRIAGE.

Forasmuch as many persons intangle themselves by rash and inconsiderate contracts for their future joining in marriage covenant, to the great trouble and grief of themselves and their friends; for the preventing thereof,

It is ordered by the authority of this court, that whosoever intends to join themselves in marriage covenant shall cause their purpose of contract to be published in some public place and at some public meeting, in the several towns where such persons dwell, at the least eight days before they enter into such contract whereby they engage themselves each to other, and that they shall forbear to join in marriage covenant at least eight days after the said contract.*

And it is also ordered and declared, that no person whatsoever, male or female, not being at his or her own dispose, or that remaineth under the government of parents, masters or guardians, or such like, shall either make, or give entertainment to, any motion or suit in way of marriage, without the knowledge and consent of those they stand in such relation to, under the severe censure of the court in case of delinquency, not attending this order; nor shall any third

* Enacted April, 10th, 1640. Col. Rec., i. 47, 48.

person or persons intermeddle in making any motion to any such, without the knowledge and consent of those under whose government they are, under the same penalty.*

MARRIAGES AND BIRTHS; *See* RECORDS.

MARSHAL.

It is ordered by this court, that the marshal shall be allowed for every execution he serves which is under the sum of five pounds, two shillings six pence, and four pence for every mile he goes to serve the said execution out of the town where he liveth: And for every execution he serves of or above five pounds and under the sum of ten pounds, he shall be allowed three shillings four pence, and four pence for every mile, as before: And for every execution he serves of or above the sum of ten pounds, he shall be allowed five shillings, and four pence for every mile as before. Also he is to be allowed his other just and necessary charges; only it is provided that if he be excessive therein, upon due complaint and proof made, it shall be redressed. And it is also further ordered that the marshal shall be allowed for every attachment he serves half so much as is before allowed him for executions, only he is is to have four pence for every mile he goes to serve the attachment as before.

It is further ordered by the court and authority thereof, that every officer † that shall at any time be fined for the breach of any penal law or other just cause, such person or persons so offending shall forthwith pay his or their fine or penalty or give in

* July 5th, 1643. Ibid, 92.

† In the printed revision of 1672–3, the word 'person' is substituted for 'officer.'

security speedily to do it, or else shall be imprisoned or kept to work till it be paid, that no loss may come to the commonwealth; and what other fines or debts already due or shall be due to the country, the marshal for the time being, upon warrant from the treasurer, and according to his oath, shall be faithful in doing the duty of his place in levying and returning the same, upon pain of forfeiting two shillings of his own estate for every pound, or else such fine as any court of justice shall impose on him for neglect.

MEASURES AND WEIGHTS.

Forasmuch as it is observed that there are divers of weights, yards, and measures amongst us, whereby damages many times ensueth by commerce with several persons; for the preventing whereof,

It is now ordered, that no man within these liberties, shall, after the publishing of this order, sell any commodities but by sealed weight or measure, under the penalty of twelve pence each default. The clerk is to have a penny for sealing a weight or measure each time; and no weight or measure is to be accounted authentic that is not sealed or approved by the clerk, once every year. The said clerk is to break or demolish such weights, yards, or measures as are defective.

MILITARY AFFAIRS.

It is ordered and by this court declared, that all persons that are above the age of sixteen years, except magistrates and church officers, shall bear arms, unless they have, upon just occasion, exemption granted by the court; and every male person within this jurisdiction above the said age, shall have in continual readiness, a good musket or other gun, fit for service and allowed by the clerk of the band, with a sword, rest, and bandaleers, or other serviceable provision in the room thereof where such cannot be had; as also such other military provision of powder, match, and bullets as the law requires; and if any person who is to provide arms or ammunition cannot purchase them by such means as he hath, he shall bring to the clerk so much corn or other merchantable goods as, by apprizement of the said clerk and two others of the company (whereof one to be chosen by the party) as shall be judged of a greater value by a fifth part than such arms or ammunition is of, he shall be excused of the penalty for want of arms (but not for want of appearance) until he be provided. And the clerk shall endeavor to furnish him so soon as may be by sale of such goods so deposited, rendering the overplus to the party. But if any person shall not be able to provide himself arms or ammunition through mere poverty, if he be single he shall be put to service by some magistrate, and the constable shall appoint him arms and ammunition, and shall appoint him when and with whom to earn it out.

And it is ordered that all the soldiers within this jurisdiction shall be trained at least six times yearly, in the months of March, April, May, September, October, or November, by the appointment of the captain or chief officer in the several towns. And the times of their meeting together shall be at eight of the clock in the morning. And the clerk of each band shall, twice every year at least, view the arms and ammunition of the band, to see if they all be according to law; And shall upon every training day give his attendance in the field, every day, (except he hath special leave from his captain or chief officer,) to call over the roll of the soldiers and take notice of any defect by their absence or otherwise: And he shall duly present to the governor or some of the magistrates, all defects in arms or ammunition, at least once in each year, and oftener if it be required. And it is left to the judgment of the magistrates to punish all defects in that kind according to the nature of the offence, wherein due regard is to be had of wilful neglects in any, that such may not pass without a severe censure. And whosoever shall be absent any of the days appointed for training, after the hour appointed, or shall not continue the whole time, shall forfeit the sum of two shillings six pence for every default, except such as are licensed under the hand of two magistrates. The clerks of the several bands are to distrain the delinquents, within fourteen days after the forfeiture; whereof six pence shall be to himself and the remainder for the maintenance of drums, colors, etc. And if any of the said clerks shall omit to distrain any delinquents, above the said term of fourteen days, he shall forfeit and pay to the use of the public, double the fine so neglected by him.

It is ordered, that the soldiers shall only make choice of their military officers, and present them to the particular court; but such only shall be deemed officers, as the court shall confirm.*

The state and condition of the place where we live, by reason of the Indians, and otherwise, requiring all due means to be used for the preservation of the safety and peace of the same, this court judgeth necessary that there should be a magazine of powder

---

*Enacted, May 25, 1647. The Massachusetts law of May, 1647, gave all *freemen* of the town the right of voting in the choice of military officers. (Mass. Rec., ii. 191.)

and shot provided and maintained in the country, in each town within this jurisdiction; and do therefore order and decree, that there shall be two barrels of powder and six hundred weight of lead provided by this commonwealth, before the general court in September next, which shall be maintained and continued, and accounted as the country stock. And it is also further ordered, that the several towns within this jurisdiction shall provide and maintain as followeth, viz:

Windsor, one barrel and half of powder, four hundred and fifty pound of lead, one hundred fathom of match, nine cotton coats or corselets, and sufficient serviceable pikes to either of them.

Hartford, two barrels of powder, six hundred weight of lead, and six score fathom of match, and twelve cotton coats or corselets, with serviceable pikes to either of them.

Wethersfeild, one barrel of powder, three hundred weight of lead, eighty fathom of match, and eight cotton coats or corselets, with serviceable pikes to either of them.

Seabrooke, half a barrel of powder, one hundred and fifty pound of lead, forty fathom of match, and three cotton coats or corselets, with serviceable pikes to either of them.

Farmington, the same in each particular with Seabrooke.

Fairefeild, and Stratford, in each town, one barrel of powder, three hundred weight of lead, one hundred fathom of match, and six coats or corselets, with serviceable pikes to either of them.

Southampton, and Pequett, in each town, half a barrel of powder, one hundred and fifty pounds of lead, forty fathom of match, with three coats or corselets with serviceable pikes to either of them.

Each town also shall provide so many good firelock muskets and good backswords or cutlasses, as the corselets are they are charged with by this order. All which shall be provided by the several towns by the court in September next, and maintained constantly for the future, upon the penalty of ten shillings per month for each town's defect or neglect herein.

Also it is further ordered, That every male person within this jurisdiction, that is above the age of sixteen years, whether magistrates, ministers, or any other, (though exempted from training, watching, and warding,) shall be always provided with, and have in readness by them, half a pound of powder, two pounds of serviceable bullets or shot, and two fathom of match to every matchlock, upon the penalty of five shillings a month for each person's default herein: provided notwithstanding, that if the proportions of powder laid upon each town and person either doth not at present or shall not (by reason of the increase of their numbers,) for the future, amount in all to three pound of powder for every soldier, then each town shall, upon the former penalty, provide so much more as shall be three pounds of powder for a soldier, and other provision of lead, &c., increase in each town according to the same proportion.

Whereas many inconveniences do appear, by reason that the several soldiers of the trained bands in each town within this jurisdiction have not been allowed some powder upon their training days, for their practice and exercise in their several firings:—

It is ordered by the authority of this court, that there shall be allowed to every soldier in the several trained bands in each town as aforesaid, half a pound of powder a piece for a year, and so from year to year for the future, to be provided by and at the proper costs and charges of the masters and governors of each family unto which the said soldiers do belong, to be called forth, improved, and disposed of, at the discretion of the captain or other principal leaders in each trained band.*

It is also ordered, that the captains, lieutenants, and ensigns shall be freed from watching and warding, and the sergeants from warding and half their watch.

MINISTERS' MAINTENANCE.

Whereas the most considerable persons in these colonies came into these parts of America that they might enjoy Christ in his ordinances, without disturbance; And whereas amongst many other precious mercies the ordinances have been and are dispensed amongst us with much purity and power; this court took it into their serious consideration how due maintenance, according to God, might be provided and settled, both for the present and future, for the encouragement of the ministers who labor therein; And do order, that those who are taught in the word, in the several plantations be called together, that every man voluntarily set down what he is willing to allow to that end and use: And if any man refuse to pay a meet proportion, that then he be rated by Authority in some just and equal way; and if after this any man withhold or delay due payment, the civil power to be exercised, as in other just debts.†

---

* Enacted, July 12, 1648.

† Ordered, Oct. 25th, 1644, upon the recommendation of the Commissioners of the U. Colonies. Col. Rec., i. 112.

OATHS.

[The oaths for the Governor, Magistrates, and Constables, are the same as those printed at the end of the Fundamental Orders, pages 58, 59.]

The Oath of a Freeman.

I, A. B. being by the providence of God an inhabitant within the jurisdiction of Connecticut, do acknowledge myself to be subject to the government thereof, and do swear by the great and fearful name of the everliving God, to be true and faithful unto the same, and do submit both my person and estate thereunto, according to all the wholesome laws and orders that there are or hereafter shall be there made and established by lawful authority, and that I will neither plot nor practice any evil against the same, nor consent to any that shall so do, but will timely discover the same to lawful authority there established; and that I will, as I am in duty bound, maintain the honor of the same and of the lawful magistrates thereof, promoting the public good of it, whilst I shall so continue an inhabitant there; and whensoever I shall give my vote or suffrage touching any matter which concerns this commonwealth, being called thereunto, will give it as in my conscience I shall judge may conduce to the best good of the same, without respect of persons or favor of any man. So help me God in our Lord Jesus Christ.

Oath for the Jury.

You shall swear that you A. B., shall duly try the cause or causes now given you in charge, between the plaintiff and defendant, (or plaintiffs and defendants,) according to your evidence given in court, and accordingly a true verdict give; your own counsel and your fellows' you shall duly keep; you shall speak nothing to any one, of the business and matters in hand, but amongst yourselves, nor shall you suffer any to speak unto you about the same, but in court: when you are agreed of any verdict you shall keep it secret till you deliver it up in court: So help you God.

[The three following were inserted after the adoption of the code, and are in the handwriting of Secretary Clark.]

Commissioner's Oath.

You do swear by the great and dreadful name of the everlasting God, that for this year ensuing and until new be chosen, you shall faithfully execute the place and office you are chosen unto, according to the extent of your commission: So help you God, in the name of the Lord Jesus Christ.

Secretary's Oath.

A. B. You being chosen Secretary for this jurisdiction, during this year, do swear by the great name of God, that you shall keep the secrets of the court and shall carefully execute the place of a Secretary, and shall truly and faithfully record all orders of the court; and (fix the seal unto the orders sent forth to the respective towns, and*) shall deliver true copies and certificates when they shall be necessarily required. So help you God, in our Lord Jesus Christ.

Grand Jury's Oath.

You do swear, by the great and dreadful name of God, that you will with all due care and faithfulness make presentment according to order, at the Quarter Court in September next, such misdemeanors and

* The words in the parenthesis are interlined in the record.

transgressions of the laws and orders of this commonwealth as shall come to your cognizance; as also to do your endeavor to find out such things as are contrary to religion and peace: so help you God, in our Lord Jesus Christ.

PEAG.

It is ordered by this Court and decreed, that no peag, white or black, be paid or received, but what is strung and in some measure strung suitably, and not small and great, uncomely and disorderly mixed, as formerly it hath been.*

POOR.

It is ordered by this Court and authority thereof, that the court of magistrates shall have power to determine all differences about lawful settling and providing for poor persons, and shall have power to dispose of all unsettled persons, into such towns as they shall judge to be most fit for the maintenance and employment of such persons and families for the ease of the country.

POUND; POUND BREACH.

For prevention and due recompense of damage in cornfields and other inclosures done by swine and cattle, It is ordered by this Court and authority thereof, that there shall be one sufficient pound or more made and maintained in every town and village within this

---

* Recommended by the Commissioners of the U. Colonies, and approved by the Gen. Court, March, 1649; Col. Rec., i. 179. "Peag" was a general name for the shell money made by the Indians. The "white" or cheaper sort was called *wampum*, or sometimes *wampum-peag*.

jurisdiction, for the impounding of all such swine and cattle as shall be found in any cornfield or other inclosure: and whosoever impounds any swine or cattle shall give present notice to the owners, if he be known, or otherwise they shall be cried at the two next lectures or markets. And if swine or cattle escape out of the pound, the owner, if known, shall pay all damages, according to law.

And whereas impounding of cattle in case of trespasses hath been always found both needful and profitable, and all the breaches about the same very offensive and injurious:—It is therefore ordered by this Court and authority thereof, that if any person shall resist or rescue any cattle going to the pound, or shall by any way or means convey them out of pound or custody of the law, whereby the party wronged may lose his damage and the law be deluded, that in case of mere rescues, the party offending shall forfeit to the treasury, forty shillings; and in case of pound breach, five pounds; and shall also pay all damages to the party wronged: and if in the rescue any bodily harms be done to the person of any man or other, they shall have remedy against the rescuers: and if either be done by any not of ability to answer the damage and forfeit aforesaid, they shall be [ ] whipped, by warrant from any magistrate before whom the offender is convicted, in the town or plantation where the offence was committed, not exceeding twenty stripes, for the mere rescue or pound breach; and for all damages to the party they shall satisfy by service, as in case of theft: and if it appear there were any procurement of the owners of the cattle thereunto (and that they were abettors,) they shall all pay forfeitures and damages as if themselves had done it.

PROFANE SWEARING.

It is ordered and by this court decreed, that if any person within this jurisdiction shall swear rashly and vainly, either by the holy name of God, or any other oath; [*or*] shall sinfully and wickedly curse any; he shall forfeit to the common treasure, for every such several offence, ten shillings: and it shall be in the power of any magistrate, by warrant to the constable, to call such persons before him, and upon just proof to pass a sentence, and levy the said penalty according to the usual order of justice: And if such persons be not able, or shall utterly refuse to pay the aforesaid fine, he shall be committed to the stocks, there to continue not exceeding three hours and not less than one hour.*

RATES.

It is ordered by this court and authority thereof, that every inhabitant shall henceforth contribute to all charges both in church and commonwealth, whereof he doth or may receive benefit, and every such inhabitant who doth not voluntarily contribute proportionably to his ability with the rest of the same town to all common charges, both civil and ecclesiastical, shall be compelled thereunto by assessments and distress, to be levied by the constable or other officer of the town as in other cases; And that the lands and estates of all men, wherever they dwell, shall be rated for all town charges, both civil and ecclesiastical as aforesaid, where the lands and estates shall lie, and their persons, where they dwell.

For a more equal and ready way of raising means for defraying of public charges in time to come, and for preventing such inconveniences as have fallen out

* Copied from Massachusetts law of Nov., 1646. (Rec. ii. 178.)

upon former assessments,—It is ordered and acted by the authority of this court, that the treasurer for the time being shall, from year to year, in the first month, without expecting any other order, send forth his warrants to the constables of every town within this jurisdiction, requiring the constable to call together the inhabitants of the town, who being so assembled shall choose three or four of their able inhabitants, whereof one to be a commissioner for the town, who shall, some time or times in the sixth month then next ensuing, make a list of all the male persons in the same town from sixteen years old and upwards, and a true estimation of all personal and real estates being (or reputed to be) the estate of all and every the persons in the same town, or otherwise under their custody or managing, according to just valuation, and to what persons the same belong, whether in their own town or other where, so near as they can by all lawful ways and means which they may use, viz: of houses, lands of all sorts, as well unbroken up as other (except such as doth or shall lie common, for free feed of cattle, to the use of the inhabitants in general, whether belonging to the towns or particular persons, but not to be kept or herded upon it to the damage of the proprietors), mills, ships and all small vessels, merchantable goods, cranes, wharves, and all sorts of cattle, and all other known estate whatsoever, as also all visible estate either at sea or on shore; all which persons and estates are by the said commissioners and selectmen to be assessed and rated as here followeth, viz: Every person aforesaid (except magistrates and elders of churches), two shillings six pence by the head, and all estates both real and personal, at one penny for every twenty shillings, according to the rates of cattle hereafter mentioned. And for a more certain rule in rating of cattle, every cow of four year old and upward shall be valued at five pounds; every heifer and steer, between three and four year old, four pounds, and between two and three year old, fifty shillings, and between one and two year old, thirty shillings; every ox and bull of four year old and upwards, six pounds; every horse and mare of four year old and upwards, twelve pounds; of three year old, eight pounds; between two and three years old, five pounds; of one year old, three pounds; every sheep of one year old, thirty shillings; every goat above one year old, eight shillings; every swine above one year old, twenty shillings; and all cattle of all sorts under a year old, are hereby exempted, as also all hay and corn in the husbandman's hand, because all meadow, earable ground and cattle are rateable as aforesaid. And for all such persons as by the advantage of their arts and trades are more able to help bear the public charge then common laborers and workmen, as butchers, bakers, brewers, victualers, smiths, carpenters, tailors, shoemakers, joiners, barbers, millers, and masons, with all other manual persons and artists, such are to be rated for their returns and gains proportionably unto other men for the produce of their estates. Provided that in the rate by the poll, such persons as are disabled by sickness, lameness or other infirmities shall be exempted; and for such servants and children as take not wages, their parents and masters shall pay for them, but such as take wages shall pay for themselves.

And it is further ordered, that the commissioners for the several towns upon this River shall yearly meet upon the third Thursday in the sixth month at

Hartford, and the commissioners for the towns of Fairefeild and Stratford shall meet the same day in one of those towns, (and two days before the General Court in September they shall meet the commissioners upon the River, in Hartford,*) and bring with them, fairly written, the just number of males listed as aforesaid, and the assessment of estates made in their several towns according to the rules and directions in this present order expressed; And the said commissioners being so assembled shall duly and carefully examine all the said lists and assessments of the several towns, and shall correct and perfect the same, according to the true intent of this order, and the same so perfected they shall transmit under their hands to the General Court, the second Thursday in September, and then, directions shall be given to the treasurer for gathering of the said rate, and every one shall pay their rate to the constable of the town where it shall be assessed; nor shall any land or estate be rated in any other town but where the same shall lie, is or was improved to the owner's, reputed owner's, or other proprietor's use or behoof, if it be within this jurisdiction. And for all peculiars, viz: such places as are not yet laid within the bounds of any town, the same lands, with the persons and estates thereupon, shall be assessed by the rates of the town next unto it; the measure or estimation shall be by the distance of the meeting houses.

And if any of the said commissioners or of the select men shall willingly fail or neglect to perform the trust committed to them by this order, in not making, correcting, perfecting, or transmitting any

* The clause in parenthesis is interlined.

of the said lists or assessments, according to the intent of this order, every such offender shall be fined forty shillings for every such offence, or so much as the country shall be damnified thereby, so as it exceeds not forty shillings for one offence; provided that such offence or offences be complained of and prosecuted, in due course of law, within six months.

And it is further ordered, that upon all distresses to be taken for any of the rates and assessments aforesaid, the officer shall distrain goods or cattle, if they may be had; and if no goods, then lands or houses; if neither goods nor lands can be had within the town where such distresses are to be taken, then upon such returns to the treasurer he shall give warrants to attach the body of such persons, to be carried to prison, there to be kept till the next court, except they put in security for their appearance there, or that payment be made in the mean time.

And it is further ordered, that the prices of all sorts of corn to be received upon any rate by virtue of this order, shall be such as the court shall set from year to year, and in default thereof they shall be accepted at the price current, to be judged by the said commissioners.

And it is further ordered, that all estates of land in England shall not be rated in a public assessment.

It is also provided and ordered, that all town rates shall be made after the same manner and by the same rule as the country rate.

Whereas much wrong hath been done to the country by the negligence of constables, in not gathering such levies as they have received warrants from the treasurer, during their office:—It is therefore ordered, that if any constable shall not have gathered the levies committed to his charge by the treasurer then being, during the time of his office, that he shall, notwithstanding the expiration of his office, have power to levy by distress all such rates and levies; and if he bring them not in to the old treasurer, according to his warrants, the treasurer shall distrain such constable's goods for the same; and if the treasurer shall not so distrain the constable, he shall be answerable to the country for the same. And if the constable be not able to make payment, it shall be lawful for the treasurer, old or new respectively, to distrain any man or men of that town where the constables are unable, for all arrearages of levies; and that man or men, upon petition to the General Court, shall have order to collect the same again, equally, of the town, with his just damages for the same.

It is further ordered by this court, that all collectors and gatherers of rates shall appoint a day and place and give reasonable warning to the inhabitants to bring in their proportions, upon which every man so warned shall duly attend to bring in his rate, or upon neglect thereof shall forfeit two pence in the shilling for what he falls short; and the said collector shall have authority hereby to distrain the delinquents, or be accountable themselves for the rates and penalties so neglected by them.

RECORDS.

It is ordered by this court and authority thereof, that the town clerk or register, in the several towns of this jurisdiction, shall record all births and deaths of persons in their town: And that all parents, masters of servants, executors and administrators, respectively, shall bring in to the register of their several towns, the names of such persons belonging to them or any of them, as shall either be born or die; and also that every new married man shall likewise bring in a certificate of his marriage, under the hand of the magistrate which married him, to the said register; And for each neglect the person to whom it doth belong shall forfeit as followeth, viz: If any person shall neglect to bring in a note or certificate as aforesaid, together with three pence a name, to the said registers, for all births and deaths, and six pence for each marriage, to be recorded, more than one month after such birth, death, or marriage, shall forfeit for every default five shillings, and the penalty further increased upon longer neglect, according to the judgment of the court. And the register of each town shall yearly convey to the secretary of the court a true transcript of the births, deaths, and marriages, given under their hands, with a third part of the aforementioned fees, under the penalty of forty shillings for every such neglect, all which forfeits shall be returned in to the treasury; Also the grand jurors may present all neglects of this order.

It is ordered by the authority aforesaid, that the several towns within this jurisdiction shall each of them provide a ledger book, with an index or alphabet unto the same; also shall choose one who shall be a town clerk or register, who shall, before the General Court in September next, record every man's house and lands already granted and measured out to him, with the bounds and quantity of the same. And whosoever shall neglect three months after notice given, to bring in to the said town clerk or register a note of his house and land, with the bounds and quantity of the same by the nearest estimation, shall forfeit ten shillings; and so ten shillings a month for every month he shall so neglect; the like to be done for all lands hereafter granted and measured to any. And if any such grantor, being required by the grantee, his heirs or assigns, to make an acknowledgment of any grant, sale, bargain, or mortgage by him made, shall refuse so to do, it shall be in the power of any magistrate to send for the party so refusing and commit him to prison without bail or mainprise, until he shall acknowledge the same: And the grantee is to enter his caution with the recorder, and shall save his interest in the meantime. And all bargains or mortgages of lands whatsoever shall be accounted of no value until they be recorded, for which entry the register shall receive six pence for every parcel, delivering every owner a copy of the same under his hand, whereof four pence shall be for himself, and two pence for the secretary of the court. And the said register shall, every general court in May and September, deliver into the same a transcript fairly written of all such grants, bargains, or engagements recorded by him in the town book; and the secretary of the court shall record it in a book fairly written, provided for that purpose, and shall preserve the copy brought in under the hand of the town clerk. Also the said town clerk shall have for every search of a parcel, one penny, and for every copy of a parcel, two pence; and a copy of the same under the hand of the said register or town clerk and two of the men chosen to govern the town, shall be a sufficient evidence to all that have the same.*

For the better keeping in mind those passages of God's Providence which have been remarkable since

---

* Oct. 10th, 1639. Col. Rec., i. 37.

our first undertaking of these plantations, Mr. Deputy, Capt. Mason, Mr. Stone, with Mr. Goodwin, are desired to take the pains severally in their several towns, and then jointly together, to gather up the same and deliver them into the general court in September next, and if it be judged then fit, they may be recorded, and for future times, whatsoever remarkable passages shall be, and if they be public, the said parties are desired to deliver in the same to the general court: But if any particular person do bring in anything, he shall bring it under the hands of two of the aforementioned parties, that it is true, then present it to the general court, that if it be there judged requisite it may be recorded: provided that any general court for the future may alter any of the parties before mentioned or add to them, as they shall judge meet.*

It is also ordered by this court and decreed, that after the death and decease of any person possessed of any estate, be it more or less, and who maketh a will in writing or by word of mouth, those men which are appointed to order the affairs of the town where any such person deceaseth, shall within one month after the same at furthest, cause a true inventory to be taken of the said estate in writing; as also take a copy of the said will or testament and enter it into a book or keep the copy in safe custody; as also enter the names upon record of the children and legatees of the testator or deceased person. And the said orderers of the affairs of the town are to see every such will and inventory to be exhibited into the public court, within one quarter of a year, where the same is to be registered. And the said orderers of the affairs of the town shall do their

* Oct. 10th, 1639. Col. Rec., i. 39, 40.

endeavors in seeing that the estate of the testator be not wasted nor spoiled, but improved for the best advantage of the children or legatees of the testator, according to the mind of the testator, for their and every of their use, and by their and every of their allowance and approbation. But when any person dieth intestate, the said orderers of the affairs of the town shall cause an inventory to be taken, and then the public court may grant the administration of the goods and chattels to the next of kin, jointly or severally, and divide the estate to wife (if any be), children or kindred, as in equity they shall see meet. And if no kindred be found, the court to administer for the public good of the common: provided there be an inventory registered, that if any of the kindred in future time appear, they may have justice and equity done unto them. And all charges that the public court or the orderers of the affairs of the town are at, about the trust committed to them, either for writing or otherwise, is to be paid out of the estate.*

Whereas also, It was recommended by the Commissioners, that for the more free and speedy passage of justice in each jurisdiction, to all the confederates, if the last will and testament of any person be duly proved in, and duly certified from any one of the colonies, it be without delay accepted and allowed in the rest of the colonies, unless some just exception be made against such will or the proving of it, which exception to be forthwith duly certified back to the colony where the said will was proved, that some just course may be taken to gather in and dispose the estate without delay or damage. And also that if any

* Oct. 10th, 1639. Col. Rec., i. 38, 39.

known planters or settled inhabitants die intestate, administration be granted by that colony unto which the deceased belong, though dying in another colony. And the administration being duly certified, to be of force for the gathering in of the estate in the rest of the colonies, as in the case of wills proved, where no just exception is returned. But if any person possessed of an estate, who is neither planter nor settled inhabitant in any of the colonies, die intestate, the administration (if just cause be found to give administration,) be granted by that colony where the person shall die and depart this life, and that care be taken by that government to gather in and secure the estate, until it be demanded and may be delivered according to rules of justice:—Which upon due consideration was confirmed by this court, and in behalf of this colony, and ordered to be attended in all such occasions for the future: provided the general courts of the other colonies yield the like assent thereunto.*

SCHOOLS.

It being one chief project of that old deluder Satan, to keep men from the knowledge of the Scriptures, as in former times [by] keeping them in an unknown tongue, so in these latter times by persuading them from the use of tongues, so that at least the true sense and meaning of the original might be clouded with false glosses of saint-seeming deceivers; and that learning may not be buried in the grave of our forefathers in church and commonwealth, the Lord assisting our endeavors,—It is therefore ordered by this court and

* Recommended by Commissioners of the U. Colonies, Sept. 1648, and confirmed by the General Court, Mar. 14th, 1648-9.

authority thereof, that every township within this jurisdiction, after the Lord hath increased them to the number of fifty householders, shall then forthwith appoint one within their town to teach all such children as shall resort to him, to write and read, whose wages shall be paid either by the parents or masters of such children, or by the inhabitants in general, by way of supply, as the major part of those who order the prudentials of the town shall appoint; provided that those who send their children be not oppressed by [paying] more then they can have them taught for in other towns. And it is further ordered, that where any town shall increase to the number of one hundred families or householders, they shall set up a grammar school, the masters thereof being able to instruct youths so far as they may be fitted for the University. And if any town neglect the performance hereof above one year, then every such town shall pay five pounds per annum, to the next such school, till they shall perform this order.*

The proposition concerning the maintenance of scholars at Cambridge, made by the Commissioners, is confirmed. And it is ordered, that two men shall be appointed in every town, within this jurisdiction, who shall demand what every family will give, and the same to be gathered and brought into some room, in March, and this to continue yearly as it shall be considered by the Commissioners.†

---

* From Massachusetts order of Nov. 1647. (Mass. Rec., ii. 203.)

† Confirmed by the general court, Oct. 25th, 1644. Col. Rec., i. 112. This "proposition of a general contribution for the maintenance of poor scholars at the college at Cambridge," was presented to the commissioners of the N. E. Colonies, at their meeting in September, 1644, by the Rev. Thomas Shepard,—"and fully approved by them,

SECRETARY.

It is ordered and decreed, that within twenty days after the session of every general court, the secretary thereof shall send forth copies of such laws and orders as are or shall be made at either of them, which are of general concernment for the government of this commonwealth, to the constables of each town within this jurisdiction, for them to publish within fourteen days more, at some public meeting in their several towns, and cause to be written into a book and kept for the use of the town. And once every year the constables in each town shall read or cause to be read in some public meeting all the capital laws, and give notice to all the inhabitants where they may at any time see the rest of the laws and orders and acquaint themselves therewith: And the secretary of the court shall have twelve pence for the copy of the orders of each session aforesaid, from each of the towns.*

---

and agreed to be commended to the several general courts as a matter worthy of due consideration and entertainment for the advancement of learning, which we hope will be cheerfully embraced." Mr. Shepard, after requesting the commissioners to consider "some way of comfortable maintenance for that school of the prophets which now is," suggests that "If therefore it were commended by you, and left to the freedom of every family which is able and willing to give, throughout the plantations, to give yearly but the fourth part of a bushel of corn or something equivalent thereunto,—and for this end, if every minister were desired to stir up the hearts of the people once in the fittest season of the year, to be freely enlarged therein, and one or two faithful men appointed in each town, to receive and seasonably to send in what shall be thus given by them,—it is conceived that as no man could feel any grievance hereby, so it would be a blessed means of comfortable provision for the diet of divers such students as may stand in need of some support, and be thought meet and worthy to be continued a fit season therein." Records of U. Colonies, Sept., 1644.

* Altered from an order made, Oct. 1639. (Col. Rec., i. 39.)

And it is further ordered that the secretary of the court shall record such wills and inventories as are exhibited into the said court, and shall file the original of them, and give a copy thereof to such as desire it, for which he shall have for every record of any will or inventory, or both, which is above the sum of forty pounds, three shillings four pence; and for every copy of them or either of them, one shilling eight pence; and for every search or supervising of them, six pence: also for recording of every will or inventory, or both, which is above the sum of thirty pounds and under the sum of forty pounds, two shillings six pence; and for every copy of them, or either of them, fifteen pence; and for every search or supervising of them, four pence: Also for every attachment, twelve pence, and for every bond or recognizance in or about the same, six pence: Also for every execution above five pounds, the secretary shall have twelve pence, and for every execution under five pounds, six pence: Also for the entry of every or any recognizance in court, six pence, and for the withdrawing of it, twelve pence, which shall be paid before the bounden be freed from his said recognizance.

It is also ordered, that whosoever shall take out any warrant from the secretary of the court, that concerns an action, shall, before he hath a warrant, enter his action with the secretary, and then take out his warrant for summons to answer the same; for which they shall pay for every entry twelve pence, and for every warrant, four pence, though they agree with their defendants before the court. Also if any other magistrate shall grant a warrant which concerns an action, they shall enter the action in a small book for that purpose, before they grant the warrant, and shall make a due return at every court to the secretary thereof, what such warrants and to whom they have granted; and all such persons shall be as liable to pay twelve pence for every such action to the secretary of the court as if they should have had their warrants of him.

STRAYS.

It is ordered by this court and authority thereof, that whosoever shall take up any stray beast or find any goods lost, whereof the owner is not known, he shall give notice thereof to the constable of the same town, within six days, who shall enter the same in a book, and take order that it be cryed at their next lecture day or general meeting, upon three several days, and if it be above twenty shillings value, at the next market, or two next towns' public meetings, where no market is within ten miles, upon pain that the party so finding and the said constable having such notice and failing to do as is here appointed, to forfeit, either of them, for such default one third part of the value of such stray or lost goods.

And if the finder shall not give notice as aforesaid, within one month, or if he keep it more than three months, and shall not apprize it by sufficient men and also record it with the register of the town where it is found, he shall then forfeit the full value thereof. And if the owner appear within one year after such publication he shall have restitution of the same or the value thereof, he paying all necessary charges, and to the constable for his care and pains, as one of the next magistrates or one of the townsmen shall adjudge; and if no owner appear within the time prefixed, the said stray or lost goods shall be thus divided, one fourth part thereof with his reasonable charge shall be to the finder, one fifth part thereof or ten shillings to the constable, at the choice of the court, and the rest to the commonwealth; provided there be three streaks clipped in the hair of the near buttock, six inches long, that they may be known.

SWINE.

It is ordered by this court, that all the swine, either hogs or shoats, in the several plantations, that are kept at home within the town, shall by September next be ringed or yoked, or kept up in their yards, under the penalty of four pence for every such swine, to be paid by the owner to the party that shall take the swine so defective and impound them; also all such as are kept by herds in the woods, shall not be suffered to abide above one night in the town, but that it shall be lawful to impound them, in case they come at any time home from the middle of March to the middle of November. Fairfield and Stratford desire to be included in this order.*

For the better preserving corn and meadow on the east side of the Great River, It is ordered by this court, that there shall no hogs nor swine of any sort be put over thither or kept there at any time, after the publishing of this order, except they be kept out of the bounds of the several towns, or in their yards, under the penalty of two shillings a head for every hog or swine, for every time they shall be found there contrary to this order.

TIMBER.

It is ordered by this court, that no timber shall be felled within three miles of the mouth of Mattabeseck

* Ordered, Sept. 1645. (Col. Rec., i. 131.)

River, nor at unseasonable times, viz: from the beginning of April to the end of September, and that it be improved into pipestaves or some other merchantable commodity, within one month after the felling thereof, or carted together: and that the timber so improved shall not be transported from the River but for discharge of debts or fetching in some necessary provision.*

TOBACCO.

Forasmuch as it is observed that many abuses are crept in and committed by frequent taking of tobacco, It is ordered by the authority of this court, that no person under the age of twenty years, nor any other that hath not already accustomed himself to the use thereof, shall take any tobacco, until he hath brought a certificate under the hands of some who are approved for knowledge and skill in physic, that it is useful for him, and also that he hath received a license from the court for the same. And for the regulating of those who either by their former taking it have to their own apprehensions made it necessary to them, or upon due advice are persuaded to the use thereof, It is ordered, that no man within this colony, after the publication hereof, shall take any tobacco publicly in the street, highways, or any barn yards, or upon training days in any open places, under the penalty of six pence for each offence against this order in any the particulars thereof, to be paid without gainsaying, upon conviction by the testimony of one witness that is without just exception, before any one magistrate. And the constables in the several towns are required to make presentment to each particular court of such

* Ordered, Sept. 1641. (Col. Rec., i. 67.)

as they do understand and evict to be transgressors of this order.*

TRESPASSES.

It is ordered by this court and authority thereof, that if any horse, or other beast, trespass in corn or other inclosure, being fenced in such sort as secures against cows, oxen, small calves, and such like orderly cattle, the party or parties trespassed shall procure two able men of good report and credit to view and adjudge the harms, which the owner of the beast shall satisfy (when known) upon reasonable demand, whether the beast were impounded or not; but if the owner be known and near residing, as in the same town or the like, notice shall be left at the usual place of his abode, of the trespass, before an estimation be made thereof, to the end he, or any others appointed by him, may be present when the judgment is made; the like notice also shall be left for him of the damage charged upon him, that if he approve not thereof he may repair to the select townsmen, or some of them, who shall in such case nominate and appoint two able and indifferent men, to review and adjudge the said harms, which being discharged, together with the charge of the notice, former and latter view, and determination of damages, the first judgment to be void, or else to stand in law.

TREASURER.

It is ordered, that the treasurer shall deliver no money out of his hands to any person, without the hands of two magistrates, if the sum be above twenty

* Enacted May, 1647. (Col. Rec., i. 153.) A law against the public use of tobacco was passed by Massachusetts the year previous. To "take" tobacco meant, at this period, to *smoke* it. The viler habit of *chewing* was not yet introduced.

shillings; if it be under, then the treasurer is to accept of the hand of one; but if it be for the payment of some bills to be allowed, which are referred to some committees to consider of, whether allowed or not, that such bills as they allow and set their hands unto, the treasurer shall accept and give satisfaction.

VOTES.

It is ordered by this court and decreed, that if any person within these liberties have been or shall be fined or whipped for any scandalous offence, he shall not be admitted after such time to have any vote in town or commonwealth, nor to serve on the jury, until the court shall manifest their satisfaction.

VERDICTS.

That love and peace, with truth and righteousness may continue and flourish in these confœderated colonies, It was, upon the recommendation of the Commissioners, ordered, that any verdict or sentence of any court within the colonies, presented under authentic testimony, shall have a due respect in the several courts of this jurisdiction, where there may be occasion to make use thereof, and shall be accounted good evidence for the party, until better evidence or other just cause appear to alter or make the same void: and that in such case, the issuing of the cause in question be respited for some convenient time, that the court may be advised with where the verdict or sentence first passed. Provided notwithstanding, that this order shall be accounted valid and improved only for the advantage of such as live within some of the confœderated colonies, and where the verdicts in the courts of this colony may receive reciprocal respect by a like order established by the General Court of that colony.*

WINE AND STRONG WATER.

Whereas many complaints are brought into the court, by reason of divers abuses that fall out by several persons that sell wine and strong water, as well in vessels on the river as also in several houses; for the preventing hereof, It is now ordered by the authority of this court, that no person or persons, after the publishing of this order, shall neither sell wine nor strong water by retail, in any place within these liberties, without license from the particular court or any two magistrates,† or where there is but one magistrate, by a magistrate and one of those appointed to order the affairs of the town.

WATCHES.

It is ordered by this court and decreed, that there shall be a sufficient watch maintained in every town, and that the constable of each town shall duly warn the same and see that the inhabitants or residents do severally in their turns observe the same, according as the inhabitants do agree.‡ And this court doth explain themselves and order that whosoever within this jurisdiction, that is liable to watch, shall take a journey out of the town wherein he liveth after he hath had timely notice and warning to watch, he shall provide a watchman for that turn, though himself be absent; and if any man that takes a journey, or goes out of the town wherein he liveth, if he return home within a week after the watch is past his house, he

* Approved by the General Court, Oct. 25th, 1644. Col. Rec. i. 113.

† Feb. 14th, 1643-4. *Ibid.* 100. The last clause was subsequently added.

‡ June, 1636. Col. Rec., i. 2.

shall be called back to watch that turn past a week before.*

And for the better keeping watches and wards by the constables in time of peace, It is ordered by this court and authority thereof, that every constable shall present to one of the next magistrates the name of every person who shall upon lawful warning refuse or neglect to watch or ward, either in person or by some other fit for that service: And if, being convented, he cannot give a just excuse, such magistrate shall grant warrant to levy five shillings on every such offender, for every such default: the same to be employed for the use of the watch of the same town. And it is the intent of the law that every person of able body (not exempted by law), or of estate to hire another, shall be liable to watch and ward, or to supply it by some other, when they shall be thereunto required. And if there be in the same house divers such persons, whether sons, servants, or sojourners, they shall all be compellable to watch as aforesaid.† Provided that all such as keep families at their farms, being remote from any town, shall not be compellable to send their servants or sons from their farms to watch and ward in the towns.

WOLVES.

Whereas great loss and damage doth befall the commonwealth by reason of wolves, which destroy great numbers of our cattle, notwithstanding provision formerly made by this court for suppressing of them; therefore, for the better encouragement of any to set about a work of so great concernment, It is ordered by this court and authority thereof, that any person,

*** Sept. 1649. Col. Rec., i. 196.**

† From Massachusetts order of 1646. (Mass. Rec., ii. 151.)

either English or Indian, that shall kill any wolf or wolves, within ten miles of any plantation within this jurisdiction, shall have for every wolf by him or them so killed, ten shillings paid out of the treasury of the country: provided, that due proof be made thereof unto the plantation next adjoining where such wolf or wolves were killed, and also bring a certificate under some magistrate's hand, or the constable of that place, unto the treasurer.

WRECKS OF THE SEA.

It is ordered and decreed and by this court declared, that if any ships, or other vessels, be it friend or enemy, shall suffer shipwreck upon our coasts, there shall be no violence or wrong offered to their persons or goods, but their persons shall be harbored and relieved, and their goods preserved in safety, till authority may be certified and shall take further order therein.

VESSELS.

It is ordered by this court and authority thereof, that no vessel nor boat shall have liberty to go from any port in any town within this jurisdiction, before they have entered with the register or recorder in each town what quantity of powder and shot they carry forth with them in their said vessels, and shall take a certificate, under the said register's or recorder's hand, of the same, paying to him for every certificate, four pence: And if any vessel shall attempt to go from the said town or port, or towns and ports, before he hath entered as aforesaid, or shall be found with any more or greater quantity of powder and shot aboard the vessel or vessels than they had a certificate to show they had entered, shall forfeit and pay for each default the true value of all such powder and shot as they should have entered as aforesaid. And all such persons or masters of such vessels shall give a true account, upon their return, to the said recorder where they have entered the premises, how they have disposed thereof, upon the former penalty: And if the said town register or recorder shall have just cause to conceive that he or they carry forth more of the premises than in an ordinary way is requisite for their necessary defence and safety in their intended voyage, then the said persons or masters of vessels shall give in security unto the said recorder (if by him required thereunto), that he shall give a due account to this commonwealth of the same, upon his return.

FOREIGNERS.

It is ordered by this court, that no foreigners, after the twenty-ninth day of September next shall retail any goods, by themselves, in any place within this jurisdiction, nor shall any inhabitant retail any goods which belong to any foreigner, for the space of one whole year after the said twenty-ninth of September next, upon penalty of confiscation of the value of one half of the goods so retailed, to be paid by the seller of them.*

HOME LOTS.

Whereas there is creeping in, in several towns and plantations within this jurisdiction, a great abuse of buying and purchasing home lots and laying them together, by means whereof great depopulations are like to follow, It is ordered that all dwelling or mansion houses that are or shall be allowed in any plantation or town within this jurisdiction, shall be upheld,

* Enacted, May 16, 1650. (Col. Rec., i. 207.)

repaired and maintained sufficiently in a comely way: As also, whosoever shall possess and enjoy any home lots within any such plantation or town, that is not yet built upon, shall, within twelve months after the making of this order, erect and build a house there, fit for an inhabitant to dwell in, unless the court, upon knowledge of the case, find cause to abate, or give longer time for building.

It is ordered, that the prices of corn for the year ensuing [1650-51], for all country rates (except where engagements to the contrary are expressed), shall be as followeth:

Wheat, four shillings six pence per bushel; pease three shillings six pence per bushel; rye, three shillings six pence per bushel; Indian, three shillings per bushel; and that there shall be liberty for all men to pay one third part of such rates, in good wampum.

IV.

SOME ORDERS OF THE GENERAL COURT AND COURT OF MAGISTRATES, 1636–1665.

[From the first volume of the Colony Records.]

A Corte holden att Newton, 26 Apr. 1636.*

Roger Ludlowe Esqr.,	Mr. Westwood,
Mr. Steele,	Mr. Warde.
Mr. Phelpes,	

It was now complayned that Henry Stiles or some of the ser[vants] had traded a peece with the Indians for Corne. It is ordered that [the] said Henry Stiles shall, betweene & the next Cort, regaine [the] saide peece from the saide Indians in a faire & legall waye, or els this Corte will take it into further consideracon.

It is ordered that from henceforth none that are within the Jurisdiction of this Cort, shall trade with the natiues or Indians any peece or pistoll or gunn or powder or shott, vnder such heavie penalty as vppon such misdemeanor the Corte shall thinke meete.

Constables sworne, for Dorchester, Newtowne & Watertowne, for this next yeere and vntill newe be

* Newton, or New Town,—now Hartford. The record of the first three sessions is given entire, preserving the original spelling, but not the abbreviations. A few words and parts of words lost by mutilations of the record, or illegible, are restored in *brackets*.

chosen, are Henry Walcott for Dorchester, Samuell Wakeman for Newtowne, & Daniell Finch for Watertowne.

Whereas there be divers strange Swine in the seuerall plantacons that their owners are not knowen & yet doe & are likelie to Comitt many trespasses. It is therefore ordered that the saide plantacons shall forthwith take notice of them & their markes, & giue speedy notice amonge the plantacons both of them & their markes & if in a fortenight noe owners come forth then the saide plantacons or plantacon where such Swine are, may appraise them att a value & sell them & take the money to some publicke vse of the saide plantacon, vnlesse their doe within one whole yeere after appear a true owner & then the money it was sould for is to be restored, prouided alwaies that when the owner appear before the money or Swine be redeliuered, there be deducted such Somes & Chardges & trespasses as haue beene comitted & expended in & aboute him or them.

It is likewise ordered if any Swine stray from oute their owne Plantacon into another they shalbe subiect [to] the orders that are there made concerninge Swine.

Whereas there was a dismission granted by the C[hurch] of Waterton in the Masachusetts, dated 29th of May last, to Andrewe Warde, Jo: Sherman, Jo: Stickland, Rob'te Coo, Rob'te Reynold & Jonas Weede, with intent to forme a newe in a Ch: Covenant, in this River of Conectecott, the saide parties haue soe accordingly done with the publicke allowance of the rest of the members of the saide Churches, as by certificate nowe produced appears. It is therefore in this present Cort ratified & confirmed, they promissing shortlie publicquely to renewe the [said] Covenante vppon notice to the rest of the Churches.

(pp. 1, 2.*)

A CORTE HELD ATT DORCHESTER† JUNE 7th, 1636.

Mr. Ludlowe, Mr. Westwood,
Mr. Steele, Mr. Warde.
Mr. Phelpes,

Whereas, the last Corte Henry Stiles was ordered to regaine [a] peece he had traded with the Indians which doth not appear that he hath done, It is ordered that a warrant shalbe directed to him to performe the same by the next Cort and then personally to appear [&] answere his neglect.

It is ordered that there shalbe a sufficient Watch maynte[ined] in every towne & that the Constable of each Towne shall d[uly] warne the same & see that the inhabitants or residents doe seuerally in their Turne observe the same accordinge as [the] Inhabitants doe agree, which said watch shall begin & end when the Courte or magistrates shall thinke meete.

It is ordered that Samuell Wakeman & Geo: Hubberd shall [survey] the breadth of the plantacon of Dorchester howe farre [it] shall extend aboue Mr. Stiles & shall certifie vnto the [next] Corte their proceedinges herein to the end it may be then confirmed, and that they shall haue from the saide Towne satisfaccon for their paines. And the saide Samuell Wake[man] shall doe the like for Watertowne in their bredth toward [the] mouth of the River & have the

* The references are to the pages of the first *printed* volume of Colonial Records, 1636–1665.

† Now Windsor.

like satisfaccon. And this done without faile before the next Corte vppon peine [of] 40 shillinges of each heade that shall faile therein.

It is ordered that every souldier in each plantacon shall haue in his howse in a readines before the end of August next, twoe pounde of powder, and that they shall shew it to the Constable whenever he shall call them vnto it vppon the penalty of X *s*. for every failure, which is presentlie to be le[vied] by the saide Constable without [resistance] as alsoe 20 bul[letts of leade in the like readines vppon the same penalty and in the same manner to be levied.]

A Corte held att Watertowne* 1° 7br, 1636.

Roger Ludlowe Esq.,	Mr. Wm. Phelps,
Mr. Jo: Steele,	Mr. Wm. Westwoode,
Mr. Wm. Swaine,	Mr. Andr: Warde.

It is ordered that the order concerninge Powder and Bulletts, of the 7th of June last be nowe presentlie published in the seueral plantacons and that there be respite given vntill th'end of this instant moneth and then to be putt in execucon without faile.

Whereas there was tendered to vs an Inventory of the estate of Mr. Jo: Oldam which seemed to bee somewhat vncerteinely valued, wee therefore thinke meete to, and soe it is ordered, that Mr. Jo: Plum and Rich: Gildersleeue togeather with the Constable shall survey the saide Inventory and perfect the same before the next Corte and then to deliuer it into the Corte.

It is ordered that Thurston Rayner as he hath

* Now Wethersfield.

hitherto done soe shall continue to looke to and preserue the Corne of Mr. Oldam and shall inn* the same in a seasonable tyme and shall bringe an Accompt the next Cort what quantitie there is of it as alsoe of his labor and then the Cort will out of the same alott vnto him soe many bushells as shalbe reasonable for his paines and labor. And in the meane if he hath vse of some for his owne spendinge to take some which shalbe then deducted out of what wilbe due to him. And then the Cort will give finall order concerninge the same.

It is ordered that every plantacon shall traine once in every moneth, and if vppon complainte of their military officer it appear that there bee divers very vnskilfull, the sayde plantacon may appointe the officer to traine oftener the saide vnskillfull. And that the saide military officer take veiwe of their seueral Armes whether they be seruiceable or noe. And for default of every souldiers absent the absent to paye 5*s.* for every tyme without lawfull excuse within 2 dayes after, tendered to the Commissioners or one of them in the saide plantacon. And for any default in Armes vppon warnings to them by the saide officer to amend the same and a tyme sett and if not then amended by the tyme appointed, 1*s.* every tyme. And where Armes are wholly wantinge to be bounde over to answere it at the next Corte.

Whereas it appeared by a wrytinge vnder hand of Mr. Oldam that twoe of the mares that are nowe seized vppon by Daniell Finch Constable of Watertowne, as Mr. Oldames goodes, are the goodes of Mr. Tho: Allen. And therefore it is ordered that the said mares

* Inn ; to house, to put under cover.

shalbe deliuered to the saide Mr. Allen into his owne possession or his assignes.

It is ordered by consent of Serieant Seely plaintiffe against the inhabitants of the Towne of Watertowne defendants, that a Jurer shalbe withdrawen, and that the defendants doe vndertake to produce an order wherein they will make it appear that it was ordered that if the inhabitants of the saide Towne did not remoue with their Families to Conectecott by the end of this instant moneth or els there was noe propriety due to them in the devident of the lands of the saide Towne and that the hand or the consent of the saide Willm. Bassum is herevnto. And if the saide order be not produced here to the Corte by the 2d Cort after this the Inhabitants are to pay the plaintiffe damages.

(pp. 2-4.)

---

21 Febr. 1636.*

Mr. Ludlowe, Mr. Phelps,
Mr. Steele, Mr. Westwoode.
Mr. Swaine,

Whereas it was ordered that Samuel Wakeman, Geo: Hubbert, & Anncient Stoughton were to consider of the boundes of Dorchester towarde the Falls & of Watertowne towards the mouth of the River; The saide Samuell Wakeman & [Geo:] Hubberd thinkes meete that the plantacon of Dorchester shall extend towards the Falls, on the same side the plantacon standes, to a Brooke called Kittle Brooke & soe over the greate River vppon the same line that Newe Towne & Dorchester doth betweene them. And soe it is ordered by the Corte.

* 1637, by our present mode of dating.

It is ordered that the plantacon nowe called Newtowne shal be called & named by the name of Harteford Towne, likewise the plantacon now called Watertowne shalbe called and named Wythersfeild.

Samuell Wakeman & Ancient Stoughton doe thinke meete that the boundes of Wythersfeild shalbe extended toward the Rivers mouth, in the same side it standes in, to a Tree sixe miles downeward from the boundes between them & Harteford [marked with] N: F: & to [runn in an east] & west line, [& over] the great River, the saide Wythersfeild to begin att the mouth of Pewter pott Brooke & there to runn due east into the Countrey 3 miles & downeward sixe miles in breadth, which is ordered accordingly.*

It is ordered that the plantacon called Dorchester shalbee called Windsor.

The boundes betweene Weathersfeild & Harteford are agreed on the side wherein they stand to be att a Tree marked N: F: & to which the Pale of the saide Harteford is fixed, to goe into the Countrey due east, and on the other side of the greate River from Pewter pott Brook att the lower side of Hocannom due east into the Countrey, which is nowe ordered accordingly.

The boundes betweene Harteford & Windsor is agreed to be att the vpper end of the greate meadowe of the said Harteford toward Windsor att the Pale that is nowe there sett vpp by the saide Harteford, which is abuttinge vppon the great River, vppon a due east line, & into the Countrey from the saide Pale vppon a due west line as paralell to the saide east line as farr as they have now paled & afterward the

---

* The words in brackets (now illegible in the original Record) are here supplied from a certified copy of this and the next preceding order, made in 1708.

boundes to goe into the Countrey vppon the same west line. But it is to be soe much shorter towards Windsor as the place where the Girte that comes alonge att the end of the saide meadowe & falls into the saide greate River is shorter then their Pale, & over the saide greate Riuer the saide Plantacon of Windsor is to come to the * Riveretts mouth that falls into the saide greate River of Conectecott, and there the said Harteford is to runn due east into the Countrey, which is ordered accordingly.

It is ordered that noe yonge man that is neither maried nor hath any servaunte, & be noe publicke officer, shall keepe howse by himself, without consent of the Towne where he liues first had, vnder paine of 20*s*. per week.

It is ordered that noe Master of a Family shall giue habitacon or interteinment to any yonge man to soiourne in his family, but by the allowance of the inhabitants of the saide Towne where he dwelles, vnder the like penalty of 20*s*. per weeke. These 2 last orders to take effect the first of Aprill next.

(pp. 7, 8.)

1637.—It is ordered that Mr. Frances Stiles shall teach Geo. Chapple, Thos. Cooper and Thos. Barber, his servants, in the trade of a carpenter, according to his promise for the service of their term behind, four days in a week only, to saw and slit their own work that they are to frame themselves with their own hands, together with himself or some other master

*[*In margin*] "The Riuerett on the other side by the Indians is called Podanke."

workmen, the time to begin for the performance of this order fourteen days hence without fail.*

1638, Mar. 9° die.—It is ordered that whosoever doth disorderly speak privately during the sitting of court, with his neighbor, or two or three together, shall presently pay one shilling, if the court so think meet.

1638.—It is thought meet that the corselets that were in the last service shall be made good to the commonwealth, and made as serviceable as before, and that Richard Lord shall take such corselets into his custody as are in the meeting house of Harteford and make them up, and when they be fitted up the said Lord is to bring in his note and the court to appoint one to view the same, and when they are certified to be in good condition there must be speedy course taken by the court for the speedy payment of the said Lord.

1639.—Jno. E——, A. S——, and Jno. W——, were censured for unclean practices as follows: Jno. E—— to be whipped at a cart's tail upon a lecture day at Harteford. Jno. W—— to stand upon the pillory from the ringing of the first bell to the end of the lecture, then to be whipped at a cart's [tail,] and to be whipped in like manner at Windsore within eight days following. A. S—— to stand upon the pillory and be whipped as W——, and to have the letter R burnt upon his cheek, and in regard of the wrong done to Mary H—— to pay her parents ten pounds, and in defect of such to the commonwealth, and when both are fit for that condition, to marry her.

---

* In this extract, and in most of those which follow, the spelling is modernized, except *proper names*.

It is the mind of the court that Mr. Ludlow and Mr. Phelps see some public punishment inflicted upon the girl for concealing it so long.

1639.—Jno. B—— and Mary H—— were both censured to be whipped for unclean practices, and the girl's master is enjoined to send her out of this Jurisdiction before the last of the next month.

1639-46.—Wm. C——, servant to Jno. Crow, was fined forty shillings for misdemeanor in drinking, and corporal punishment was remitted upon his promise of his care for the future to avoid such occasions.

1640.—Ed. Veare of Wethersfyeld is fined ten shillings for cursing and swearing, and also he is to sit in the stocks at Wethersfyeld, two hours the next training day.

N. O——, for his lascivious carriage and foul misdemeanors at sundry times with Mary B——, is adjudged to pay twenty pound fine to the country, and to stand upon the pillory at Hartford the next lecture day during the time of the lecture. He is to be set on, a little before the beginning and to stay thereon a little after the end.

1640.—It is ordered, that what person or persons within this jurisdiction shall, after September, 1641, drink [i. e. smoke] any other tobacco but such as is or shall be planted within these liberties, shall forfeit for every pound so spent five shillings, except they have license from the court.

1641.—Notwithstanding the late order concerning the restraint of excess in apparel, yet divers persons of several ranks are observed still to exceed therein: It is therefore ordered that the constables of every town within these liberties, shall observe and take notice of any particular person or persons within their several limits, and all such as they judge to exceed their condition and ranks therein, they shall present and warn to appear at the particular court; as also the said constables are to present to the said court all such persons who sell their commodities at excessive rates; And the said court hath power to censure any disorder in the particulars before mentioned.

1641.—Whereas it was ordered that every family should plant a spoonful of hempseed, at a foot distant every seed: upon complaint that the said hempseed cannot be procured, It is ordered, that such persons who have above the quantity of a spoonful, and deny to sell to others that are unprovided, they shall plant so many spoonfuls themselves, according to the said order, as they deny to sell to others that want and desire to buy it of them at a reasonable rate.

1641.—For the preventing and avoiding that foul and gross sin of lying, it is ordered, that when any person or persons shall be accused and proved guilty of that vice, it shall be lawful for the particular court to adjudge and censure any such party, either by fine or bodily correction according as they shall judge the nature of the fault to require; this to hold to the next court.

1641.—Forasmuch as the court having lately declared their apprehensions to the country concerning the excess in wages amongst all sorts of artificers and workmen, hoping thereby men would have been a law unto themselves, but finding little reformation therein, The said court hath therefore ordered, that sufficient able carpenters, plow-wrights, wheelwrights, masons, joiners, smiths, and coopers, shall not take above twenty pence for a day's work from the tenth of March to the eleventh of October, nor above eighteen pence a day for the other part of the year, and to work eleven hours in the day the summer time, besides that which is spent in eating or sleeping, and nine hours in the winter: also, mowers, for the time of mowing shall not take above twenty pence for a day's work.

It is ordered, also, that all other artificers, or handi-crafts-men and chief laborers shall not take above eighteen pence a day for the first half year as aforesaid, and not above fourteen pence a day for the other part of the year; and whatsoever work is let or taken by the great or parcel, by any workmen, laborers or artificers whatsoever, shall be valued by the proportion aforesaid.

1642.—For the better furnishing the River with cordage towards the rigging of ships, It is ordered, that what hempseed any person hath within these liberties, that they shall either sow it themselves, or sell it to some others within the River that may sow the same.

1642.—It is ordered, that there shall be a guard of forty men to come complete in their arms to the meeting every Sabbath and lecture day, in every town within these liberties upon the River.

1643.—To prevent or withstand such sudden assaults as may be made by Indians upon the Sabbath or lecture days, It is ordered, that one person in every several house wherein is any soldier or soldiers, shall bring a musket, pistol or some piece, with powder and shot to each meeting, except some one magistrate dispense with any one, and appoint some other to supply his room.

1643.—Whereas that is observed that the late order for one in a family to bring his arms to the meeting house every Sabbath and lecture day, hath not been attended by divers persons; It is now ordered, that whosoever hereafter shall at any time neglect the same, shall forfeit twelve pence for every neglect, whereof, six pence to the party that shall inform and six pence to the country.

1643.—Whereas, the prosperity and well-being of common weals doth much depend upon the well government and ordering of particular families, which in an ordinary way cannot be expected where the rules of God are neglected in laying the foundation of a family state: For the prevention therefore of such evils and inconveniences, which by experience are found not only to be creeping in but practiced by some in that kind, It is ordered, that no person whatsoever, male or female, not being at his or her own dispose, or that remaineth under the government of parents, masters or guardians or such like, shall either make, or give entertainment to any motion or suit in way of marriage, without the knowledge and consent of those they stand in such relation to, under the severe censure of the Court, in case of delinquency not attending this order; nor shall any third person or persons intermeddle in making any motion to any such without the knowledge and consent of those under whose government they are, under the same penalty.

1647.—It is the mind of the court that there should be provision made for entertaining the magistrates during the sitting of the court, and the deputies of Hartford are desired to find out a fit man.

1647.—For the preventing that great abuse which is creeping in by excess in wine and strong waters, It is ordered, that no inhabitant in any town of this jurisdiction shall continue in any common victualing house in the same town where he liveth, above half an hour at a time in drinking wine, beer, or hot waters, neither shall any who draweth and selleth wine suffer any to drink any more wine at one time than after the proportion of three to a pint of sack. And it is further ordered, that no such wine drawer deliver any wine, or suffer any to be delivered out of his house, to any who come for it, unless they bring a note under the hand of some one master of some family and allowed inhabitant of that town, neither shall any such Ordinary keep, sell or draw any hot waters to any but in case of necessity, and in such moderation for quantity as they may have good grounds to conceive it may not be abused; and shall be ready to give an account of their doings herein when they are called thereto, under censure of the Court, in case of delinquency.

1645.—Susan C., for her rebellious carriage toward her mistress, is to be sent to the house of correction and be kept to hard labor and coarse diet, to be brought forth the next lecture day to be publicly corrected, and so to be corrected weekly, until order be given to the contrary.

Robert B——, for his loathsome and beastly demeanor, is adjudged to be brought forth the next lecture day, to be severely scourged, and to be kept in the house of correction a fortnight longer, and then brought forth again to be publicly whipped, and then to be bound to appear at every quarter court to be whipped, until the court see some reformation in him, and shall see cause to release him.

Walter G——, for his misdemeanor in laboring to inveigle the affections of Mr. Hoocker's maid, is to be publicly corrected the next lecture day.

1646.—Robert B., for his gross misdemeanor in slandering Mrs. Mary Fenwicke, is to stand on the pillory, Wednesday, during the lecture, then to be whipped, and fined five pound, and half year's imprisonment.

1648.—John Drake complains against John Bennett for saying he had enticed and drawn away the affections of his daughter.

1648.—The court adjudgeth Peter Bussaker, for his filthy and profane expressions (viz., that he hoped to meet some of the members of the church in hell ere long, and he did not question but he should,) to be committed to prison, there to be kept in safe custody till the sermon, and then to stand in the time thereof in the pillory, and after sermon to be severely whipped.

1649.—J. J., for his filthy and profane speeches and carriages, is adjudged to lie in prison till next Thursday morning after the catechising, and then to be publicly whipped, and so return to prison again for a month after that, except he find bail to appear when he is called for again to receive second correction, which the court appoints and thinks meet to be next Thursday come month, except the Governor judges the weather unseasonable.

1652.—Thomas Lord, having engaged to this court to continue his abode in Hartford for the next ensuing year, and to improve his best skill amongst the inhabitants of the towns upon the River within this

Jurisdiction, both for setting of bones and otherwise, as at all times occasions and necessities may or shall require; This court doth grant that he shall be paid by the country the sum of fifteen pounds for the said ensuing year, and they do declare that for every visit or journey that he shall take or make, being sent for to any house in Hartford, twelve pence is reasonable; to any house in Wyndsor, five shillings; to any house in Wethersfeild, three shillings; to any house in Farmington, six shillings; to any house in Mattabeseck, eight shillings; (he having promised that he will require no more;) and that he shall be freed for the time aforesaid from watching, warding and training; but not from finding arms, according to law.

1654.—This court grants Mr. Cullick liberty to draw and sell one hogshead of claret and a quarter cask of red wine to his friends and neighbors, free from the country's excise. And this court doth also futher grant unto the said Mr. Cullick, free license and liberty for the future to draw out or sell to his friends and neighbors what wine and liquors he shall see cause, free from the country's excise.

1656.—That no butcher, by himself or any other person, gash or cut any hide of ox, bull, steer or cow, in flaying thereof, whereby the same shall be impaired, under the penalty of twelve [pence] for every such gash in hide or skin.

Nor shall any person or persons using or which shall use the mystery of tanning, at any time or times hereafter, offer or put to sale any kind of leather which shall be insufficiently or not thoroughly tanned, or which shall not then have been after the tanning thereof well and thoroughly dried, upon pain of forfeiture so much of his or their said leather as by any searcher or sealer of leather lawfully appointed shall be found insufficiently tanned or not thoroughly dried as aforesaid.

1658.—This court orders that there shall be no ministry or church administration entertained or attended by the inhabitants of any plantation in this colony, distinct and separate from and in opposition to that which is openly and publicly observed and dispensed by the settled and approved minister of the place, except it be by approbation of the general court, and neighbor churches: *provided always* that this order shall not hinder any private meetings of godly persons to attend any duties that Christianity or religion call for, as fasts or conference, nor take place upon such as are hindered by any just impediments on the Sabbath day, from the public assemblies, by weather or water and the like.

1659.—It is ordered by this court, that if any person be found drunk, and convicted so to be, in any private house, he shall pay twenty shillings for every transgression of this nature, unto the public treasury, and the owner of the house where the person is found and proved to be made drunk, shall pay ten shillings.

It is ordered and required by the authority of this court, that the constables in each town shall make diligent search upon all occasions when there is suspicion of miscarriages by disordered meetings of persons in private houses to tipple together; and having discovered they are to make presentment thereof to public authority, and such as are convicted to be guilty of the breach of this order shall pay five shillings, one half to the public treasury, the other half to the person discovering.

1660.—This court doth order, that no man or woman within this colony who hath a wife or husband in foreign parts, shall live here above two years, upon penalty of forty shillings per month upon every such offender; and any that have been above three years already, not to remain within this colony above one year longer, upon the same penalty, except they have liberty from the general court.

1662.—This court orders, that the Bible that was sent to goodwife Williams be by Sergt. John Not delivered to goodwife Harrison, who engageth to this court to give unto the children of the said Williams, a bushel of wheat apiece, as they shall come out of their time. And John Not doth engage to give each of the children two shillings apiece as they come out of their time, to buy them Bibles; and John Not hath hereby power granted him as is ordered, to dispose of the rest of the books, to the children of the said Williams.

1662, Oct. 9.—The PATENT or CHARTER was this day publicly read in audience of the Freemen, and declared to belong to them and their successors, and the freemen made choice of Mr. Willys, Capt. John Talcot and Lieut. John Allyn to take the Charter into their custody, in behalf of the freemen, who are to have an oath administered to them by the General Assembly, for the due discharge of the trust committed to them.

It is enacted and decreed by the Freemen, that the town of Hartford for future shall be the settled place for the convocation of the General Assembly, at all times, unless it be upon occasion of epidemical diseases, sickness, or the like.

This court appoints that Wednesday come fortnight be set apart, throughout this colony, for a solemn day of Thanksgiving for the mercies that God hath extended to this colony the year past, and particularly for the good success God hath given to the endeavors of our Honored Governor in obtaining our charter of his Majesty our Sovereign; as also for his gracious answer of our prayer in the late drought, in sending rain; and for abatement of the sickness; and for the hopes we have of settlement in the ways of peace and righteousness.

This court doth order and declare, that the seal that formerly was used by the general court shall still remain and be used as the seal of this colony until the court see cause to the contrary, and the secretary is to keep the seal, and to use it on necessary occasions, for the colony.

Aug., 1663.—This court doth desire that those friends appointed to keep the Charter do also receive the duplicate into their custody, and keep it in behalf of the freemen of this corporation; and the worshipful Governor is desired to deliver the said duplicate to the said friends, or either of them.

V.

THE FUNDAMENTAL AGREEMENT AT NEW HAVEN, JUNE 4th, 1639.

[From New Haven Colony Records, i. 11-17.]

The fourth day of the fourth month called June 1639, all the free planters assembled together in a general meeting* to consult about settling civil government according to God, and about the nomination of persons that might be found by consent of all fittest in all respects for the foundation work of a church which was intended to be gathered in Quinipieck. After solemn invocation of the name of God in prayer for the presence and help of his spirit, and grace in those weighty businesses, they were reminded of the business whereabout they met, viz., for the establishment of such civil order as might be most pleasing unto God, and for the choosing the fittest men for the foundation work of a church to be gathered. For the better enabling them to discern the mind of God, and to agree accordingly concerning the establishment of civil order, Mr. John Davenport propounded

* "This meeting took place according to tradition, in a large barn belonging to Mr. Newman. Dr. Bacon, Hist. Disc. 20, has shown that it was most probably Robert Newman's, and pointed out its location as being near Temple St., between Elm and Grove streets."—Hoadly's N. H. Col. Records, i. 11, note.

divers queries to them, publicly praying them to consider seriously in the presence and fear of God the weight of the business they met about, and not to be rash or slight in giving their votes to things they understood not, but to digest fully and thoroughly what should be propounded to them, and without respect to men, as they should be satisfied and persuaded in their own minds, to give their answers in such sort as they would be willing they should stand upon record for posterity.

This being earnestly pressed by Mr. Davenport, Mr. Robt. Newman was entreated to write in characters and to read distinctly and audibly in the hearing of all the people what was propounded and accorded on, that it might appear that all consented to matters propounded according to words written by him.

Quær. 1. Whether the Scriptures do hold forth a perfect rule for the direction and government of all men, in all duties which they are to perform to God and men, as well in the government of families and commonwealths as in matters of the church.

This was assented unto by all, no man dissenting, as was expressed by holding up of hands. Afterward it was read over to them that they might see in what words their vote was expressed: They again expressed their consent thereto by holding up their hands, no man dissenting.

Quær. 2. Whereas there was a covenant solemnly made by the whole assembly of freeplanters of this plantation the first day of extraordinary humiliation which we had after we came together, that as in matters that concern the gathering and ordering of a church, so likewise in all public offices which concern civil order, as choice of magistrates and officers, making and repealing of laws, dividing allotments of inheritance, and all things of like nature, we would all of us be ordered by those rules which the Scripture holds forth to us. This covenant was called a plantation covenant to distinguish it from a church covenant which could not at that time be made, a church not being then gathered, but was deferred till a church might be gathered according to God: It was demanded whether all the free planters do hold themselves bound by that covenant in all businesses of that nature which are expressed in the covenant, to submit themselves to be ordered by the rules held forth in the Scripture.

This also was assented unto by all, and no man gainsaid it, and they did testify the same by holding up their hands both when it was first propounded, and confirmed the same by holding up their hands when it was read unto them in public. John Clarke being absent when the covenant was made, doth now manifest his consent to it: also Richard Beach, Andrew Low, Goodman Banister, Arthur Halbidge, John Potter, Robert Hill, John Brockett and John Johnson, these persons being not admitted planters when the covenant was made, do now express their consent to it.

Quær. 3. Those who have desired to be received as free planters, and are settled in the plantation with a purpose, resolution and desire that they may be admitted into church fellowship according to Christ as soon as God shall fit them thereunto, were desired to express it by holding up of hands: Accordingly all did express this to be their desire and purpose by holding up their hands twice, viz., both at the proposal of it, and after when these written words were read unto them.

Quœr. 4. All the free planters were called upon to express whether they held themselves bound to establish such civil order as might best conduce to the securing of the purity and peace of the ordinances to themselves and their posterity according to God. In answer hereunto they expressed, by holding up their hands twice as before, that they held themselves bound to establish such civil order as might best conduce to the ends aforesaid.

Then Mr. Davenport declared unto them by the Scripture what kind of persons might best be trusted with matters of government, and by sundry arguments from Scripture proved that such men as were described in Exodus, xviii. 2, Deuteronomy, i. 13, with Deuteronomy, xvii. 15, and 1 Corinthians, vi. 1 to 7, ought to be intrusted by them, seeing they were free to cast themselves into that mould and form of commonwealth which appeareth best for them, in reference to the securing of the pure and peaceable enjoyment of all Christ his ordinances in the church according to God, whereunto they have bound themselves as hath been acknowledged. Having thus said, he sat down, praying the company freely to consider, whether they would have it voted at this time or not. After some space of silence Mr. Theophilus Eaton answered it might be voted, and some others also spoke to the same purpose, none at all opposing it. Then it was propounded to vote.

Quœr. 5. Whether free burgesses shall be chosen out of church members, they that are in the foundation work of the church being actually free burgesses, and to choose to themselves out of the like estate of church fellowship; and the power of choosing magistrates and officers from among themselves, and the power of making and repealing laws according to the word, and the dividing of inheritances and deciding of differences that may arise, and all the businesses of like nature are to be transacted by those free burgesses.

This was put to vote and agreed unto by the lifting up of hands twice as in the former it was done. Then one man stood up after the vote was past, and expressing his dissenting from the rest in part, yet granting, First, that magistrates should be men fearing God; Second, that the church is the company whence ordinarily such men may be expected; Third, that they that choose them ought to be men fearing God: only at this he stuck, that free planters ought not to give this power out of their hands. Another stood up and answered that in this case nothing was done but with their consent. The former answered that all the free planters ought to resume this power into their own hands again if things were not orderly carried. Mr. Theophilus Eaton answered that in all places they choose committees; in like manner the companies of London choose the liveries by whom the public magistrates are chosen. In this the rest are not wronged, because they expect in time to be of the livery themselves, and to have the same power. Some others entreated the former to give his arguments and reasons whereupon he dissented. He refused to do it and said they might not rationally demand it, seeing he let the vote pass on freely and did not speak till after it was past, because he would not hinder what they agreed upon. Then Mr. Davenport, after a short relation of some former passages between them two about this question, prayed the company that nothing might be concluded by them in this weighty question but what themselves were persuaded to be agreeing with the mind of God; and they had heard what had been said since the voting; entreated them again to consider of it, and put it again to vote as before. Again all of them by holding up their hands did shew their consent as before, and some of them professed that whereas they did waver before they came to the assembly, they were now fully convinced that it is the mind of God. One of them said that in the morning, before he came, reading Deuteronomy, xvii. 15, he was convinced at home; another said that he came doubting to the assembly, but he blessed God by what had been said he was now fully satisfied that the choice of burgesses out of church members, and to intrust those with the power before spoken of, is according to the mind of God revealed in the Scriptures. All having spoken their apprehensions, it was agreed upon, and Mr. Robert Newman was desired to write it as an order whereunto every one that hereafter should be admitted here as planters should submit and testify the same by subscribing their names to the order, namely, that church members only shall be free burgesses, and that they only shall choose magistrates and officers among themselves, to have the power of transacting all the public civil affairs of this plantation, of making and repealing laws, dividing of inheritances, deciding of differences that may arise, and doing all things or businesses of like nature.

This being thus settled as a fundamental agreement concerning civil government, Mr. Davenport proceeded to propound some things to consideration about the gathering of a church. And to prevent the blemishing of the first beginnings of the church work, Mr. Davenport advised that the names of such as were to be admitted might be publicly propounded, to the end that they who were most approved might be chosen, for the town being cast into several private meetings wherein they that dwelt nearest together gave their accounts one to another of God's gracious work upon them, and prayed together and conferred to their mutual edification, sundry of them had knowledge one of another, and in every meeting some one was more approved of all than any other; for this reason, and to prevent scandals, the whole company was entreated to consider whom they found fittest to nominate for this work.

Quær. 6. Whether are you all willing and do agree in this, that twelve men be chosen that their fitness for the foundation work may be tried, however there may be more named, yet it may be in their power who are chosen to reduce them to twelve, and it be in the power of those twelve to choose out of themselves seven that shall be most approved of the major part to begin the church.

This was agreed upon by consent of all, as was expressed by holding up of hands, and that so many as should be thought fit for the foundation work of the church shall be propounded by the plantation, and written down and pass without exception unless they had given public scandal or offence, yet so as in case of public scandal or offence, every one should have liberty to propound their exception at that time publicly against any man that should be nominated, when all their names should be writ down, but if the offence were private, that men's names might be tendered, so many as were offended were entreated to deal with the offender privately, and if he gave not satisfaction, to bring the matter to the twelve that they might consider of it impartially and in the fear of God. The names of the persons nominated and agreed upon were Mr. Theophilus Eaton, Mr. John Davenport, Mr. Robert Newman, Mr. Matthew Gilbert, Mr. Richard Malbon, Mr. Nathaniel Turner, Ezekiel Chevers, Thomas Fugill, John Ponderson, William Andrewes, and Jeremiah Dixon. No exception was brought against any of those in public, except one about taking an excessive rate for meal which he sold to one of Pequanack in his need, which he confessed with grief and declared that having been smitten in heart and troubled in his conscience, he restored such a part of the price back again with confession of his sin to the party, as he thought himself bound to do. And it being feared that the report of the sin was heard farther than the report of his satisfaction, a course was concluded on to make the satisfaction known to as many as heard of the sin. It was also agreed upon at the said meeting that if the persons above named did find themselves straitened in the number of fit men for the seven, that it should be free for them to take into trial of fitness such other as they should think meet, provided that it should be signified to the town upon the Lord's day who they so take in, that every man may be satisfied of them according to the course formerly taken.

Whereas there was a fundamental agreement made in a general meeting of all the free planters of this town, on the fourth of the fourth month called June, namely, that church members only shall be free burgesses, and they only shall choose among themselves magistrates and officers to have the power of transacting all public civil affairs of this plantation, of making and repealing laws, dividing inheritances, deciding of differences that may arise, and doing all things and businesses of like nature. It was therefore ordered by all the said free planters that all those that hereafter should be received as planters into this plantation should also submit to the said fundamental agreement, and testify the same by subscribing their names under the names of the aforesaid planters as followeth:—

Mr. Theoph. Eaton,	Mr. Nath. Turner,
Mr. John Davenport,	Mr. Richard Malbon,
Mr. Samuel Eaton,	Mr. Browninge,
Mr. Robert Newman,	[and the others.]
Mr. Matthew Gilbert,	

A General Court held at Newhaven the 23d of October, 1643.

Whereas this plantation at first with general and full consent laid their foundations that none but members of approved churches should be accounted free burgesses, nor should any else have any vote in any election, or power, or trust in ordering of civil affairs, in which way we have constantly proceeded hitherto in our whole court, with much comfortable fruit through God's blessing: And whereas Stamforde, Guilforde, Yennicock, have upon the same foundations and engagements entered into combination with us, this court was now informed, that of late there have been some meetings and treaties between some of Milforde and Mr. Eaton, about a combination, by which it appeareth, that Milforde hath formerly taken in as free burgesses, six planters who are not in church fellowship, which hath bred some difficulty in the passages of this treaty, but, at present, it stands thus: the deputies for Milforde have offered, in the name both of the church and town, First, that the present six free burgesses who are not church members, shall not at any time hereafter be chosen, either deputies, or into any public trust for the combination. Secondly, that they shall neither personally, nor by proxy, vote at any time in the election of magistrates. And, thirdly, that none shall be admitted freemen or free burgesses hereafter at Milforde, but church members, according to the practice of Newhaven. Thus far they granted, but in two particulars they and their said six freemen desire liberty, first that the said six freemen being already admitted by them, may continue to act in all proper particular town business wherein the combination is not interested. And, secondly, that they may vote in the election of deputies to be sent to the general courts for the combination or jurisdiction, which deputies so to be chosen and sent, shall always be church members.

The premises being seriously considered by the whole court, the brethren did express themselves as one man, clearly and fully, that in the foundations laid for civil government they have attended their light, and should have failed in their duty had they done otherwise, and professed themselves careful and resolved not to shake the said groundworks by any change for any respect, and ordered, that this their understanding of their way, and resolution to maintain it, should be entered with their vote in this business, as a lasting record. But not foreseeing any danger in yielding to Milforde with the before-mentioned cautions, it was, by general consent and vote, ordered that the consociation proceed in all things according to the premises.

A General Court Held at Newhaven for the Jurisdiction, the 27th of October, 1643.

Present:

Magistrates.	Deputies.	
Theoph. Eaton, Gov.,	Geo. Lamberton,	Newhaven.
Steph. Goodyear, Dep.	John Astwood John Shirman	Milforde.
Thomas Gregson,		
William Fowler,	Will Leete Sam. Disbrough	Guilforde.
Edward Tapp,		
	R. Gildersleeve John Whitmore	Stamforde.

It was agreed and concluded as a fundamental order not to be disputed or questioned hereafter, that none shall be admitted to be free burgesses in any of the plantations within this jurisdiction for the future, but such planters as are members of some or other of the approved churches in New England, nor shall any but such free burgesses have any vote in any election, (the six present freemen at Milforde enjoying the liberty with the cautions agreed,) nor shall any power or trust in the ordering of any civil affairs be at any time put into the hands of any other than such church members, though as free planters, all have right to their inheritance and to commerce, according to such grants, orders and laws as shall be made concerning the same.

2. All such free burgesses shall have power in each town or plantation within this jurisdiction to choose fit and able men, from amongst themselves, being

church members as before, to be the ordinary judges, to hear and determine all inferior causes, whether civil or criminal, provided that no civil cause to be tried in any of these plantation courts in value exceed twenty pounds, and that the punishment in such criminals, according to the mind of God, revealed in his word, touching such offences, do not exceed stocking and whipping, or if the fine be pecuniary, that it exceed not five pounds. In which court the magistrate or magistrates, if any be chosen by the free burgesses of the jurisdiction for that plantation, shall sit and assist with due respect to their place, and sentence shall pass according to the vote of the major part of each such court, only if the parties, or any of them, be not satisfied with the justice of such sentences or executions, appeals or complaints may be made from and against these courts to the court of magistrates for the whole jurisdiction.

3. All such free burgesses through the whole jurisdiction, shall have vote in the election of all magistrates, whether Governor, Deputy Governor, or other magistrates, with a Treasurer, a Secretary, and a Marshal, etc. for the jurisdiction. And for the ease of those free burgesses, especially in the more remote plantations, they may by proxy vote in these elections, though absent, their votes being sealed up in the presence of the free burgesses themselves, that their several liberties may be preserved, and their votes directed according to their own particular light, and these free burgesses may, at every election, choose so many magistrates for each plantation, as the weight of affairs may require, and as they shall find fit men for that trust. But it is provided and agreed, that no plantation shall at any election be left destitute of

a magistrate if they desire one to be chosen out of those in church fellowship with them.

4. All the magistrates for the whole jurisdiction shall meet twice a year at Newhaven, namely, the Monday immediately before the sitting of the two fixed general courts hereafter mentioned, to keep a court called the court of magistrates, for the trial of weighty and capital cases, whether civil or criminal, above those limited to the ordinary judges in the particular plantations, and to receive and try all appeals brought unto them from the aforesaid plantation courts, and to call all the inhabitants, whether free burgesses, free planters or others, to account for the breach of any laws established, and for other misdemeanors, and to censure them according to the quality of the offence, in which meetings of magistrates, less than four shall not be accounted a court, nor shall they carry on any business as a court; but it is expected and required, that all the magistrates in this jurisdiction do constantly attend the public service at the times before mentioned, and if any of them be absent at one of the clock in the afternoon on Monday aforesaid when the court shall sit, or if any of them depart the town without leave, while the court sits, he or they shall pay for any such default, twenty shillings fine, unless some providence of God occasion the same, which the court of magistrates shall judge of from time to time; and all sentences in this court shall pass by the vote of the major part of magistrates therein, but from this court of magistrates, appeals and complaints may be made and brought to the general court as the last and highest for this jurisdiction; but in all appeals or complaints from, or to, what court soever, due costs and damages shall be

paid by him or them that make appeal or complaint without just cause.

5. Besides the plantation courts and court of magistrates, there shall be a general court for the jurisdiction, which shall consist of the Governor, Deputy Governor and all the Magistrates within the jurisdiction, and two Deputies for every plantation in the jurisdiction, which deputies shall from time to time be chosen against the approach of any such general court, by the aforesaid free burgesses, and sent with due certificate to assist in the same, all which, both Governor and Deputy Governor, Magistrates and Deputies, shall have their vote in the said court. This general court shall always sit at Newhaven (unless upon weighty occasions the general court see cause for a time to sit elsewhere), and shall assemble twice every year, namely, the first Wednesday in April, and the last Wednesday in October, in the later of which courts, the Governor, the Deputy Governor, and all the magistrates for the whole jurisdiction, with a Treasurer, a Secretary, and Marshal, shall yearly be chosen by all the free burgesses before mentioned: besides which two fixed courts, the Governor, or in his absence, the Deputy Governor, shall have power to summon a general court at any other time, as the urgent and extraordinary occasions of the jurisdiction may require, and at all general courts, whether ordinary or extraordinary, the governor and deputy governor, and all the rest of the magistrates for the jurisdiction, with the deputies for the several plantations, shall sit together, till the affairs of the jurisdiction be dispatched or may safely be respited, and if any of the said magistrates or deputies shall either be absent at the first sitting of the said general court,

(unless some providence of God hinder, which the said court shall judge of,) or depart, or absent themselves disorderly before the court be finished, he or they shall each of them pay twenty shillings fine, with due considerations of further aggravations if there shall be cause; which general court shall, with all care and diligence provide for the maintenance of the purity of religion, and shall suppress the contrary, according to their best light from the word of God, and all wholesome and sound advice which shall be given by the elders and churches in the jurisdiction, so far as may concern their civil power to deal therein.

Secondly, they shall have power to make and repeal laws, and, while they are in force, to require execution of them in all the several plantations.

Thirdly, to impose an oath upon all the magistrates, for the faithful discharge of the trust committed to them, according to their best abilities, and to call them to account for the breach of any laws established, or for other misdemeanors, and to censure them, as the quality of the offence shall require.

Fourthly, to impose an oath of fidelity and due subjection to the laws upon all the free burgesses, free planters, and other inhabitants within the whole jurisdiction.

Fifthly, to settle and levy rates and contributions upon all the several plantations, for the public service of the jurisdiction.

Sixthly, to hear and determine all causes, whether civil or criminal, which by appeal or complaint shall be orderly brought unto them from any of the other courts, or from any of the other plantations, In all which, with whatsoever else shall fall within their cognizance or judicature, they shall proceed according to the Scriptures, which is the rule of all righteous laws and sentences, and nothing shall pass as an act of the general court but by the consent of the major part of magistrates, and the greater part of deputies.

These generals being thus laid and settled, though with purpose that the circumstantials, such as the value of causes to be tried in the plantation courts, the ordinary and fixed times of meetings, both for the general courts, and courts of magistrates, how oft and when they shall sit, with the fines for absence or default, be hereafter considered of, continued or altered, as may best and most advance the course of justice, and best suit the occasions of the plantations, the court proceeded to present particular business of the jurisdiction.

Nevv-Haven's

SETTLING IN

NEW-ENGLAND.

AND SOME

LAWES

FOR

GOVERNMENT:

Publifhed for the Ufe of that Colony.

Though fome of the Orders intended for prefent convenience, may probably be hereafter altered, and as need requireth other Lawes added.

LONDON:

Printed by *M. S.* for *Livewell Chapman*, at the *Crowne* in *Popef-head*-Alley.
1656.

VI.

NEW HAVEN'S SETTLING IN NEW ENGLAND, AND SOME LAWS FOR GOVERNMENT, &c.

It hath pleased the only wise, and all-sufficient God, who ruleth all the world, determines times, and sets the bounds of all men's habitations, but is the rich, and precious portion of them that fear and trust in him, at sundry times, and upon weighty occasions, to bring several companies of his people, over the great deeps, into this part of America, called New England, a place far remote from their dear Native Country, and hath here planted, protected, and graciously provided for them.

The first adventurers (before they had conveniency for travel, and opportunity to consider, and compare one place with another) sat down at Plymouth, and have had much experience of God's goodness and compassion in a wilderness, now betwixt thirty and forty years.

In some years after, the Lord bringing over more of his people, they planted in, and about the Massachusetts Bay, and grew a large colony, and after them the English in Connecticut and New Haven, for the conveniency of the sea, and rivers, planted more westerly. And for a while continued, though united in nation, religion, and affection, yet otherwise several and distinct jurisdictions, free from any express engagement one to another. In this time the enemy slept not, but was at work, to disturb the peace of the English, both in sowing tares within, among themselves, and stirring up the Indians from abroad against them; but He that is wonderful in counsel, and excellent in working, overpowered Satan, and his instruments, and gave good issues to his people, in those their uncomfortable exercises.

A while after, upon the motion of the Massachusets colony, a treaty was begun, and in process of time comfortably finished; solemn covenants were agreed, and concluded betwixt the said jurisdictions, in the following words.

Articles of Confederation betwixt the Plantations under the government of the Massachusets, the Plantations under the government of Plimouth, the Plantations under the government of Connectecut, and the government of New Haven, with the Plantations in combination therewith.

[The articles of confederation between the four colonies, adopted in 1643, need not be re-printed here. They may be found in Hazard's Collection of State Papers, ii. 1-6; Winthrop's History of New England ii. 101; New Haven Col. Records (edited by Mr. Hoadly) ii, 562-566; and elsewhere.]

When the Plantations within this Colony first treated to be one Jurisdiction, and to settle themselves under one Government, these following particulars were solemnly and unanimously approved and concluded as a fundamental Agreement, upon which the Combination was framed.

That none shall be admitted freemen, or free burgesses within this jurisdiction, or any part of it, but such planters as are members of some one, or other of the approved churches of New England; nor shall any but such be chosen to magistracy, or to carry on any part of civil judicature, or as deputies or assistants to have power, or vote in establishing lawes, or in making or repealing orders, or to any chief military office, or trust, nor shall any others, but such church members, have any vote in any such elections. Though all others admitted to be planters, have right to their proper inheritances, and doe and shall enjoy all other civil liberties and priviledges, according to all lawes, orders, or grants, which are, or hereafter shall be made for this colony.*

That all such freemen of this jurisdiction, shall yearly without any summons, upon the election day, which is to be the last fourth day in the week, commonly called Wednesday, in May (till by the generall court some other time be ordered and published), either in person, or by proxy, attend that service: And according to their best light from the word of God, shall vote in the election of Governour, Deputy Governour, Magistrates, Commissioners for the United Colonyes, Treasurer, Secretary, Marshall, or any other officer, then chosen for the jurisdiction. And for the ease of the said freemen (especially such as dwell remote) it is agreed, That when any of them cannot conveniently come, they may send their votes, either written, or in some other way sealed up in the presence of the rest of the freemen in the plantation where they dwell, or the greater part of them. And further, if any of them purposing to be present at the election, when the other votes were sealed up, should after be hindred, and then want opportunity to seale up his

*In this reprint, the marginal references to texts of scripture which authorize the several articles of the Agreement and the provisions of law, are omitted. For this first clause (restricting to church-members the privileges of freemen) the texts cited are: Deut. i. 13; Ex. xviii. 21; Deut. xvii. 15; Jer. xxx. 21.

vote, in the presence of the major part of the freemen; in such case he may seale it up in the presence of two such freemen as knew he sent no vote before, and (upon their testimony or certificate) it shall be accepted, that so the liberty of the freemen may be preserved, they may have means to attend their duty, and their votes may be directed according to their particular light. And the said freemen may at the election court yearly, choose so many magistrates for the jurisdiction in each plantation, as the weight of affaires shall require, and as they shall there find freemen fit for such a trust; provided that when any man of what plantation soever, shall be first propounded for magistracy within this jurisdiction, seasonable notice shalbe first given to all the plantations, of such a purpose, or desire, that all the freemen may duely consider or informe themselves, and that such as cannot be present, but send their votes, may proceed accordingly, and that each freeman whether present or absent, at the election, may the better improve his liberty, It is ordered, that he may give or send his vote, as he finds cause, either in the affirmative, by putting in an Indian corne, or in the negative, by putting in a beane, or in such other manner, as the generall court shall iudge more convenient.

That the affaires of this jurisdiction, may be the better carried on, and that the inhabitants may know whom to obey, and from whom to seek redresse of injuiries, it is agreed, that there be severall courts for severall purposes, and of different constitutions and power.

First, a General Court, which shall consist of the Governor, Deputy Governor, all the Magistrates, and of two Deputies for each Plantation in the Jurisdiction (where there is a church duely gathered, and freemen orderly admitted), which deputies shall be chosen either yearly, or against the approach of any such generall court, by the freemen of each plantation, or the greater number of them, and shall be sent at each generall court with full power (as having the power and voyces of all the said freemen derived to them) to consult of, and determine, all such matters, as concerne the publick welfare of this colony, and with due certificate thereof, all which both Governor, Deputy Governor, magistrates, and plantation deputies shall have vote in the said court.

This generall court and all the members thereof, shall from time to time meete and sitt at Newhaven (unlesse upon weighty cause, the major part of the court see cause for a time to alter the place), at least once every yeare, namely the last fourth day in the weeke commonly called Wednesday in May; first to carry on the elections, and after to consider and order, all such other affaires of the jurisdiction, as fall within their cognizance, trust, and power, beside which fixed courts, the Governor, or in his absence, the Deputy Governor, and in their absence, any two Magistrates of this jurisdiction, shall have power to summon a generall court, at any other time, as the urgent and extraordinary occasions of the jurisdiction, or any part thereof, may require, and at all such generall courts, whether ordinary, or extraordinary, the Governor, Deputy Governor, Magistrates, with all the before-mentioned deputies, shall sitt together till the affaires of the jurisdiction be dispatched, or may (as they conceive) be safely respited; And if any of the said magistrates, or deputies, shall either be absent at the first sitting of the said court, or without leave depart, or disorderly absent him or themselves from the service, before the court be finished (though the absence of a lesse part, either of magistrates, or deputies, when the court is either fixed, or with due notice, called extraordinarily, shall neither stop proceedings nor abate the force of what is ordered, by the major part both of magistrates, and deputies, yet) he, or they, shall each of them pay twenty shillings for a fine to the jurisdiction, for such absence, or departure; But if any Plantation send no deputy, or if the absence, or departure, be mingled with contempt, or willfull neglect, which may either hinder the publick service, or prove an ill example, the fine shall be increased, as the court upon due consideration of the offence, with the agravations, shall judge meete, or if the absence &c. grow by any overruling providence of God, the same is also duely to be considered by the court, for sparing or mitigating the fine.

This court thus framed, shall first with all care, and diligence from time to time provide for the maintenance of the purity of religion, and suppresse the contrary, according to their best light, and directions from the word of God.

Secondly, though they humbly acknowledge, that the Supreame power of making lawes, and of repealing them, belongs to God onely, and that by him this power is given to Jesus Christ as Mediator, Matt. xxviii. 19, John v. 22: And that the lawes for holinesse, and righteousnesse, are already made, and given us in the Scriptures, which in matters morall, or of morall equity, may not be altered by humane power, or authority; Moses onely shewed Israel the lawes, and statutes of God, and the Sanedrim the highest court, among the Jewes, must attend those lawes: Yet civill rulers, and courts, and this Generall Court in particular (being intrusted by the freemen as before) arethe ministers of God, for the good of the people; And have power to declare, publish, and establish, for the plantations within their jurisdictions, the lawes he hath made, and to make and repeale orders for smaller matters, not particularly determined in Scripture, according to the more generall rules of righteousnesse, and while they stand in force, to require due execution of them.

Thirdly, to require an oath from all the magistrates, deputies, or assistents, &c., in every court of judicature, for the faithfull discharge of the trust committed to them, according to their best abilities. And to call them to account for the breach of any lawes established, or for other misdemeanours in their places, and to censure them as the quality of the offence may require; and here the vote to passe as in the Law of Appeals.

Fourthly, to impose an oath of fidelity and due subjection to the just lawes standing in force, upon all the freemen, planters, and inhabitants fit to take an oath, with due penalty for obstinate refusall, after some convenient time hath been given for due consideration.

Fifthly, to order and appoint such works and fortifications as they conceive may tend to the better defence of this colony; with guns, ammunition, and all other provisions and furniture suitable thereunto: And to provide that the same be kept and preserved in a condition fit for present service, whether against Indians, or other enemies. And to order all affairs of war and peace, levying of men, &c. with due respect to the former articles of confederation.

Sixthly, to order and regulate trade, both with

Indians and others, according to the rules of righteousness and prudence, for the publick good; and to settle and levy rates, contributions and impositions upon all sorts of persons, lands and goods, within this jurisdiction, as the publick service, and occasions of church or commonwealth may from time to time require.

Seventhly, to hear and determine all causes, whether civil or criminall, which by appeal or complaint shall be orderly brought unto them, either from any inferiour court, or from any of the plantations.

In all which, with what ever else falls within their cognizance, trust or judicature (as the highest court within this jurisdiction) they shall proceed according to Scripture light, and lawes, and orders, agreeing therewith. And nothing shall be concluded, and passe as an act of the general court (unlesse in cases expressly excepted) but by the consent and vote of the major part of the magistrates, together with the consent and vote of the greater part of the deputies.

Secondly, there shall be a court, called the Court of Magistrates, wherein all the magistrates for the jurisdiction, shal meete and sitt at New-haven, at least twice a year; namely, the second day of the weeke, commonly called Munday, before the court of elections in the third month called May, and the third fourth day in the weeke, commonly called Wednesday, in the eight month called October, to heare, examine, and determine, all weighty and capitall causes civill, and criminall, above those limited to plantation courts, and to receive, and try all appeales duely brought unto them, from plantation courts, and to call all the inhabitants, freemen, planters, and others to account for breach of any lawes, or orders, established, or for other misdemeanours, and to censure them, as the quality of the offence shall require, in which meetings of the magistrates, lesse than foure magistrates, shall not be accounted a court, nor shall they carry on any buisnesse as a court of magistrates. But it is expected, and required, that all, and every of the magistrates for this jurisdiction, doe constantly attend the publick service; at every court of magistrates, whether fixed, or upon speciall occasion duely summoned, either by the Governor, or in his absence, by the Deputy Governor, or in their absence, by any two magistrates of this jurisdiction, and if any of them (having had due warning) be absent at the first sitting of any such court, or after without leave depart, or disorderly absent himselfe from the service, before the court be finished, he, or they shall pay for every such default, twenty shillings fine to the jurisdiction, or more as the case may require, unlesse some providence of God (whereof the court of magistrates shall from time to time judge) did necessarily cause the same, and all sentences in this court, shall passe by the vote of the major part of the magistrates present, onely the Governor, and in his absence the Deputy Governor, when votes in other respects are equall, shall in this court, and when they or either of them sitt in a plantation court, have a casting voyce, but from this court, appeales and complaints may be made, and brought to the generall court, the plaintiff in point of security, first duely attending the Law of Appeales.

Thirdly, beside the generall court, and court of magistrates, for the ease of the inhabitants, there shall be Plantation Courts, to heare and determine inferiour causes, which courts may be of two sorts, namely, in every plantation within this jurisdiction, where there is a magistrate, one, or more, the freemen from among themselves, shall choose at least two deputies, but three or fower if they see cause, to assist the magistrate, or magistrates, and in such courts they may try any civill cause betwixt party and party, in valew not exceeding twenty pounds, and any criminall cause, when the punishment by Scripture light, exceeds not stocking, and whipping, and if the fine be pecuniary, when the fine exceeds not five pounds, and in all such courts, the sentance shall passe according to the vote of the major part of the court, onely when votes in their number are equall, the casting voyce shall be in the Governor, or Deputy Governor, or magistrates present. But to expedite justice with as little inconvenience as may be to magistrates more remote, it is agreed, and ordered, that any such plantation court, calling in two other magistrats, from any other neighbouring plantation, or plantations, within this jurisdiction, may try any civill cause, though of the highest valew, and any criminall cause, provided it be not capitall, extending to the life of the offendor, but in such plantations, if the magistrate upon any occasion be absent, the deputies alone have no such power of judicature, onely to prevent inconveniences, they may order the marshall to stay any malefactor or suspitious person, or seize, or stop the estate of any man, or part of it, upon case shewn, when the case will not admit delay, till the magistrate come home, provided that sufficient security be taken of him, or them, causing such stay or seizure, to pay just damages, if the proceedings prove unwarantable, and in case of remove, or death of such magistrate, the deputies fall in with other plantations, where there is no magistrate, till further order be taken, and in such plantations deputies being chosen, either by the generall court, or with their allowance, by the freemen from among themselves, they may keepe courts to issue smaller causes, and to order other affaires, in all respects, as the general court shall from time to time appoint and limit, but from all these courts, and in all tryals, and proceedings in them, appeals and complaints may be brought to the court of magistrates, the plaintiff putting in security, according to the Law of Appeales.

These generalls were at first laid, as a foundation for government, though it was foreseene, and agreed, that the circumstantialls therein, such as the ordinary, and fixed times both for elections, and for the meeting of the generall court, and court of magistrates, how oft, and when they shall sit, the fines for absence, or disorderly departing, and the valew of causes to be tryed in plantation courts, with other particulars in their proceedings, might after be further considered, continued or altered, as may best suite the course of justice, and the conveniency of the plantations.

Certaine Lawes, Liberties, and Orders, made, granted, and established, at severall times, by the Generall Court of New-haven Colony, for and to the Inhabitants of that Jurisdiction, now collected, and further published, for the use of such as are concerned in them, wherein they have made use of the Lawes published by the Honourable Colony of the Massachusets.*

* The first edition of the "Laws and Liberties" of Massachusetts was published, by authority, in 1649. No copy of this edition is known to be extant. The Massachusetts "Body of Liberties" was established in 1641.

It is ordered by this court, and the authority thereof, that no man's life shall be taken away, no man's honour, or good name, shall be stained, no man's person shall be imprisoned, banished, or otherwise punished, no man shall be deprived of his wife, or children, no man's goods, or estate shall be taken from him, under colour of law, or countenance of authority, unlesse it be by vertue, or equity of some expresse law of this jurisdiction, established by the generall court, and sufficiently published, or for want of a law in any particular case, by the word of God, either in the court of magistrates, or some plantation court, according to the weight and valew of the cause, onely all capitall causes, concerning life or banishment where there is no expresse law, shall be judged according to the word and law of God, by the generall court.

That no man shall be put to death, for any offence, or misdemeanour in any case, without the testimony of two witnesses at least, or that which is equivalent thereunto; provided, and to prevent, or suppresse much inconvenience which may grow, either to the publick, or to particular persons, by a mistake herein, it is ordered, and declared, by the authority aforesaid, that two, or three single witnesses, being of competent age, of sound understanding, and of good reputation, and witnessing to the case in question (whither it concerne the publick peace, and welfare, or any one, and the same particular person) shall be accounted (the party concerned, having no just exception against them) sufficient proofe, though they did not together see, or heare, and so witnesse to the same individuall, and particular act, in reference to those circumstances of time, and place.

Actions.

It is ordered by this court and the authority thereof, that every person impleading another, in the court of magistrates, or in any plantation court, when the debt or damage he demands, or the action he layeth, is above twenty pounds, so that it cannot be tryed by a plantation court unless two magistrates of some other plantation, be called in to assist, he shall pay the sum of ten shillings, before his case be entred, or any part of it heard, unlesse the court see cause to admit the plaintiff to sue, *in forma pauperis.* But in all actions, brought to any court, the plaintiff shall have liberty to withdraw his action, or to be non-suited, before sentence passe, in which case, he shall alwayes pay full cost and charges to the defendent, and may after renew his suite at another court.

Age.

It is ordered, &c. that the age for passing away of lands, or such kinds of hereditaments, or ingagements of like nature, as for giving of votes, passing sentences in publick meetings, civil courts, or causes, shall be at least twenty and one years, but in cases admitting the choyce of guardians, any age above fourteen may be sufficient.

Appeales.

It is ordered, &c. that if any man cast, or sentenced in his cause, be unsatisfied with the proceedings and issue, it shall be in his liberty (the cause not being criminall) to make his appeal from any plantation court, to the court of magistrates; and in like case, from the court of magistrates, to the general court. But in such case, when the magistrates, or some of them, have already exprest themselves, to prevent difference and inconvenience, it is ordered, that the major part of the general court, consisting of magistrates and deputies, taken joyntly shall issue it. But to prevent, or provide against unnecessary trouble to courts, charge to the jurisdiction, and other inconveniencies which may follow, if the course of justice be delayed, or evaded, it is further ordered, that whosoever shall so appeal, doe tender his appeal, and put in sufficient security before the judges of the court from which he appeales, the secretary, or other person or persons authorized to admit appeals, effectually by himself, his deputy or attorney to prosecute his appeal, at the next usuall fixed time of that court's sitting, to which the appeale is made; and to observe, perform, and pay to the defendant, as shall be there adjudged; but every such appeal shall be entred, and security as before put in, within three days after sentence in the cause was given, and the same at the charge of the party appealing, to be recorded, and certified to the court, unto which the appeale is made. And lastly, it is ordered, that if in the review it appear, the plaintiff had no cause to appeale, petition, or complain, he shall pay such further charge, as the court shall judge hath been expended in their sitting to re-examine his cause, that no unnecessary charge fall upon the Colony.

Appearance. Non-Appearance.

It is ordered, &c. that no man shall be punished for not appearing at or before any civil assembly, court, magistrate, or officer, nor for omission of any office or service, to be performed in his own person only, if he shall be necessarily hindred by any apparent providence of God, which he could neither foresee, nor avoid, and by giving or sending notice, hath done what was in his power. Provided, that this law shall not prejudice any person of his just cost and damage, in any civil action.

Arrests. See *Imprisonment.*

Attachment. See further in the Title *Distresse.*

It is ordered, &c. that no attachment shall be granted in any civil action to any forraigner, against a setled inhabitant of this jurisdiction, before he hath given sufficient security, or caution, duly to prosecute his action, and to answer the defendant such costs and damages, as the court shall award. And it is further ordered, that in all attachments of goods and chattels, of lands or hereditaments, whether by forraigners, or setled inhabitants, legall notice shall be given to the party concerned, or left in writing at his house, or place of usuall abode, before the suit proceed; but if he be out of the jurisdiction, the cause shall proceed to tryall, but judgement shall not be entred till another court at least a month after. And if the defendant doe not then appear, judgement shall be entred, but execution shall not be granted before the plaintiff hath given sufficient security to be responsall to the defendant, if he shall reverse the judgement within one year, or such further time as the court shall see cause to order.

Bakers.

It is ordered, &c. that every person within this jurisdiction, who shall bake bread for sale, shall have a distinct mark for his bread, and keep the true assizes hereafter expressed and appointed.

When wheat is ordinarily sold by the bushell, at

the severall rates hereafter mentioned, the penny white loaf, penny wheaten loaf, and penny household loaf shall weigh severally and respectively by *aver dupoyse* weight as followeth.

When the bushell of wheat is

s.d.	the			
at 3.0,	penny white loaf	11 1-4 oz.	wheaten 17 1-4 oz.	houshold 23 oz.
at 3.6,	penny white loaf	10 1-4 oz.	wheaten 15 1-4 oz.	houshold 20 1-2 oz.
at 4.0,	penny white loaf	9 1-4 oz.	wheaten 14 oz.	houshold 18 1-2 oz.
at 4.6,	penny white loaf	8 1-4 oz.	wheaten 12 3-4 oz.	houshold 16 1-2 oz.
at 5.0,	penny white loaf	7 3-4 oz.	wheaten 11 1-2 oz.	houshold 15 1-2 oz.
at 5.6,	penny white loaf	7 oz.	wheaten 10 1-2 oz.	houshold 14 1-4 oz.
at 6.0,	penny white loaf	6 1-2 oz.	wheaten 10 oz.	houshold 13 oz.
at 6.6,	penny white loaf	6 oz.	wheaten 9 1-2 oz.	houshold 12 1-4 oz.

And so proportionably under the penalty of forfeiting all such bread, as shall not answer the before-mentioned severall assizes. And for the better execution of this order there shalbe in every plantation, as occasion may require, an officer yearly chosen, who shal be sworn at the next plantation court, or by the next magistrate, or officer for taking oaths, unto the faithfull discharge of his office, who is hereby authorized to enter into any house, either with the constable, or marshall, or without, where he understands that any bread is baked for sale, and to weigh such bread, as often as he seeth cause: and after once notice, or warning, to seize all such bread as he findeth defective in weight, or not marked according to this order. And all such forfeitures shall be divided, one third part to the officer for his care and paines, and the rest to the poor of the place.

Ballast.

It is ordered, &c. that no ballast shall be cast out of any ship or other vessel in the channel, or other place inconvenient, in any harbour within this jurisdiction, under the penalty of ten pounds to be levied upon the owners, mariners, seamen, or others offending, to the use of the said plantation. The ship or vessel to be stayed till payment be made.

Barratry.

It is ordered, &c. That if any person be proved, and judged a common barrater, vexing others with unjust, frequent, and troublesome suites, it shall be in the power of any court, both to reject his cause, and to punish him for his barratry. *

Bills and Specialties.

It is ordered, &c. That any debt, or debts, due upon bill, or other specialty, being duly assigned to another, shall be as good a debt, and estate to the assignee, as it was, or could be, to the assigner. And that it shall be lawfull for the said assignee to sue for, and recover the said debt, due upon bill, or other specialty, and so assigned, as fully as the original creditor might have done. Provided the assignation be either made upon the back of the specialty, or to the court some other way cleared, that future questions may be stopped, or duly answered. †

Burglary and Theft.

It is ordered, &c. That if any person shall commit burglary, or break up any dwelling house, or any thing equi[va]lent, or rob any person by force, or by using any threatning gestures, or other actions, in the fields, high-wayes, or other place, the party so offending, shall for the first offence (beside such restitution and damage as the court to which the cognizance be-

---

* Mass. Body of Liberties, §34, amended; and Conn. Code.

† Conn. Code, (see page 65,) with verbal amendments.

longs, shall see cause to order) be branded on the right hand with the letter (B); if he shall offend in the like kind a second time (beside restitution and damage) he shall be branded on the left hand, and also be severely whipt; and if he fall into the like offence the third time, (beside restitution and damage out of his estate) he shall be put to death as incorrigible. And if any person shall commit such burglary, or so rob in any place on the Lord's day, he shall (beside restitution and damage) for the first offence, be burnt on the right hand, as before, and severely whipt; for the second offence, he shall be burnt on the left hand, stand on the pillory, be severely whipt, and wear a halter in the day time constantly and visibly about his neck, as a mark of infamy, till the court of magistrates see cause to release him from it; but if he fall into the same offence the third time, he shall be put to death as incorrigibly unrighteous, and presumptuously profane.*

And to prevent or suppresse other thefts, and pilfrings, it is ordered, That if any person shall be taken, or proved to have stollen, assisted, or any way have been accessary to the stealing of any cattel of what sort soever, or swine, he shall by way of forfeit make such restitution to the owner, as the court considering all circumstances, shall judge most agreeable to the word of God. And if any person shall be proved to have stollen any goods of what sort soever, out of any man's dwelling-house, warehouse, barn, or other outhouse, or left out in court, yard, garden, orchard, highway, from the water-side, or out of any boat or vessel, or other place, or to have robbed any garden, or orchard, or stollen, or hurt, any grafts, or fruit-trees,

* Massachusetts law of 1646.

or fruit, he shall forfeit and pay double damages to the owner, beside such further fine and punishment, as the court considering all aggravating circumstances of time, manner &c., shall judge meet.* If the thief in any part of the premisses be not able to make restitution (if the case require it) he is to be sold for a servant, till by his labour he may make due restitution. And if any children, or servants, who cannot pay for themselves, shall transgresse, and trespasse in any part of the premisses, if their parents or masters will not pay the penalty for them, they shall be publickly whipt, or further proceeded against as the case may require, and all servants, and workemen, imbezeling, pilfring, or stealing the goods of their masters, or such as set them on worke, shall make such restitution, and be liable to all lawes and penalties as other men, and if any person shall be proved to pilfer or steale a second or third time, his punishment shall be increased by whiping or otherwise, as the court shall see cause.

And forasmuch as small thefts, trespasses, or other offences of a criminall nature, are sometimes committed by the English or others in townes or places remote from prisons, or it may prove inconvenient to defer the tryall, or to make stay of the persons offending, or hard to get security for appearance at a court, it is therefore ordered, that any magistrate, or deputy intrusted to assist in judicature, calling in such other help as the place affords for a plantation court (which help is hereby required to attend the service upon due warning), may upon complaint brought to him, when the case so requires, with the first conveniency, heare, and upon due proofe determine any such offence (the valew whereof

---

* **Massachusetts law of 1646.**

either in point of fine, damage, or other punishment exceeds not the limits of that plantation court, according to the lawes here established) and may give warrant to the marshall, or other officer, for answerable execution, but if the offendor refuse to pay or have nothing to satisfie, the magistrate, or deputy with the help aforesaid, may punish by stocking, whiping, or otherwise; according to the nature of the offence, and import of this law.

Capitall Lawes.

It is ordered, &c., That if any person after legall, or other due conviction, shall have, or worship any other God, but the Lord God, he shall be put to death. Exod. 22. 20. Deut. 13. 6, 10. Deut. 17. 2, 3, 4, 5, 6.

If any person be a witch, he or she shall be put to death, according to Exod. 22. 18. Levit. 20. 27. Deut. 18. 10, 11.

If any person within this jurisdiction, professing the true God, shall wittingly and willingly presume to blaspheme the holy name of God, Father, Son, or Holy Ghost, with direct, expresse, presumptuous, or high-handed blasphemy, either by willfull or obstinate denying the true God, or his creation, or government of the world, or shall curse God, Father, Son, or Holy Ghost, or reproach the holy religion of God, as if it were but a politick device to keep ignorant men in awe; or shall utter any other kind of blasphemy of like nature, and degree, such person shall be put to death. Levit. 24. 15, 16.

If any person shall commit any wilfull murder, if he shall kill any man, woman, or child, upon premeditated malice, hatred, or cruelty (not in a way of necessary and just defence, nor by meer casualty against his will) he shall be put to death. Exod. 21. 12, 13. Numb. 35. 31.

If any person slayeth another suddenly in anger, or cruelty of passion, he shall be put to death. Lev. 24. 17. Numb. 35. 16, 17, 18, 19, 20, 21.

If any person come presumptuosly to slay another with guile, whether by any kinde of force, poyson, or other wicked practice, every such person shall be put to death. Ex. 21. 14. Agreeing with Deut. 19. 19. By parity of reason.

If any man or woman, shall lye with any beast, or bruite creature by carnall copulation, he, or she, shall surely be put to death, and the beast shall be slaine, buried, and not eaten. Lev. 20. 15, 16.

If any man lyeth with mankinde, as a man lyeth with a woman, both of them have committed abomination, they both shall surely be put to death. Levit. 20. 13. And if any woman change the naturall use, into that which is against nature, as Rom. 1. 26. she shall be liable to the same sentence, and punishment, or if any person, or persons, shall commit any other kinde of unnaturall and shamefull filthines, called in Scripture the going after strange flesh, or other flesh then God alloweth, by carnall knowledge of another vessel then God in nature hath appointed to become one flesh, whether it be by abusing the contrary part of a grown woman, or child of either sex, or unripe vessel of a girle, wherein the naturall use of the woman is left, which God hath ordained for the propagation of posterity, and Sodomiticall filthinesse (tending to the destruction of the race of mankind) is committed by a kind of rape, nature being forced, though the will were inticed, every such person shall be put to death. Or if any man shall act upon himself, and in the sight of others spill his owne seed, by example, or counsel, or both, corrupting or tempting others to doe the like, which tends to the sin of Sodomy, if it be not one kind of it; or shall defile, or corrupt himself and others, by any other kind of sinfull filthinesse, he shall be punished according to the nature of the offence; or if the case considered with the aggravating circumstances, shall according to the mind of God revealed in his word require it, he shall be put to death, as the court of magistrates shall determine. Provided that if in any of the former cases, one of the parties were forced, and so abused against his or her will, the innocent person (crying out, or in due season complaining) shall not be punished, or if any of the offending parties were under fourteen year old, when the sin was committed, such person shall onely be severely corrected, as the court of magistrates considering the age, and other circumstances, shall judge meet.

If any man married, or single, commit adultery with a marryed or espoused wife, the adulterer and adulteresse shall surely be put to death. Lev. 18. 20. Lev. 20. 10. Deut. 22. 23, 24.

If any person steale a man, or mankind, that person shall surely be put to death. Exod. 21. 16.

If any person rise up by false witnesse, wittingly and of purpose to take away any man's life, that person shall be put to death. Deut. 19. 16, 18, 19.

If any person shall conspire, and attempt any invasion, insurrection, or publick rebellion against this jurisdiction, or shall endeavour to surprize, or seize any plantation, or town, any fortification, platform, or any great guns, provided for the defence of the jurisdiction, or any plantation therein; or shall treacherously and perfidiously attempt the alteration and subversion of the frame of policy, or fundamentall government laid, and setled for this jurisdiction, he or they shall be put to death. Numb. 16. 2 Sam. 18. 2 Sam. 20. Or if any person shall consent unto any such mischievous practice, or by the space of foure and twenty houres conceale it, not giving notice thereof to some magistrate, if there be any magistrate in the plantation, or place where he liveth, or if none, to some deputy for the jurisdiction, or to the constable of the place, that the publick safety may be seasonably provided for, he shall be put to death, or severely punished, as the court of magistrates weighing all circumstances shall determine.

If any child, or children, above sixteen year old, and of competent understanding, shall curse, or smite, his, her, or their naturall father, or mother, each such child shall be put to death, Exod. 21. 17. Levit. 20. 9. Exod. 21. 15, unlesse it be proved, that the parents have been very unchristianly negligent in the education of such child, or children, or so provoked them by extream and cruell correction, or usage, that they have been urged or forced thereunto, to preserve themselves from death or maiming.

If any man have a stubborn rebellious son, of sufficient age and understanding, namely sixteen year old, or upward, which will not obey the voyce of his father, or the voyce of his mother; and that when they have chastned him, will not hearken unto them, then shall his father and his mother (being his naturall parents) lay hold on him, and bring him to the magistrates assembled in court, and testifie unto them, that their son is stubborn and rebellious, and will not obey their voyce and chastisement, but lives in sundry notorious crimes; such a son shall be put to death. Deut. 21. 18, 19, 20, 21.

If any man shall ravish any maid, or single woman, who is above the age of ten years, committing carnall copulation with her by force, against her own will, he shall be severely and grievously punished, as the court of magistrates considering all circumstances shall determine.

Caske and Cooper.

It is ordered, &c. That all cask, whether pipes, hogsheads, barrels, quarter cask, or other sorts used in trade, whether for any liquor, fish, pork, beef, or other commodity put to sale, shall be of London assize. And that in each plantation within this jurisdiction, where cask is made or used for trade, the plantation court, or the constable, with the present or last deputies for the generall court, where there is no plantation court, shall from time to time appoint some fit person, or persons, to view and gage all such vessel or cask: and such as shall be found of due assize and made of sound, and well seasoned stuffe, (and none but such shall be marked with the gager's mark) who shall have for his paines eight pence for every tun, and proportionably for what he so marketh. And every cooper shall have, and set a distinct brand-mark of his own, upon each cask, upon paine of forfeiting after the rate of twenty shillings a tun, for what he sells, either without the gager's mark, or not marked with his own constant brand mark.

Cattell, Corn Fields, Fences.

To prevent, or remedy much inconvenience, and many differences which may grow about fencing, planting, sowing, feeding, and improving of common fields, inclosed for corn, or other necessary use, it is ordered, That every person interessed in any such field shall from time to time, make and keep his part of the fence, sufficiently strong and in constant repaire, according to all orders in force in each plantation, to secure the corn, and other fruits therein. And shall not put, cause, or permit any cattel to be put in, so long as any corn, or other fruit shall be growing, or remain upon any part of the land so inclosed. Unlesse by some generall expresse agreement of such as are interessed. And if at any time the owners or occupiers of any such inclosed land cannot, or doe not agree, in any part of the premises, it is ordered, That upon due and seasonable notice given to the select men or towns men, appointed for prudentiall affaires, proper to their care and trust, by any concerned, and unsatisfied, they shall appoint a convenient time to hear and order such differences, and settle a due way of fencing, improving, and preserving such fields, and the fruits of them. And whosoever shall oppose or transgresse, shall be liable to all damages proved to grow thereby, and to such further fine for breach of order, as the plantation court, or authority there setled for such purposes, shall judge meet. But in any plantation, where there are yet no such select, or towns men, the freemen from among themselves, shall yearly choose a convenient number to order such occasions, that peace and righteousnesse may be the better preserved therein. And these select, or towns men, shall from year to year appoint one, two, or more, of the planters, for all or each common field, belonging to the plantation where they dwell, to view the common fences within their trust and to take due notice of the reall defects and insufficiency thereof, and shall forthwith acquaint the owners with the same. And if the said owners or occupiers doe not at furthest within six working dayes, or sooner if the said select men see cause, and so appoint, sufficiently repaire, or cause the same to be repaired, he, or they, shall forthwith upon the demand of the appointed viewer or viewers (beside other just damages) pay as a fine to the plantation, twelve pence for every rod (if there be a considerable quantity of such defective fence together), or for every single defect, in such faulty fence, or the said viewer or viewers, taking due witnesse of the defects, may if it suite their conveniency forthwith repaire or renew them, or cause them to be repaired or renewed, and shall have double recompence for the same, to be paid (beside other just damages) by the owners, or occupiers of the said insufficient fence, or fences. And in either case if payment be denyed or delayed, such viewer, or viewers, shall have warrant from the said select men, directed to the marshall, or constable, to levy the same forthwith upon the estate of the delinquent.

And when lands lye in common unfenced if one man shall improve his land by fencing in severall, and others, one, or more shall not, he who shall so improve, shall secure his land from other men's cattel (unruly cattle excepted), who shall compell no man to make any fence with him, except he also improve in severall, and where one man shall improve before his neighbour, and so make the whole fence, if his said neighbour shall after improve, he shall then satisfie for half the other's fence against him, according to the present value, and shall maintaine the same: and if the said first man shall after lay open his said field, or land, then the said neighbour shall both enjoy his said half fence so purchased, and shall have liberty to buy the other half fence against his land, paying according to the present worth as it shall be rated by two men indifferently chosen. And the like order shall be, when any man shall improve land, against, or adjoyning to a town common. Provided this extend not to house-lots, in which, if one shall improve, his neighbour or neighbours shall be compellable to make, and maintaine one half of the fence between them, whether he or they improve, or not. Provided also, that no man shall be liable to damage done in any ground not sufficiently fenced, and himself not interessed in the defective fence, or some part of it, except the damage were done by prohibited or unruly cattel of any sort (in which swine are included) which cannot be restrained by ordinary fences, or where any shall unwarrantably put in cattel, of what sort, or under what colour or pretence soever, or otherwise willfully trespasse upon his neighbour's ground.

It is further ordered, That whatsoever swine, or greater cattel (horses excepted, which are particularly mentioned hereafter,) shall be found in the woods, or commons unmarked, are lyable to poundage, and being either pounded, or otherwise prosecuted and proved, the owner shall pay for each swine unmarked, three shillings and four pence, of which half the fines to the pounder, or prosecutor, and the rest to the plantation. And for each of the greater sort of cattel, six shillings, whereof half shall be ordered to the pounder, or prosecutor, and the rest to the plantation; but if the owners be not known, or found, then every such swine or beast of a greater kind, to be duly cryed, that the owner may take notice, claim his interest, and pay the fine, and charges; but if yet no owner be found, then after due apprisement by indifferent men chosen by authority in the place, and the same recorded by the secretary, sale to be so far made, that the fine and charges may be fully paid, and the remainder kept by the treasurer, till the owner be knowne, and the rest of such swine, or cattel, being first marked with a publick town mark, or brand, with some distinction from the mark of particular men, to be again turned into the woods.

Lastly, it is ordered, That no owner of cattel, of what kind soever, after knowledge, or notice given, that any cattel of his, whether horse, other beast, or swine, is unruly in respect to fences, shall suffer any such to goe at liberty, either in common, or against corn fields, or other impropriate enclosed grounds fenced as aforesaid, but shall either constantly keep them upon his own ground, within sufficient fences, all his own, or put and keep upon each of them, such shackles and fetters, or yoaks and rings, as may sufficiently from time to time, restrain and prevent trespasse, or shall pay all damages and charges, whether in corne, or other fruits, with hurt in fences, expence of time, and help in catching, pounding, driving out, and bringing home, any such unruly cattel, of what kind soever, with such further fine for breach of order, and court charges, if the plaintiff be put to recover it that way, as the court shall judge meet.

Charges Publick.

That publick charges may be defrayed in a ready and just way, it is ordered by this court, and the authority thereof, That in each plantation within this jurisdiction, the select or towns men,* or some others

*"It seems that Townsmen were chosen in New Haven for the first time, November 17, 1651, that the town meetings, 'which spends

thereunto deputed, doe yearly the first week of the third month called May, require, procure, and make a full and just list of all the male persons within their limits, from sixteen years old, and upwards; and a true estimation of all personall and reall estates, being or reputed to be the estate of all and every the persons belonging to the plantation, or in their present possession, viz. of houses, lands of all sorts, meadow and upland, as well unbroken up, as other (except such as doth and shall lye common for free feed of cattel at all times to the use of the inhabitants in generall), mills, ships, and all small vessels, merchantable goods, cranes, wharfs, and all sorts of cattel and other estate (houshold stuff, and goods of that kind, provided and kept for that use, and not for trade, onely excepted), whether at sea, or on shoar, with a due consideration and estimate of the advantage men may have by their severall and respective arts, or trades. Which list, and particular account, of males and estates in reference to rates, shall by the deputies chosen by each plantation, and sent to assist at the generall court, be presented yearly when they sit, in the latter end of May, under such penalty for default, as the court considering the hindrance in the jurisdiction affaires, shall see cause to inflict. All which persons and estates, are to be assessed and rated, by such as are thereunto appointed, for one single rate, as followeth, viz. every male person above sixteen years of age (except magistrates and elders of churches) at twenty pence by the head, and all estates both reall and personall, at one penny for every twenty shillings. And that houses (wherein there is much difference)

---

the towne much time, may not be so often.' Town Rec. ii. 76."—C. J. Hoadly, in note to N. H. Col. Rec. ii. 581.

may be the more equally rated, according to their worth, it is ordered, That the deputies from the severall plantations within this jurisdiction now assembled at this generall court, doe before their return, rate two houses in New-haven, which shal be as patterns for the other plantations to rate by. That all lands, whether meadow, or upland, and whether the upland be better, or worse, broken up, or not (except it lye common as before), be rated at twenty shillings an acre; and for that a considerable part of men's estates in these parts, lyeth in cattel, to avoyd many questions which may grow about their age, it is ordered, That all sorts of cattel from year to year, though any of them should not be a year old till the last of July, yet in reference to rates, be accounted, and pay as if they were a year old the first of May. And in like manner for two years old, or elder; and in lieu thereof, cattel though near three quarters of a year old the first of May, shall not be rated, and cattel of a year and almost three quarters, shall be rated but a year old, and so upward. And it is further ordered, That till this court find some considerable alteration in prises, every cow of four year old (the age reckoned as before) or upward, shall be rated at five pounds; every heifer, or steer, three year old, reckoned as before, at four pounds; and betwixt two and three years old, at fifty shillings; and of one year old, thirty shillings. Every ox, and bull of four year old, or upward, at six pounds; every horse of three year old (after the former account) or more, shall be valued at ten pounds; every mare of three year old, or upward, at twelve pounds; those of two year old, or upward, according to the former account, whether horse, or mares, each of them at five pounds ten shillings; and those of three-quarters of a year old, or above, till they come to be a year and three-quarters, shall be rated at three pounds and ten shillings; every yew sheep of a year old, or above, at thirty shillings; every weather sheep, or ram, of a year old, or above, at sixteen shillings; every goat of a year old, or above, at eight shillings; every swine of a year old, or above, at twenty shillings; every asse of a year old, or above, at forty shillings. And all hey, and corn in the husbandman's hand, is hereby exempted from rates, because all meadow, arrable land, and cattel, are rateable as aforesaid. And for all such persons, as by the advantage of their arts and trades, are more enabled to bear publick charges, then common labourers and workmen, as butchers, bakers, victuallers, smiths, carpenters, taylors, shoomakers, joyners, barbers, millers, masons, with other artists, such are to be rated for their returns and gaines in proportion to other men, for the produce of their estates. Provided that in the rate by the poll, such persons as are disabled by sicknesse, lamenesse, or other infirmity, shall be so long exempted. And for such servants and children, as take not wages, their parents and masters shall pay for them; but such as take wages, shall pay for themselves. And it is ordered, That all rates assessed by this court, be duly paid in, to the jurisdiction treasurer, at such time, or times, in such pay, and at such prises, as this court shall appoint, and under such penalties for default, as shall from time to time be ordered. And power is hereby given and granted to each plantation within this jurisdiction, to gather all rates from time to time, from the severall inhabitants, as they grow due; and for want, or delay of payment in an orderly way, to distreyn within their own limits, to prevent further inconveniences. But that the jurisdiction suffer not by the neglect or delay of any plantation, or plantations herein, it is further ordered, That at any time hereafter, upon the complaint of the jurisdiction treasurer, any magistrate may send the marshall alone, or with others to distreyn the cattel, corn, or any other goods belonging to any of the inhabitants within such plantation, as shall be defective in the payment of rates due, for the whole sum behind and unpaid, with addition of all penalties incurred, and due charges for the marshall, and others imployed in seizing, and bringing away such distresse, every inhabitant in such case, having liberty to require, and recover his damage, from the plantation, or officers, there intrusted for civil affaires, according to justice. Provided that if any person now, or hereafter, having taken up a lot, or lots in any plantation, be removed, or shall withdraw himself, and his moveable estate, or any considerable part of it, still keeping such lot, or lots, in his own possession, or power, without due improvement, by which means the plantation wants his personall service, besides other inconveniences, it is hereby ordered, That in such case, every such person shall in all respects, pay his rates by lands only, as was ordered, and done before rating by heads, and estates, but in due proportion to a whole rate, as then it was. And if the plantation find no other means to recover the said rates, they may distreyn houses, or lands, or both, upon a true account, that what advantage they shall make, by selling or letting the same, or any part thereof, over and above what is due for the said rates, with just damages, and necessary charges, shall be returned to the owner, if he demand the same, within three years.

Children's Education.

Whereas too many parents and masters, either through an over tender respect to their own occasions, and businesse, or not duly considering the good of their children, and apprentices, have too much neglected duty in their education, while they are young, and capable of learning, it is ordered, That the deputies for the particular court, in each plantation within this jurisdiction for the time being; or where there are no such deputies, the constable, or other officer, or officers in publick trust, shall from time to time, have a vigilant eye over their brethren, and neighbours, within the limits of the said plantation, that all parents and masters, doe duly endeavour, either by their own ability and labour, or by improving such schoolmaster, or other helps and means, as the plantation doth afford, or the family may conveniently provide, that all their children, and apprentices as they grow capable, may through God's blessing, attain at least so much, as to be able duly to read the Scriptures, and other good and profitable printed books in the English tongue, being their native language, and in some competent measure, to understand the main grounds and principles of Christian Religion necessary to salvation. And to give a due answer to such plain and ordinary questions, as may by the said deputies, officers, or others, be propounded concerning the same. And where such deputies or officers, whether by information or examination, shall find any parent or master, one or more negligent, he or they shall first give warning, and if thereupon due reformation follow, if the said parents or masters shall thenceforth seriously and constantly apply themselves to their duty in manner before expressed, the former neglect may be passed by; but if not, then the said deputies, or other officer or officers, shall three months after such warning, present each such negligent person, or persons, to the next plantation court, where every such delinquent upon proof, shall be fined ten shillings to the plantation, to be levied as other fines. And if in any plantation, there be no such court kept for the present, in such case, the constable or other officer, or officers, warning such person or persons, before the freemen, or so many of them as upon notice shall meet together, and proving the neglect after warning, shall have power to levy the fine as aforesaid: but if in three months after that, there be no due care taken and continued for the education of such children or apprentices as aforesaid, the delinquent (without any further private warning) shall be proceeded against as before, but the fine doubled. And lastly, if, after the said warning, and fines paid or levied, the said deputies, officer, or officers, shall still find a continuance of the former negligence, if it be not obstinacy, so that such children or servants may be in danger to grow barbarous, rude and stubborn, through ignorance, they shall give due and seasonable notice, that every such parent and master be summoned to the next court of magistrates, who are to proceed as they find cause, either to a greater fine, taking security for due conformity to the scope and intent of this law, or may take such children or apprentices from such parents or masters, and place them for years, boyes till they come to the age of one and twenty, and girles till they come to the age of eighteen years, with such others, who shall better educate and govern them, both for publick conveniency, and for the particular good of the said children or apprentices.

Conveyances fraudulent.

To prevent or avoyd the mischievous inconveniences which may grow by fraudulent conveyances, and that every man may the better know what estate or interest other men may have in any houses, lands, or other hereditaments which he purposeth to deale in, it is ordered, that no morgage, bargaine, sale, grant, or conveyance, made of any house or houses, lands, rents, or other hereditaments, within this jurisdiction, where the granter remains in possession, shall be hereafter in force, against any other person or persons, then the granter and his heirs, unlesse the same be acknowledged before some court or magistrate within this jurisdiction, and recorded as hereafter expressed. And that no such grant, bargain, or sale already made in way of morgage, &c. where the granter remains in possession, shall be of force against any other but the granter and his heirs, except the same shall be entred (as here expressed) within one month after the first publishing of this order, if the party concerned be within this jurisdiction, or else within three months after he shall return. And if any such granter be required of the grantee, his heirs or assigns, to make an acknowledgement accordingly, of any grant, sale, bargain, or morgage, by him made, and shall refuse so to doe, it shall be in the power of any court or magistrate, to send for the party so refusing, and upon evidence of his injuriousnesse therein, to commit him to prison, without baile or mainprize, untill he shall acknowledge the same. And the grantee in such case is to enter his caution with the secretary, or other officer appointed to record such deeds, and this shall save his interest in the mean time. But if it be doubtfull whether it be the deed or grant of the party, he shall be bound with sureties to the next court of magistrates, and the caution shall remain good as aforesaid. Lastly, it is ordered, that in each plantation, either the secretary, or some other officer, be appointed duly to enter and record, in a book kept for that purpose, all and every such grants, sales, bargaines, morgages of houses, lands, rents, and other hereditaments, as aforesaid, with all and every such caution, together with the name of the granter and grantee, thing, and estate granted, with the date thereof; the grantee paying six pence to the secretary or officer, for each such entry or record.

Cooper, see *Caske*.

Courts for Strangers.

For the ease and conveniency of strangers, who sometimes cannot stay to attend the ordinary courts of justice, it is ordered, that the Governour, Deputy Governour, or any magistrate within this jurisdiction, may call a speciall court, and that in such cases, any three magistrates, calling in such of the deputies for the plantation court, as may be had, shall have power to hear and determine all causes civil and criminal (triable in plantation courts, when two magistrates are called in) which shall arise betwixt such strangers; or when any such stranger or strangers, shall be a party, whether plaintiff or defendant, the secretary of the place (as in other ordinary trialls) duly recording the proceedings, all which shall be at the charge of the party, or parties, as the court shall determine; so that neither the jurisdiction nor plantation be charged by such courts.

Cursing, see *Prophane Swearing*.

Damages pretended, and Vexatious Suites.

It is ordered, &c. That if any person or persons in

any suit, shall falsely pretend great damages or debts, to discredit, trouble, or vex his, her, or their adversary, the court upon discovery and proof, shall have power to set a reasonable fine upon the head of any such offendor; and that in all cases, where it appears to the court, that the plaintiff hath willingly and wittingly done wrong to the defendant, in commencing and prosecuting any action, suit, complaint, or indictment, in his own name, or in the name of others, he shall beside just damages to the party wronged, be fined forty shillings, or any lesse sum to the jurisdiction or plantation treasury. as the case may require.

Distresse.

It is ordered, &c. That no man s corn or hey that is in the field, or upon the cart, nor his garden stuff, nor any thing subject to present decay, shall be taken in distresse, or by way of attachment, unlesse it be first duly prized, by order of some magistrate, or other officer; and that he that takes it, first put in due security to satisfie the worth of it, if it come to any harm, with other damages, according to the course of justice.

Disturbers of the Public Peace.

It is ordered, &c. That whosoever shall disturb or undermine the peace of this jurisdiction, or of any of the plantations, churches, families, or persons within the same, whether by conspiring, or plotting with others, or by his own tumultuous and offensive carriage, traducing, reproaching, quarrelling, challenging, assaulting, battery, or in any other way, tending to publick disturbance, in what place soever it be done, or shall defame any court of justice, or any of the magistrates, or other judges of any such court within this jurisdiction, in respect of any act, or sentence therein passed;

every such offender upon due proof made, either in the generall court, court of magistrates, or particular court (if the tryall, and issuing of the case exceed not their limits), shall be punished by fine, imprisonment, binding to the peace, or good behaviour, disfranchisement or banishment, according to the quality and measure of the offence, or disturbance.*

Divorce, or a Marriage declared a Nullity. Desertion, &c.

It is ordered, &c. That if any marryed person proved an adulterer, or an adulteresse, shall by flight, or otherwise, so withdraw or keep out of the jurisdiction, that the course of justice (according to the mind and law of God here established) cannot proceed to due execution, upon complaint, proof, and prosecution, made by the party concerned, and interessed, a separation or divorce, shall by sentence of the court of magistrates be granted and published, and the innocent party shall in such case have liberty to marry again. Mat. 19. 9.

And if any man marrying a woman fit to bear children, or needing and requiring conjugall duty, and

---

*The following clause was added by the General Court, Feb. 24, 1656-57 :

"And for that designes or practises tending to publique inconuenienc and mischeife, are vsually mannaged by letters or writings in a cunning secret way, the conspirators or actors not thinking it safe to meete often, it shall be in the power of the gouernor, or any magistrate, or other officer where there is no magistrate, vpon just or probable grounds, to search or cause to be searched any man's house, study, closset, or any other place, for bookes, letters, wrightings, or anything else, to discouer and preuent such danger, and the like in case of murder, theft, and other enormioss crimes, that wee may liue a quiet and peaceable life, in all godlines and honesty, which is the vse and end of magistracy." (N. H. Col. Rec., ii. 198.)

due benevolence from her husband, it be found (after convenient forbearance and due tryall) and satisfyingly proved, that the husband, neither at the time of marriage, nor since, hath been, is, nor by the use of any lawfull means, is like to be able to perform or afford the same, upon the wive's due prosecution, every such marriage shall by the court of magistrates, be declared voyd, and a nullity, the woman freed from all conjugall relation to that man, and shall have liberty in due season, if she see cause, to marry another; but if in any such case, deceipt be charged and proved, that the man before marriage knew himself unfit for that relation, and duty, and yet proceeded, sinfully to abuse an ordinance of God, and in so high a measure to wrong the woman, such satisfaction shall be made to the injuried woman, out of the estate of the offendor, and such fine paid to the jurisdiction, as the court of magistrates shall judge meet. But if any husband after marriage, and marriage duty performed, shall by any providence of God be disabled, he falls not under this law, nor any penalty therein. And it is further declared, that if any husband shall without consent, or just cause shewn, willfully desert his wife, or the wife her husband, actually and peremptorily refusing all matrimoniall society, and shall obstinately persist therein, after due means have been used to convince and reclaim, the husband or wife so deserted, may justly seek and expect help and relief, according to 1 Cor. 7. 15. And the court upon satisfying evidence thereof, may not hold the innocent party under bondage.

Dowryes.

It is ordered, &c. That every marryed woman (living with her husband in this jurisdiction, or other where absent from him, with his consent, or through his meer default, or inevitable providence, or in case of divorce where she is the innocent party) that shall not before marriage be estated by way of joynture (according to agreement) in some housing, lands, tenements, hereditaments, or other means for tearm of her life, shall immediately after the death of her husband, have right and interest by way of dower, in and to one third part of all such houses, lands, tenements and hereditaments, as her said husband was seized of to his own use, either in possession, reversion, or remainder, within this jurisdiction, at any time during the marriage, to have and enjoy for tearm of her naturall life, according to the estate of such husband, free, and freely discharged of and from all titles, debts, rents, charges, judgements, executions, and other incumbrauces whatsoever, had, made, or suffered by her said husband, during the said marriage between them, or by any other person claiming by, from, or under him, otherwise then by any act, or consent of such wife, as this court shall ratifie, and allow. And if the heir of the husband, or other person interessed, shall not within one month after lawfull demand made, assign, and set out to such widow, her just third part with conveniency, or to her satisfaction, according to the intent of this law, then upon due complaint, and prosecution either before the court of magistrates, or plantation court, as the case may require, her dower, or third part, shall be assigned and set forth by such persons as the court shall appoint, with due costs and damages. provided that this law shall not extend to any houses, lands, tenements, or other hereditaments, sold or conveyed away by any husband *bona fide*, for valuable consideration before this law was published. And it is further ordered, That every such wife, as before expressed, immediately after the death of her husband, shall have interest in, and unto, one third part of all such money, goods, and chattels, of what kind soever, whereof her husband shall dye possessed, (so much as shall be sufficient for the discharge of his funerall, and just debts, being first deducted) to be allowed, and, set out to her (as before appointed) for her dower; provided alwayes, that every such widow endowed as aforesaid, shall from time to time, maintain all such houses, fences, inclosures, with what else shall be for her life assigned to her of such estate, for her dowry, and shall in all respects leave the same in good and sufficient repaire, neither committing nor suffering any strip, or wast.

Ecclesiasticall Provisions.

Forasmuch as the word of God, as it is contained in the Holy Scriptures, is a pure and precious light, by God in his free and rich grace given to his people, to guide and direct them in safe paths to everlasting peace: And for that the preaching of the same, in a way of due exposition and application, by such as God doth furnish and send, is through the presence and power of the Holy Ghost, the chief ordinary means appointed of God for conversion, edification, and salvation, It is ordered, That if any Christian (so called) shall within this jurisdiction, behave himself contemptuously toward the word preached, or any minister thereof, called, and faithfully dispensing the same in any congregation, either by interrupting him in his preaching, or falsely charging him with errour, to the disparagement and hindrance of the work of Christ in his hands, every such person or persons, shall be duly punished, either by the plantation court or court of magistrates, according to the quality and measure of the offence, that all others may fear to break out into such wickednesse.

And it is further ordered, that wheresoever the ministry of the word is established within this jurisdiction, according to the order of the gospel, every person according to the mind of God, shall duly resort and attend thereunto, upon the Lord's days at least, and also upon days of publick fasting, or thanksgiving, ordered to be generally kept and observed. And if any person within this jurisdiction, shall without just and necessary cause, absent or withdraw from the same, he shall after due means of conviction used, for every such sinfull miscarriage, forfeit five shillings to the plantation, to be levied as other fines.

It is further ordered, that all the people of God within this jurisdiction, who are not in a church way, being orthodox in judgement, and not scandalous in life, shall full have liberty to gather themselves into a church estate, provided they doe it in a Christian way, with due observation of the rules of Christ, revealed in his word; provided also that this court doth not, nor hereafter will approve of any such company of persons, as shall joyn in any pretended way of church fellowship, unlesse they shall first in due season, acquaint both the magistrates, and the elders of the churches within this colony, where and when they intend to joyn, and have their approbation therein. Nor shall any person being a member of any church, which shall be gathered without such notice given, and approbation had; or who is not a member of some church in New England, approved by the magistrates, and churches of this colony, be admitted to the freedome of this jurisdiction.

And that the ordinances of Christ may be upheld, and comfortable provision made and continued for a due maintenance of the ministry according to the rule, 1 Cor. 9. 6. to 12, Gal. 6. 6, It is ordered, that when, and so oft as there shall be cause, either through the perversnesse, or negligence of men, the particular court in each plantation, or where no court is held, the deputies last chosen for the generall court with the constable, or other officer for preserving peace, &c. shall call all the inhabitants, whether planters, or sojourners before them, and desire every one particularly to set down what proportion he is willing and able to allow yearly, while God continues his estate, towards the maintenance of the ministry there. But if any one, or more, to the discouragement or hindrance of this work, refuse or delay, or set down an unmeet proportion, in any and every such case, the particular court, or deputies and constable as aforesaid, shall rate and assesse every such person, according to his visible estate there, with due moderation, and in equall proportion with his neighbours. But if after that, he deny, or delay, or tender unsuitable payment, it shall be recovered as other just debts. And it is further ordered, that if any man remove from the plantation where he lived, and leave or suffer his land there, or any part of it, to lye unimproved, neither selling it nor freely surrendring it to the plantation, he shall pay one third part of what he paid before, for his movable estate and lands also. And in each plantation where ministers maintenance is allowed in a free way without rating, he shall pay one third part of what other men of the lowest rank, enjoying such accommodations, doe pay: but if any removing settle near the said plantation, and continue still to improve his land, or such part of it as seems good to himself, he shall pay two third parts of what he paid before, when he lived in the plantation, both for moveable estate, and land, or two third parts of what others of like accommodation pay.

Escheates.

It is ordered, &c. That where no heire, or owner of houses, lands, tenements, goods, or chattels, can be found upon the decease of the late testator or proprietor, a true inventory of every such estate, in all the parts, and parcels of it, shall with the first conveniency be duly taken, and a just apprisement made upon oath, by fit men thereunto appointed by the magistrate, or such authority as at that time is in the plantation, where the said estate is; and the whole estate to be seized to the publick treasury, till the true heires or owners shall make due claime thereto, unto whom the same shall be restored, upon just and reasonable tearms.

Falsifying, see *Forgery*.
Fences, see *Cattell*.
Fines, see *Rates*.

Fire.

It is ordered &c. That whosoever shall kindle any fire in woods, or grounds, lying in common, or inclosed, so as the same shall burn fences, buildings, or cause any other damage, in any season or manner, not allowed by the authority in that plantation, or on the last day of the week, or on the Lord's day, such person shall pay all damages, and half so much more, for a fine to the plantation, and if not able to, shall be corporally punished, as the court shall judge meet. But whosoever shall wittingly and willingly burn, or destroy any farm, or other building, timber hewed, sawn, or riven, heaps of wood, charcoal, corn, hey, straw, hemp, flax, or other goods, he shall pay double or treble damages, as the court shall judge meet; or if not able to make such restitution, he shall be either sold for a servant till by his labour he may doe it, or be severely punished, as the case may require.

Forgery, or *Falsifying.*

It is ordered, &c. That if any person shall forge or falsifie any deed or conveyance, testament, bond, bill, release, acquittance, letter of attorney, or any writing to pervert equity and justice, he shall stand on the pillory three severall lecture dayes, or other dayes of most publick resort, as the plantation court or court of magistrates (according to the value of the cause) shall appoint, and shall render double damages to the party wronged; and further, he shall be disabled to give any evidence to any court, or magistrate in this jurisdiction, till upon his repentance satisfyingly manifested to the court of magistrates, he be by sentence released from it.

Fornication.

It is ordered, &c. That if any man shall commit fornication with any single woman, they shall be punished, either by enjoyning marriage, or fine, or corporall punishment, any, or all these, as the court of magistrates, or plantation court duly considering the case with the circumstances, shall judge most agreeable to the word of God.

Fraudulent Conveyances. See *Conveyances.*

Gaming.

To prevent much inconvenience which may grow by gaming, It is ordered, That no person who either as an inn-keeper, or seller of strong liquors, wine or beer, entertaines strangers or others, to lodge, or eat, or drink, shall permit or suffer any to use the game of Shuffleboard, or any other gaming, within his house, or limits, under the penalty of twenty shillings for every time so offending. And whatever person or persons shall so play or game, in any such house, or place, or in any other gaming-house, where there is a common resort to such play, or gaming, shall forfeit for every such offence five shillings. And whosoever shall so play, or game for money, or money-worth, shall further forfeit double the value thereof, one-half, to the informer, and the rest to the plantation, within the limits whereof he so played or gamed.

Heresie.

Although no Creature be Lord, or have power over the faith and consciences of men, nor may constreyn them to believe, or professe, against their consciences, yet to restreyn, or provide against such as may bring in dangerous errours or heresies, tending to corrupt and destroy the soules of men, It is ordered, &c. That if any Christian within this jurisdiction, shall goe about to subvert or destroy the Christian faith, or Religion, by broaching, publishing, or maintaining any dangerous errour, or heresie, or shall endeavour to draw, or seduce others thereunto, every such person so offending, and continuing obstinate therein, after due means of conviction, shall be fined, banished, or otherwise severely punished, as the court of magistrates duly considering the offence, with the aggravating circumstances, and danger like to ensue, shall judge meet.

Horses.

Whereas many questions, and sometimes troublesome suites grow betwixt men, about horses running together in the woods unmarked, It is ordered, That each plantation in this jurisdiction shall have a marking iron, or flesh-brand, for themselves in particular, to distinguish the horses of one plantation from another; namely, New-haven, an iron made to set on the impression of an H, as a brand-mark, Milford an M, Guilford a G, Stamford an S, Southold an S with an O in the middle of it, Brainford a T. Which plantation brand-mark, is to be visibly and as sufficiently as may be, set upon the near buttock of each horse, mare, and colt, belonging to that plantation. Beside which, every owner is to have, and mark his horse or horses, with his own particular flesh-brand having some letter, or letters of his name, or such distinguishing mark, that one man's horses may be known from another's. And that in each plantation there be an officer appointed, to record each particular man's mark, and to see each particular man's horse, mare, and colt, branded, and to take notice, and record the age of each of them, as near as he can, with the colour, and all observable marks, whether naturall or artificiall; and what artificiall marks it had before the branding, whether on the ear, or elsewhere, with the year and day of the month when branded. And in each plantation, the officer for his care and pains, to have six pence of the owner, for each horse, mare, or colt, so branded and recorded. And that after the publishing hereof, every one who hath any horse or horses, of what age or kind soever, doe duly attend this order, at his perill; the officer also is to require as satisfying evidence of his right, who presents any such horse, &c. as may be had, or to record any defect of due evidence, that a way may be open to other claimes.

Impost upon Wines, and strong Liquors.

For the better support of the government of this jurisdiction, &c. That every person, merchant, seaman, or other, who shall bring any wine into any harbour, or place within this colony (except it come directly from England, or out of some other harbour within this jurisdiction, where they have already paid custome, and that certified by the officer who received it, before he or they land or dispose any of it, more or lesse) shall first make entry of so many buts, pipes, or other vessels, as he, they, or any of them shall put, take on shore, or any way dispose, by a note in writing, delivered to the jurisdiction treasurer at his house, or to some other officer, appointed by each plantation, who is to be upon his oath for the said service, under the penalty of forfeiture and confiscation of all such wines as contrary to this order are or shall be landed or sold before such entry made, wheresoever found, or some lesse penalty, as the court shall judge meet, upon proof that the errour was committed through ignorance. And the first buyer, under the same penalty, shall see the same be done, the one half to the jurisdiction, and the other half to him that informs, and prosecutes in the case. And the merchant, or owner of such wines of any kind, as soon as he imports, lands, and sells them, or any of them, shall deliver and pay to the said treasurer, or officer, for every but or pipe of Fiall wines, or any other wines of those Islands, five shillings; for every pipe of Madary wines, six shillings and eight pence; for every but or pipe of Sherris Sack, Maligo,or Canary wines, ten shillings; for Bastards, Tents, and Alligants, ten shillings: and proportionably for greater or lesser vessels of each kind. And for every hogshead of French wines, two shillings and six pence, and proportionably for greater or lesser vessels. And upon proof that any the forementioned wines, have been imported or landed, without such entry and payment, if neither the seller nor wine can be found, then double the value of the said customes, by this order due to the jurisdiction, are to be recovered by way of action, as other debts, of the first buyer of the said wines, if it will not be paid otherwise.

And it is further ordered, that whosoever shall bring any strong liquor, of what kind soever, into any harbour or other part of this colony (unlesse directly out of England, or out of some other part of this jurisdiction, where custome hath been paid, and certified, as in the case of wines) before he or they land or dispose of any of it, more or lesse, shall first make a true and full entry, of the quantity he shall so import, or cause to be imported or landed, by a note in writing delivered to the jurisdiction treasurer at his house, or to some other officer, as in the case of wines, under the like penalty of forfeiture, with mitigation if the case require it, as there, the one half to the jurisdiction, the other half to him that informs and prosecutes. And the owner, or importer of any such strong liquor, as soon as he lands, imports, and sells it or any part of it, shall deliver and pay to the said treasurer, or officer, for every anchor containing ten gallons, six shillings and eight pence, and so for greater or lesser quantities, namely after the rate of eight pence a gallon. And the first buyer shall under the same penalty, see that such entry and payment be duly made. And that whosoever within this colony, shall at any time for sale or merchandize, distill any sort of strong liquor, he or she shall within eight days after the same is distilled, and so ready for use, or sale, give in a like true note in writing, of the full quantity so distilled, to the treasurer, or other officer, under the like penalty, and shall within three months after, duly pay, or cause to be paid to the said treasurer, or officer, after the rate of eight pence a gallon, for the full quantity so distilled, and upon proof, that any such strong liquor hath been distilled and sold without such entry and payment, the value thereof shall be forfeited to the jurisdiction, unlesse cause of mitigation appear, as in the wines. And that no person at any time retaile any sort of strong liquor within this jurisdiction, without expresse license from the authority of the plantation, within the limits whereof he so sells, wherein the selling of lesse then three gallons at a time, is to be accounted retaile, and that due moderation be attended in prises, when it is so retailed. But that none of any sort, be at any time sold, above three shillings and six pence a wine quart. Lastly, it is ordered, that if any distilling such strong liquor, within this colony, shall by way of trade or merchandize, after he hath paid such custome, ship and send forth out of this jurisdiction, any quantity of the same, he shall for so much, have the said custome repayed, by the treasurer, or officer, who received it.

Imprisonment.

It is ordered, That no man's person shall be imprisoned either for fine, or debt, to the jurisdiction or plantation, or particular person, if any competent means of satisfaction from his estate, doe otherwise appear; but if no such estate be known, nor can presently be found, or if contempt or other proud and offensive behaviour against the court, or any authority here setled, be mingled with his cause, he may be imprisoned, and kept in prison at his own charge, if he be able, till satisfaction be made, or till the court which committed him, or some superiour court, see cause to release him. Provided neverthelesse, that no man's person shall be kept in prison for debt, at the will of the creditor, but when there appears some estate which he will not produce, in which case, any court, or commissioners authorized by the generall court, may administer an oath to the party, or any others, suspected to be employed, or privy to the conveying away, or concealing of such estate, or some of it; but if any such person or persons, in such case, being so required, shall refuse to discover the truth by oath, he shall be liable to such fine, as the court duly weighing the case shall judge meet; but if no estate can be found, to pay or satisfie such just debt, or debts, every such debtor shall satisfie by service, if the creditor, or creditors, require it, for such time, as the court considering the debt, shall with due moderation judge meet; but shall not be sold to any out of the United English Colonyes, if the debt grow by any ordinary way of borrowing, contract, or other engagement, and not by sinfull and heynous miscarriages, which disturb the publick peace, which the court to whose cognizance such cases are proper, will duly weigh and consider.

Incest.

It is ordered, &c. That if any persons shall commit

incest, which is, when being near of kin, within the degrees by God forbidden, they wickedly defile themselves one with another, they shall be put to death. Levit. 20. 11, 12, 14, 17, 19, 20, 21.

Indians.

It is ordered, &c. That no planter, inhabitant, or sojourner within this jurisdiction, shall directly, or indirectly for himself, or any other, purchase, or truck any plantation, or land, upland, or meadow more or less, of any Indian, Indians, or others from them, either upon the Maine between Connecticut River, and Hudson's River, or upon Long Island, nor shal receive any land by way of gift or upon any other tearms, for his or their, or any either private or publick use, or advantage, or as agent for others who may pretend to begin a plantation without express license, either from the court of magistrates for this jurisdiction, or at least from some one of the plantation courts, where there is a magistrate, and deputies. And in the latter case, the land to lye so as neither in point of title, nor conveniency may concern any other plantation, but onely the plantation so licensing, under the penalty of losing and forfeiting all the right and title purchased, or obtained in any such land, with such further punishment for contempt as the court shall judge meet. And if any person or persons within this jurisdiction, by what way or means soever be already justly possest, or interessed of or in any land within the limits before mentioned, he or they shal neither directly nor indirectly by gift, sale, or upon any other consideration or respect, alienate or return the right he or they have in the same, or any part of it, to the Indians, or any of them without license from this court; and if any plantation within this jurisdiction shal hereafter purchase, or upon any tearms receive, or obtaine title or right to any land from the Indians, or others from them, which may concerne, or be convenient to another plantation within this jurisdiction also; and so there grow any question or difference either in reference to the land, or this order; it shall be heard and determined by this Court, that peace may be continued, and the conveniency of each plantation provided for.

And the better to suppress or restrain the inconveniences or mischiefs which may grow by a general and unlimited furnishing of the Indians with guns, powder, shot, or any other weapons or instruments proper or useful in or for war. It is ordered, That whosoever of, or within this jurisdiction, or any part thereof shal directly or indirectly, by himself or any other, sel, barter, give, lend, lose, or by any means, or device whatsoever, furnish any Indian or Indians, or any for them, with any guns smal or great, by what name soever called, or with any powder shot, lead, or shot mould, or with any stocks or locks for guns, or swords, rapiers, daggers, or blades for any such, or pikes, pike-heads, halberts, arrow-heads, or any other provision or furniture for war of what kind soever, whether fully finished or not; or what smith, or other person within or belonging to this jurisdiction shal mend any gun, stock, or any thing belonging to it, or procure it to be done, or any the forementioned, or other weapons or instruments proper, or used for war, without express written license from this general court, or some one or more deputed by them to give such license with directions upon what termes, and in what manner, such a trade with a due respect to all the premises shall be managed, shal forfeit and pay to the jurisdiction twenty times the value of what shal be sold, bartered,or any way alienated, mended,or upon any contrivement or device done contrary to the tenour and true meaning of this order, or any part of it, whereof one 4th part goeth to the informer, and the rest to the jurisdiction.

And to the same purpose and end, it is further ordered, that whosoever, shal either directly or indirectly sel, bartar, or cause to be sold &c., any guns, powder, shot, lead, or any of the forementioned instruments or provisions for warr, to any person or persons inhabiting out of this jurisdiction, without license from two magistrates of this jurisdiction under their hands, or where there is but one magistrate under his hand, and the hands of two deputies for the plantation court, shal as a fine for his breach of order and contempt pay five times the value of what shal be so sold, bartered, &c.

And it is further ordered, that the magistrate or magistrates who at any time give any such license under their hands shal keep a true account in writing of all the particulars, and quantities, he or they so license, to whom and upon what grounds, that upon any question this court may receive satisfaction therein; and that every such license be limited, as to the perticular things and quantities; so to the time, that if the same or any part thereof be not within the limited time sould and delivered, the license for the whole, or such part to be altogether void, and each sale or delivery after, without a new license, to be adjudged a breach of this order.

And the better to prevent controversies and disturbance betwixt the English and Indians in this jurisdiction; it is ordered, that whosoever shal upon any occasion, trust, or take pawn or pledge of any Indian for the securing or payment of any thing sold or lent, he shal neither after take any thing from him or them by force, for, or toward satisfaction, nor dispose of any pawn, or pledg so received, though the time set for redeeming it be enquired, without either consent of the Indian, or license from the court, or from the authority setled in the Plantation where lives.

Indians, see further, into the title of Inn-keepers, Tipling, and Drunkenness.

Indictments.

If any person shall be indicted of, or legally charged with any capitall crime (who is not then in durance) and shal withdraw, or refuse to render his person to some magistrate, or officer for this jurisdiction, within one moneth, after three proclamations publickly made in the town, or plantation where he did formerly usually abide, there being a full moneth betwixt proclamation and proclamation; his lands and goods shall be seized to the use of the jurisdiction (and ordered with due respect to his family, as the court of magistrates shal judge meet) till he make his lawful appearance. And such withdrawing of himself shall stand instead of one witnesse to prove the crime charged, unlesse he can make it appeare to the court that he was necessarily hindered.

Inkeepers, Tipling, Drunkenness.

It is ordered, &c. That no person, or persons, shall at any time hereafter, under any pretence or colour whatsoever, undertake or become a common victualer, keeper of a cooke's shop, or house for common entertainment, tavern, or publick seller of wine, ale, strong beere, or strong liquor by retaile within this jurisdiction; nor shall any either directly or indirectly, sell any sort of wine privately in his house, cellar, &c. or out of doores, by a lesse quantity, or under three gallons at a time, without approbation and license of the plantation-court to which he belongeth: or where there is no such court, without the license of the constable, and major part of the free-men, under the penalty of five pounds, to be paid to the plantation for the first miscarriage complained of, and proved; and ten pounds for the second miscarriage so proved: And where payment cannot or wil not be made, imprisonment during the court's pleasure, for the first offence, and for the second offence, such further punishment as the court shall order. And that no person so licensed shal sell any beere, or ale, above three pence an ale quart, under the penalty of three shillings and four pence for such miscarriage, proved the first time, and six shillings and eight pence the second time. But it is allowed and ordered, that any man that will may sell beere or ale out of doores, at a peny a quart, or cheaper.

It is further ordered, That whosoever licensed as before, selleth any sort of wine by retaile, that is, by any lesse quantity then three gallons at a time, he shall pay to the jurisdiction treasurer over and above the custome before mentioned, after the rate of forty shillings for every but, or pipe so re-taled; and every one, that so selleth by retale, shal give a true account and notice to the said treasurer, or to some other officer appointed for that purpose in each plantation, of the true or ful quantity, which he either buyeth or receiveth into his custody, and that within one week after he is so possessed of it, upon paine of forfeiting the same, or the value thereof; and shal further every six months, truly account with the jurisdiction's treasurer, or other officer as aforesaid, for what he hath sold by re-tale as aforesaid, and discharge the same, having due allowance for what he hath sold by greater parcels, then by this order is accounted re-tale; and in case of delay, or neglect of payment after demand, the treasurer or officer shal recover it by action as other debts, provided that if any person shal give in a false account to defraud the jurisdiction, upon due proof, he shal pay double the value of what he would so have kept back.

And it is further ordered, That every person so licensed to draw and sel strong beer, ale, wine, or strong liquour, do see, and take care that good order, and all rules of sobriety be duly attended in his course, and house, and about the same; and that he neither see, nor suffer any to be drunken, or to drink excessively, or to continue tipling above the space of an hour, or at unseasonable times; or after nine of the clock at night without weighty cause; nor that any children or servants without the consent of parents, or governors be permitted to sit, or stay there drinking or unnecessarily to spend their time there, especially at late or unseasonable hours, but that he duly complain to authority, that all such disorders may be seasonably suppressed, under the penalty of five shillings for the first offence, with such increase of fine for a continued slightness or neglect as the court shal determine.

Provided notwithstanding, that such licensed persons may entertain strangers, land travellers, sea-faring men, lodgers, or others for their necessary occasions, refreshment, or during meales, when they come from their journies or voyages, or when they prepare for their journey or voyage in the night, or next day early, or such may continue in such houses of common entertainment, as their business and lawful occasions may require, so that there be no disorder among them.

But every person found drunken, namely so that he be thereby for the present bereaved, or disabled in the use of his understanding, appearing in his speech, jesture, or carriage in any of the said houses or elsewhere, shal forfeit for the first time ten shillings; and for excess of drinking, or continuing in any such place unnecessarily at unseasonable times, or after nine of the clock at night five shillings, and for continuing tipling there above the space of an hour two shillings six pence for the first offence, and for the second offence in each kind, and for all further disorder, quarrelling, or disturbance, whether a first or second time, such further fine or punishment as the court shall determine.

And for that God may be much dishonoured, and many inconveniences may grow by the Indians disorderly drinking of wine, strong water, and strong beere, unto which they are much addicted; it is ordered, That no person whatsoever shall either directly or indirectly within this jurisdiction, sel any wine, strong water, or strong beere to any Indian or Indians, or procure any for them, either to drink within this jurisdiction, or upon any pretence to carry away without special license under the hand of some magistrate of this jurisdiction, or in any plantation where there is no magistrate, under the hand of one of the deputies, or constable where he lives; and that no license so given shal serve, or be of force any longer then for that one particular time, and for the limited quantity then granted, under the penalty of five shillings for the first offence, and ten shillings for the second ; but if any shal offend the third time therein, it is left to the plantation court where the offence is committed to consider the case, and to inflict such punishment or increase of fiue as shal be meet; and in any plantation, where at present there is no court kept, the deputies last chosen for the general court, or constable, shall require the forfeitures, and for defect of payment make seizure of so much out of the delinquent's estate; but if any person shal offend the third time, every such person shal by the said deputies, or constable, be bound over to answer it before the next court of magistrates.

Laws without penalty.

It is by this court declared and ordered, That in all laws and orders formerly, now, or hereafter to be made, where no fine, or penalty is expressed and limited, all transgressors have been, are, and shall be lyable to such penalties, or punishments as the court of magistrates, or any plantation court, to which the cognizance appertains, weighing the nature of the offence, with the circumstances, shall judge meet, liberty of appeales, or complaints, as in other cases, being duly preserved.

Leather, and Shoo-makers.

Upon consideration of the damage or injury which many sustaine by the ill coming of leather, and by the shooe-makers ill making it up into shooes, and boots, it is by this court ordered, That in every plantation within this jurisdiction where either tanner, or shooe-maker is imployed in their trades, one or two sealers shall be chosen, and appointed, as the occasions reqvire, who shal be under oath, faithfully (according to their best ability) to discharge their trust; and shal seale no leather, but such as they judg sufficiently tanned, and fit to be wrought out, and sold in shooes, and boots. And that every such plantation shal have two seales, to distinguish betwixt good leather wel and sufficiently tanned, and such, as though tanned enough, is in some other respect defective, either by over-liming, or for want of being wel wrought upon the beame, or by frost, or hath received some dammage in drying; so that though it may serve for inward or middle soals, yet not for other uses without dammage to the buyer; all which leather so defective, shall be sealed with a different seale, that it may known to be faulty. But that which is not sufficiently tanned, shal neither be sealed, nor used in boots, or shooes, til it be duly tanned. The chosing and appointing of which sealer or sealers, the print or mark, which each plantation shal set upon their seals for good, or faulty leather, with the rate to be allowed for sealing, being left to the several plantations, but no tanner within this jurisdiction shal upon any pretense, sel, deliver, cause, or suffer to be delivered, or pass out of his hands, or custody, any hide, or hides, til being fully dry, they be first sealed by the officer or officers thereunto appointed, under the penalty of forfeiting the said leather, or the value of it to the plantation where the offence is committed.

And it is further ordered, That if any shooe-maker shal use, or put any unsealed leather, either in bootes, or shooes, or put any of the forementioned faulty leather (though sealed as such) in any outward soals, or upper leather, or in any other place, which may be hurtful to the buyer, or wearer; or shall use any other way of deceit in making up his ware, he shall make due and full recompence to the person or persons wronged, and complaining; and shal suffer such further punishment as his offence considered with the circumstances shal require; and whosoever shal bring hides from any other place, and shal sel or use any of them for bootes or shooes within this jurisdiction, before they be sealed by some officer here, according to the import of this order, or shal use them in bootes, or shooes, contrary to the intent thereof; the hides so sold or used, or the value of them shal be forfeited to the plantation where the offence is committed, or such recompence, or fine shal be made or paid, (if it grow only of ignorance) as the case may require; provided that if both buyer and seller be faulty, they shal pay the forfeit betwixt them; but due tenderness and respect is to be had of an innocent stranger who brings, sels, or uses good leather, though for want of means to know the law, it were unsealed.

Levies, see *Marshall.*

Lying. *

It is ordered, That if any person above the age of fourteen years shal wittingly, and willingly make, and publish any lye, tending to the damage, or injury of any particular person, or with intent to deceive and abuse the people, with false newes, or reports, or which may be any way pernicious to the publick

* Taken, in substance, from the Massachusetts law of 1645, and Connecticut law of 1650. See, before, pages 102, 103.

weale; and the same complained of, and duly proved either before any court or magistrate, or where there is no magistrate, before the constable, or other officer, he calling one or two of the freemen to him, (who are hereby inabled to hear and determine ordinary offences of this nature, according to the tenour of this law) the offender shal pay to the plantation where he is prosecuted for his lying, as it is a sin against God, for the first offence ten shillings; and if after such conviction, he offend the second time, he shal pay for that second offence twenty shillings; which fines, or penalties shal be severally levied as in other cases. But if any such person be not able, or utterly refuse to pay the said fines, or either of them, he shall in such case be committed to the stocks; and for the first offence shal continue there betwixt one and two hours; for the second offence betwixt three and four hours. But if he offend the third time, he shal be publickly whipt for the same; each person being notwithstanding left his liberty, to proceed further by action of of slaunder, defamation, or otherwise, as the case may require. But the said court, magistrate, or other officer, as before, finding weighty aggravations in the case, either in the sin against God, or disturbance, and damage to the publick, are to proceed accordingly; or if need require may bind the offender over to the court of magistrates.

Magistrates, or other Judges in relation.

To prevent occasions and jealousies of partial and undue proceedings in courts of justice: It is ordered, That no magistrate, or deputy shal sit as a Judge, or among the Judges when any cause of his own is tryed; and that in every case of civil nature between party, and party, where there shal fal out so near relation between any judg, and any of the parties, as betwixt father, and son, either by nature, or marriage, brother and brother, uncle and nephew, landlord and tennant in matters of considerable valew, wherein any of them being one of the judges is concerned; such judge though he may be present at the tryal, and may propound and hold forth light in the case, yet he shal neither sit as judg, nor shal have power to vote or pass sentence therein; and in case the court without such magistrate or deputy may not proceed, either two magistrates may be called in, or the matter referred to the court of magistrates if it be not otherwise to just satisfaction issued.

Manslaughter.

It is ordered, That if any person in the just and necessary defence of his own life, or the life of another, shal kil any person attempting to robb, or murther in the field, high-way, or other place, or to break into any dwelling house, if he cannot otherwise prevent the mischiefe, or with safety of his own person take the fellon, or assailant, and bring him to tryal, he shal be holden blameless.*

Marriage.

For the preventing of much inconvenience which may grow by clandestine and unlawful marriages: It is ordered, That no persons shal be either contracted, or joyned in marriage before the intention of the parties proceeding therein, hath been three times published, at some time of publick lecture, or town meeting in the town, or towns where the parties, or

* From Massachusetts law of 1647, and Conn. Code of 1650. See, before, p.105.

either of them dwel, or do ordinarily reside; or be set up in writing upon some post of their meeting house door, in publick view, there to stand so as it may be easily read by the space of fovrteen daies; and that no man unless he be a magistrate in this jurisdiction, or expressly allowed by the general court shall marry any persons, and that in a publick place, if they be able to go forth under the penalty of five pounds fine for every such miscarriage.

And the court considering that much sin hath been committed against God, and much inconvenience hath growen to some members of this jurisdiction by the irregular and disorderly carriage of young persons of both sexes, upon purpose or pretence of marriage, did and do order, that whosoever within this jurisdiction shal attempt, or indeavor to inveagle, or draw the affections of any maide, or maide-servant, whether daughter, kinswoman, or in other relation, for himself, or for any other person, without the consent of father, master, guardian, governor, or such other, who hath the present interest, or charge, or (in the absence of such) of the nearest magistrate, whether it be by speech, writing, message, company-keeping, unnecessary familiarity, disorderly night meetings, sinful dalliance, gifts, or any other way, directly or indirectly, every such person (beside all damages which the parent, governor or person intrusted or interessed, may sustain by such unlawful proceedings) shall pay to the plantation forty shillings for the first offence; and for the second offence towards the same party four pounds; and for the third offence he shal be further fined, imprisoned, or corporally punished, as the plantation court, or court of magistrates considering all circumstances shal determine.

And whereas some persons men or women do live, or may come to settle within this colony, whose wives, or husbands are in England or elsewhere, by means whereof they are exposed to great temptations, and some of them live under suspition of uncleanesse, if they do not fal into lewd and sinful courses: It is therefore ordered, That all such persons living within this jurisdiction, shal by the first opportunity, repair to their said relations, (unless such cause be shewen to the satisfaction of the plantation court, that further respite and liberty be given) under the penalty of paying twenty pounds fine, for contempt, or neglect herein. Provided that this order do not extend to such as are, or shal come over to make way for their families, or are in a transient way for traffick, merchandise, or other just occasions for some smal time.

Marshall.

That justice may be the better executed, the jurisdictions occasions carried on, and that the marshal and other officers may know how to demean themselves in their places; It is ordered, that in case of rates and fines to be leavied, and in case of debts, and executions in civil actions; the officer shall first demand the summ due of the party, or at his house, or place of usual abode, but upon refusal or non-payment, he shal have power (calling in such assistance as the case may require) to break up the door of any house, chest, or place where he shal conceive, or have notice, that any goods liable to such leavy or execution shal be; and if he be to take the person, he may do the like, if upon demand he shal refuse to render himself; and whatever charges the officer in any such case shal be put unto, he shal have power to leavy the same, as he doth the debt, assesment, or fine; and in case the officer be put to leavy any such goods, as cannot without considerable charge, be conveyed to the place where the treasurer, or party dwelleth, who should receive the same, he shal levy the said charge also, with the rest; provided it shall not be lawful for any such officer, to leavy any man's necessary bedding, apparel, tooles, armes, or such implements of houshold stuff, as serve for his necessity, without express direction from the court, upon whose sentence, the execution or seizure was grounded, or at least, of some magistrate of the jurisdiction, but in such cases he shal leavy his land or person. And in no case shal the officer be put to seek out any man's estate, furthur than his place of abode; but if the party wil not discover his goods, or lands to a sufficient value, the officer may take his person.

And to prevent the inconveniences which may grow by the slightness of some men's spirits, who are apt to neglect and violate wholsome orders and laws, made in the jurisdiction, or plantations, It is ordered, That whosoever shal be fined by any court for any disorder, or breach of law, every such person shal forthwith pay the fine, or penalty, or put in security speedily to do it, or else shal be imprisoned, or kept to work, if the court upon due consideration of persons, and circumstances judge it not meet to make other seizure.

Masters, and Servants, &c.

It is ordered, &c. That no servant male, or female, or other person under government, shall without license from his, her, or their masters or governors, either give, sel, or truck any commodity whatsoever, during the time of their service, or subjection, under the paine of such fine, or corporal punisnment, as the court upon a due consideration of the offence shal judg meet; and that whosoever shal receive from, or trade with any child, son, or daughter, under age, and under government, or with any servant, or servants, in a suspitious disorderly manner, or shal harbor or entertaine any such in the night, or at other unseasonable times, or shal suffer them disorderly to meet at any place within their power, or to play at shovel-board, or other game, or games, to drink, spend mony, or provisions, or shal use or suffer any offensive, sinful carriage, conference, counsel, or songs, which in their nature tend to corrupt, all such persons shal be liable to such fines, or other punishment, as the court shal judge meet.

Mayming, Wounding, &c.

If any shal in distempered passion, or otherwise, sinfully hurt, wound, or maime another, such person shal be punisht by fine, with some valuable recompence to the party; and shal pay for the cure, with losse of time, &c. And when the case requires it, the court of magistrates are duly to consider the mind of God, as it is revealed, Exod. 21. 18, to the 28. Levit. 24. 19, 20.

Military Affairs.

For as much as the well managing of the militia, is under God, in all places, of great import, and concernment, for publick peace, and safety: It is orderd, That (beside a general stock of guns, powder, shot, match, &c. provided and kept in store by each plantation in this jurisdiction, according to former agreements of the Commissioners for the United Colonies, and orders of this court, which they are hereby required to keep continually ful, and in a constant readiness for service, upon all occasions, and by their deputies to make a true certificate thereof yerely to the general court) every male within this jurisdiction from sixteen, to sixty years of age, (not freed by publick allowance) shal be, and from time to time continue wel furnished with arms, and all other suitable provision; namely a good serviceable gun, such as shal be ordered by the court, and allowed by the military officers, to be kept in a constant fitness in all respects for service, with a fit, and sufficient rest, a good sword, bandaleers, or horne, a worme, a scourer, a priming wire, shot bagg, charger, and whatsoever else is necessary for such service, with a pound of good powder, four pounds of pistol bullets, or four and twenty bullets fitted for the gun, four faddom of serviceable match, for a match-lock gun, five or six good flints fitted for every firelock gunn, under the penalty of ten shillings for any defect; and the military officers are hereby required to give or send in an account yearly in May, from each plantation, to the general court, or court of magistrates, how the inhabitants are furnished and provided.

That in each plantation within this jurisdiction, according to the number of soldiers, in their trained band, and as they are furnished with able men for such a service, and trust, military officers as need requireth, shal from time to time be chosen. And all the freemen in each plantation shal have their vote, in the nomination, and choice of them; provided that none but freemen be chosen. And that every captain, and chiefe officer, chosen in any of the plantations, for the military affairs, shal from time to time be propounded to the next general court, after he is chosen, for approbation and confirmation. And if the said court, have any just exception, against any so propounded, the freemen shall proceed to a new choice, that the jurisdiction may be furnished with such officers, as in whom they may satisfyingly confide.

That in each plantation, the captain or chief military officer shal once in each quarter of a year, at least, but oftener if there be cause, order, or take a strict view, how every male, from sixteen to sixty years of age is furnished with arms, and provisions, according to the former directions, and where any are found faulty, the clark or some other officer shal duly present their names, with each defect to the next plantation court, or to such officer (where there is no court) who hath a trust in civil affairs, that the fines and penalties may from time to time be duly leavied. And if this view of arms, &c. shall at any time be neglected, or the defects not duly presented; the captain or chief military officer, or the other officer ordered to take this view, or the clark, or officer appointed to present, &c. shall pay forty shillings each quarter when this service, or any part of it, is omitted as the fault upon examination shal joyntly or severally be justly charged.

There shal be in each plantation within this jurisdiction, every year at least six training daies, or daies of publick military exercise to teach and instruct all the males, above sixteen years of age, (who are not freed from that service) in the comly handling, and ready use, of their arms in all postures of war, to understand and attend all words of command; and further, to fit all such as are in some measure instructed for all military service, against there be occasion under the penalty of forty shillings, to be leavied of the military officers, as the court upon examination shal find them more or lesse faulty, and with respect to their places, the greater trust paying the greater fine for neglect; which dayes of training shal be some of them in the spring of the year, before harvest, and some in the latter end of the summer, before winter, as may best suit each plantation, but at no time any two of these traynings shal be within fourteen dayes one of another. And it is further ordered, That on every such training day, the captain or chief military officer present, cause the names of all the soldiers to be read, at least in the forenoone, but in the afternoon also if he see cause. And whosoever in any training day shal be totally absent, shal pay five shillings for every such default, whosoever shal at any time of the day withdraw himself from the service, without leave from the chief military officer present, he shall pay either as for total absence, or a greater or lesse fine, as the offence considered in all circumstances may require; And whosoever shal come late, shal pay for each such default one shilling; and for any other disorderly offensive carriage, according to the nature and measure of it. This court expecting from each plantation, that they suffer not men to neglect, or grow slight in a service of such import.

That a fourth part of the trained band in every plantation shal in their course, as the military officer shal order, come constantly to the publick worships of God every Lord's day, and (such as can come) on lecture dayes, to be at the meeting-house, at latest, before the second drum hath left beating, with their arms compleat, their guns ready charged, their match for their match-locks, and flints ready fitted to their fire-lock guns, with shott and powder for at least five shot, beside the charge in their guns, under the penalty of two shillings fine, for every person negligent, or defective in furniture, and for late coming one shilling. The sentinal also, and they that walk the round shal have their matches lighted, during the time of their meeting, if they use their matchlocks, and shal diligently and faithfully attend their duty under such further penalty as the breach of such a trust may require.

That a strict watch be constantly kept in the night, in all the plantations within this jurisdiction, according to all such orders, as shal from time to time be made, either by the general court, or by plantation courts, or officers intrusted for civil affairs, where there is no court; and that both for number of watchmen, in each plantation, the time of setting or beginning the watch every night, their rising, and leaving it in the morning, and all other carriage, and duties in managing this trust, they duly attend and observe all directions given. And it is left to the care and consideration of the governor, magistrates, officers, or any of them, as the case may require, to double, or further to increase the watch by night, in times of danger, and to appoint some competent number of men to ward or walk by day, with their armes, in, or about the plantation, as may best tend to the publick safety; And if any watchman, or warder do at any time neglect his duty, either in coming too late to the service, or departing too soon from it, not coming completely furnished with arms, according to order, or any other way neglecting duty, or falsfying his trust, he shal pay such fine, or receive such punishment as his neglect or unfaithfulnesse deserves, that both himselfe may be warned, and others may feare to be slight, or false in a matter of such concernment.

But upon consideration of publick service, and other

due respects, It is ordered, That all Magistrates within this jurisdiction, and teaching Elders, shal at all times hereafter, be freed, not onely in their persons, but each of them, shall have one son or servant by vertue of his place or office, freed from all watching, warding, and training. And it is further ordered, That all ruling elders, deputies for courts intrusted for judicature, all the chief military officers, as captains, lieftenants, and ensignes, the jurisdiction treasurer, deacons, and all physitians, schoolmasters, and surgeons allowed by authority in any of these plantations, all masters of ships and other vessels, above fifteen tun, all publick millers, constantly imployed, with others for the present discharged for personal weakness and infirmity, shal in their own persons, in time of peace and safety, be freed from the said services; And that all other seamen and ship carpenters, and such as hold farms, above two miles from any of the plantations, train onely twice a yeare, at such times as shal be ordered, either by the authority, or by the military officers of the plantation. But all persons freed and exempted from the respective services, as before, shall yet in all respects, provide, keep, and maintain in a constant readinesse, compleat arms, and all other military provisions as other men, magistrates and teaching elders excepted, who yet shal be constantly furnished for all such sons and servants as are hereby freed from the forementioned services.

Ministers maintenance, see *Ecclesiastical provisions.*

Oppression.

To prevent, or suppress much sin against God, and much damage to men, which doth, and may grow by such as take liberty to oppress, and wrong others, by taking excessive wages for work, or unreasonable prises for commodities: it is ordered, That if any shal offend in either of the said cases, upon complaint and proof, every such person shal be punished by fine, or imprisonment, according to the quality and measure of the offence, as the court shal judge meet.

Plantations.

Whereas the freemen of every town, or plantation, within this jurisdiction, have in sundry particulars liberty to make orders among themselves, as about fencing their land, ordering or keeping their cattel,or swine, &c. as may best suite with their own conveniency; It is by this court ordered, That if any greater cattel, of what sort soever, or swine, belonging to one plantation, be found either unmarked, or proved to have done trespass, or both, within the limits of another plantation; The damage being duly rated, the owners of such cattel, or swine, shal from time to time, pay all fines and damages, according to the just agreements, and orders, made by the plantation, where the trespass is done; provided that the orders be such, and no other, then what they make, and execute upon themselves, in like cases.

Pound, Pound breach.

For prevention, or due recompence of damages in corne-fields, or other places done by cattel, or swine; It is ordered, That there shal be one sufficient pound, or more, made, and maintained in every plantation within this jurisdiction, for the impounding of such cattel, or swine, as shal be found in any corne-field, other inclosure, or place prohibited, til it may appear, where the fault, and damage ought to be charged.

And whoso impounds any cattel, or swine, shal give present notice to the owner, if he be known, otherwise they shal be cryed at the two next lectures, or most publick meetings, but if yet the owner be not found, then fine, and damages to be recovered, as in the order about cattel, &c. And if any of them escape out of the pound; the owners if known, shal pay all just damages and charges.

But if any person, or persons, shal resist, or rescue any cattel or swine going, or driven toward the pound, or shal by any way, or meanes, get, or convey any such out of the pound, without due order from lawful authority, setled by this court, he or they, shall pay for such rescue, or disorder, forty shillings, and in case of pound breach five pounds, beside just damages to the party wronged. And if in the rescue, any bodily harme be done to any person, he, or they, may have remedy from the rescuer, or rescuers; and if any such miscarriage be committed by any not able, or refusing to answer the forfeiture and damage, every such person shal sustain such bodily punishment, as the court shal judge meet, and shal answer all damage to the party by service, if estate cannot be found, as in the case of other just debts; and if it appear there were any procurer, or abettor of any the former offences, every such person shal be liable to forfeiture, dammage, or punishment, as if himselfe had done it.

Prophanation of the Lord's Day.

Whosoever shall prophane the Lord's day, or any part of it, either by sinful servile work, or by unlawful sport, recreation, or otherwise, whether wilfully, or in a careless neglect, shal be duly punished by fine, imprisonment, or corporally, according to the nature, and measure of the sinn, and offence. But if the court upon examination, by clear, and satisfying evidence find that the sin was proudly, presumptuously, and with a high hand committed against the known command and authority of the blessed God, such a person therein despising and reproaching the Lord, shal be put to death, that all others may feare and shun such provoking rebellious courses; Numb. 15. from 30 to 36 verse.

Prophane swearing, or cursing.

If any person within this jurisdiction, shal swear rashly and vainly, either by the holy name of God, or any other oath, or shal from distempered passion, or otherwise curse another, he shal forfeit to the plantation where he so offends, for the first offence, 10*s*. And if after such conviction, he offend the second time, he shal pay for that second offence 20*s*. and it shal be in the power of any magistrate alone, or where there is no magistrate, of any constable, or deputy of a particular court, calling in to him one or two of the freemen, to warne, or cal such a person before him, and upon sufficient proof, to pass sentence, and leavy the said penalties, according to the usual order of justice in this jurisdiction. But if any such person be not able, or utterly refuse to pay the forementioned fines, or any of them, he shal in such case, be committed to the stocks, and for the first offence, shal continue there, betwixt one and two hours; for the second offence, betwixt three and four hours. But if the said person, notwithstanding such former proceedings, shal offend the third time, by such swearing, or cursing, he shal be whipped, for his incorrigible prophaneness. But if swearing and cursing go both together, or be accompanied with other sinful aggravations, such miscarriages shal be punished with a higher fine, or corporally with due severity, as the court shal judge meet.

Rates, Fines etc.

Whereas much inconvenience may arise by the neglect of officers in collecting, and seasonably paying in, all such rates, fines, and debts, as from time to time, grow due to the jurisdiction treasury; It is ordered, That in each plantation, where the officer, or collector, doth not at the time appointed for the payment of all such rates, and fines, or at furthest within one moneth after (though his office within, or after that month, be expired,) and that by distress, whereunto he is hereby inabled, when a milder course wil not serve, gather, and receive them, in some such pay, as this court hath appointed, and presently, without delay, pay them in, as each plantation hath, or shal order; that the jurisdiction treasurer may be duly furnished for the publick occasions; that then the particuler court, or constable, in each plantation, cause the said rates, and fines to be leavied by distress, out of the proper estate of such remiss collector, or officer, to prevent further inconvenience, and disturbance to the plantation. But if any such officer, or collector, be removed out of the jurisdiction, or if any of the planters be dead, removed, or grown insolvent, or if by any other meanes, the ful payment of the rates, and fines be hindred, the present authority in any such plantation by a due assessment, are to leavy, and gather the same, of the present planters, and without delay, to pay it in to the jurisdiction treasurer; otherwise the cattel,or other goods, of any planter, or planters, are to be seized by the marshal, or other officer, with, or without assistants, as in the law for publick charges is exprest.

Records.

It is ordered, That all parents, masters, housekeepers, and others who have either children, servants, sojourners, or lodgers in the house, or dwelling with them shal bring in to the secretary of the plantation, where he lives, or to such other officer in each plantation as shal be thereunto appointed, the names of such persons belonging, or in any way referring to them, or any of them, as shal either be born, or dye, with the respective time of each such birth, or death. And also that every new married man (if married within this jurisdiction) shal bring in the certificate thereof, under the hand of the magistrate or officer that married him, with the time when, to be recorded first by the officer of the plantation, where he was married; but if married in another jurisdiction, though at present or after he come to be an inhabitant in this, then to record the marriage where he liveth; and to pay for every record, whether birth, death, or marriage, three pence, whereof two pence for each such record, shal be to the officer in each plantation, who shal both record in the plantation book, and yearly deliver or send a transcript of every birth, death, or marriage, with a peny for each, to the secretary for the general court: and what person soever (to whom it doth belong) shal neglect to bring in a note, or certificate, as aforesaid, together with three pence for each record, to the said plantation-officer, more then one month, after each birth, death, or marriage, he shal pay for each six pence to the said officer; if he neglect two months, he shal pay twelve pence; if three moneths, five shillings; which forfeits shal go, two third parts to the plantation-officer, the rest to the jurisdiction-officer. And if the plantation-officer shal either neglect to record, or to deliver over the transcripts, as before; or if the secretary for the general court, shal neglect to record them, each officer for every such neglect shal pay to the jurisdiction-treasurer ten shillings.

It is further ordered and declared, That every man shal have liberty to record in the publick register of any court, any testimony given upon oath, in the same court, or before two magistrates, or any deed or evidence, legally confirmed, there to remain *in perpetuam rei memoriam;* and that every inhabitant in this jurisdiction, shal have free liberty to search, and view any such publick records or registers, and to have a copie thereof, written, examined, and signed by the secretary, or officer of the said court, paying the due charge or fees therfore. Also every trial betwixt party and party, and proceedings against delinquents in criminal causes, shal be briefly and distinctly recorded, the better to prevent after mistakes, and other inconveniences.

Replevin.

It is ordered and declared, That every man shal have liberty to replevy his cattel, or goods, impounded, distreined, or seized, unless it be upon execution after judgment, or for payment of rates, or fines; provided he put in good security to prosecute the replevin, and to satisfie such damage and charge, as his adversary shal recover against him in law.

Sabbath, see *prophanation of the Lord's day.*

Seamen, &c.

It is ordered, That if any seaman, marriner, master of ship or vessel, or other person, shal receive into any ship, pinnace, bote, cannooe, or other vessel by what name soever called, and shal carry away, or suffer to take, or have passage, out of any harbor, or plantation, within this jurisdiction, any child, servant, or other person, whether male, or female, whom he knoweth to stand in relation, or under the charge and government of another, and so not at his or her own present dispose, or any debtor, delinquent, or offender, whom he knoweth, or hath heard to be under, or liable, to any ingagement, censure, or punishment, to or from any particular person, or the authority of this jurisdiction, or any plantation therein, without express, and written license, from some magistrate, dwelling in that plantation, or from the constable, or deputies intrusted for civil affairs, where there is no magistrate, or at least from the master, or governor of the family, who hath the trust or power, where there is no other ingagement or guilt: He shal be liable (if known and apprehended in any part of this jurisdiction) to satisfie, and pay all such debts and ingagements as any such person oweth, or ought to satisfie, and to pay such damage or fine to the person or persons wronged, or to the plantation, or jurisdiction, as the court considering the case, with the circumstances, shal judge meet.

Sentences of Judgement.

It is ordered, That all sentences of Judgement, upon criminal causes, shal be executed upon the offenders, in the presence of the magistrates, or one of them at least; Deut. 25. 2, [or] of some other officer in the absence of the magistrate.

Servants, see *Masters.*

Shoomakers, see *Leather.*

Single Persons.

To prevent, or suppress inconvenience, and disorder in the course and carriage of sundry single persons, who live not in service, nor in any family relation, answering the mind of God in the fift commandement: It is ordered, That no single person of either sex, do henceforward board, diet, sojourn, or be permitted so to do, or to have lodging; or house room within any of the plantations of this jurisdiction, but either in some allowed relation, or in some approved family licensed thereunto, by the court, or by a magistrate, or some officer, or officers in that plantation, appointed thereunto, where there is no magistrate; the governor of which family, so licensed, shal as he may conveniently, duly observe the course, carriage, and behaviour, of every such single person, whether he, or she walk diligently in a constant lawful imployment, attending both family duties, and the publick worship of God, and keeping good order day and night, or otherwise. And shal then complaine of any such disorder, that every such single person may be questioned, and punished, if the case require it. And if any single person shal dyet, or lodge, or if any housekeeper shal admit, or entertaine any such, contrary to the true meaning of this order; or if any licensed to receive such, shal neglect to complain of any disorder observed, all, and every such persons, shal pay such fine, as the court, or authority appointed for the place, shal judge meet.

Sojourners, see *Strangers*.

Strayes.

It is ordered, That whosoever shal take up, or detain any stray beast, or swine, or find any lost goods, he shal within six daies, give notice thereof to the marshal, cryer, or other officer appointed for such service, by the plantation to which he belongs, who shal enter, or cause the same to be entred in a book; and take order, that it be duly cryed, on their three next lecture dayes, or upon three several dayes of the town's most general meeting which the time wil afford; and if the value exceed twenty shillings, he shal cause the like publication to be made, at the publick meetings, of the two next towns, that the owner may the better hear of, and recover what belongeth to him. And further, in the case of a stray beast, he shal within one moneth after such finding, put, and indeavour from time to time, to keep a with, or wreath about the neck of it; and within three months at furthest, (if the owner in that time appear not) he shal acquaint the next magistrate with the stray taken up, or goods found, and his due proceedings about them, that the same may be apprised by such indifferent men as the said magistrate shal nominate, and appoint. And shal within six dayes after that, cause the apprisement to be duly recorded, by the secretary of the plantation-court, or constable, or other officer there intrusted for publick affairs, with the colour, age, natural or artificial markes, or such other description, as best suits the stray, or goods, so taken up, or found. And if the owner of any such stray appeare within one yeare after such publication, he shal have restitution in kind, if with safety, and conveniency it might be so long kept, paying all just damages, and charges, to the finder, and officers, nay if he appear within three years, after the stray was first taken up, (paying as before) he shal have the ful value (according to the forementioned apprisement) restored. But if the owner shal be, and continue so negligent that neither in the first, second, nor third year, he improve the means prescribed, to assert, and clear his title; the said stray, or lost goods, (to prevent contention, and inconvenience which may after grow) shal be in reference to the first owner by sentence of the plantation-court lost, and forfeited; and the ful value, all damages, and charges to finder, officers, or others, being first deducted (wherein if there be any question, the court, or some indifferently chosen if there be no court in that plantation, shal consider and determine) shal be equally divided, one half to the plantation, and the other half to the finder. But if the said finder shal omit, or neglect his duty, or any part of it, according to the former directions, he shal pay such damage to the owner, and such fine to the plantation, as the owner, and such fine to the plantation, as the court upon consideration of the miscarriage shal judge meet; if he proceed further, to sel, kil, or any way for his own advantage dispose, or alienate the property of any such stray, without attending the said directions, he shal upon proofe, pay double the value, either to the owner, if he may be found, or to the plantation to which the finder belongs; provided also that if the owner or other person, shal injuriously, without order from authority, or consent of the finder, take off such with or wreath, or take away such stray (after such with or wreath, to his knowledg hath been put on) before he have cleared his interest, and given satisfaction for damages, or charges expended, he shal forfeit the ful value of the stray, apprised as before, to the use of the finder.

Strangers, see *Courts*.

Strangers complaining.

If any stranger, or person of another nation, complain of injury received from any within this jurisdiction; It is ordered, that due search and inquiry be made concerning the same, that justice may have a free passage; and that the stranger (if wronged) may receive due satisfaction, either out of the estate of the offender, or by his corporal punishment, as the case may require, and according to Matt: 7. 12.

Strangers, Sojourners, and Servants.

To prevent sundry inconveniences which may grow to this jurisdiction, and the plantations thereof, by the inconsiderate, and disorderly receiving and entertaining of strangers, or others, to be planters, or sojourners in any part of this colony; it is ordered, That henceforward, no person receive, or entertain any man, or woman, of what age or quality soever, coming or resorting either from forraign parts, or from other jurisdictions, or plantations, into any plantation, or farme house, or habitation within the bounds, or limits of any plantation within this jurisdiction, to settle as a planter, or sojorner, nor sel, give, nor any way alienate, or pass over, lease, or let any house, or hous-lot, or any part or parcel of any of them, or any land, of what kind or quality soever, nor shal permit any such to stay, or abide above one moneth, without a license from, and under the hand of some magistrate dwelling in that plantation, or without the consent, and express order of the major part of the freemen of such plantation where there is no magistrate, or without the consent, and order of the greater part of the inhabitants, where there is neither church nor freemen, under the penalty of ten pounds to be paid as a fine to the plantation, where this order is violated. Yet if any such violation or offence be made, or committed, only by error, or mistake, and with smal or no inconvenience to the plantation, or jurisdiction; the fine, or penalty, may be moderated, as the plantation-court, or court of magistrates, shal see cause. Provided that this order is neither intended, nor reacheth to travelers, nor such as resort hither in a way of merchandise, or trade, nor to the entertainment of friends, who in a way of love come only to visit, and walk inoffensively, nor to servants received, and entertained upon family respects. In all which cases, as every perticuler person considers his own conveniency in receiving and entertaining, so the court of magistrates, or plantation court wil consider how far they may justly free the jurisdiction, or plantatation, from inconvenience and charge. But it is by this court ordered, That if any servant fal sick, or any way diseased, or distempered, during the time of service by covenant or agreement; the governor of such servant, while that tearm lasteth, shal provide what is necessary, without putting any burden, or charge upon the plantation, or jurisdiction: And if such hurt came, or were brought upon such servant by the cruelty, or miscarriage of the family governor; such governor shal allow recompence or maintenance, after the time of relation is expired, as the plantation court shal judge meet. But if the hurt came by any providence of God, without the default of the family governor; the plantation shal dispose, or provide for such servant, after his or her time of service is expired, as the case may require.

And to prevent difference or questions which may arise, and grow within this jurisdiction: it is agreed, and ordered, that if any person, male, or femal, elder, or younger, whether with, or without license, shal hereafter sojourne, or have constant dwelling, or abode, within the limits of any plantation in this jurisdiction, for and during the tearm, or time of one whole year, every such person shal to all purposes (in reference to any plantation within this jurisdiction, but no further) be accounted an inhabitant there, and shal not be sent back, or returned (unless to some particular person standing, and continuing in relation to receive, and provide as the case may require) nor shal the jurisdiction, or any other plantation in it be liable to any charge, or burden, in reference to any such person, though he, or she, hath dwelt elsewhere in the jurisdiction before.

Stripes.

Stripes, or whipping, is a correction fit and proper in some cases, where the offence is accompanied with childish, or brutish folly, with rude filthiness, or with stubborn insolency, with bestly cruelty, or with idle vagrancy, or for faults of like nature. But when stripes are due: it is ordered, That not above forty stripse shal be inflicted at one time; Deut 25. 3.

Suits Vexatious, see *damages pretended.*
Swearing, see *prophane swaering.*
Swine, see *Cattel*, and see *Plantations.*
Thefts, see *Burgalry.*

Trespass.

It is ordered, and declared, That in any trespass,

or damage done to any man or men, if it appeare, or can be proved to be done, by the meer default of him, or them, upon whom the losse, or damage fals; it shal be judged no trespass, nor any recompence allowed for it.

Watch, see *Military affairs.*

Weights and Measures.

Whereas a considerable part of righteousnesse, between buyer, and seller, doth consist, in known, certain, and just weights, and measures, It is ordered, That every plantation, within this jurisdiction, there be several standards, procured, and sealed, that they may be uniform, and certain; viz. for weights, a set of brass weights, to 4 pounds, with the less weights included, according to the averdepois pound, consisting of sixteen ounces, with a good beam, and scales, fit to try them. And so for corn measures, the bushell, halfe bushell, peck, halfe peck, to be fitted to Winchester measure in England, and alike in all plantations. And measures for liquid things, as the ale quart, wine quart, wine pint, &c: and that there be one ell, and one yard. That all, and each may be according to the use in London, as is generally practised in these United Colonies. And that in goods sold by the ell, or yard, a thums breadth be allowed to the length of each ell, and yard. In goods sold by the hundred weight, that five-score and twelve be allowed. And in all sorts of nails sold by the hundred, six-score be allowed to the hundred, according to the course in England.

And that in each plantation within this jurisdiction, some fit man, or men, be chosen and appointed, under oath to view, and try all the forementioned weights and measures used in buying and selling, at least once a year; but oftener if there be cause, and to fit them to the forementioned standards, and then to mark them, with some such known, and approved mark, and to have such allowance for the same, as each plantation shal order, which viewer, or officers, so sworn, shal in each plantation yearly (beside extraordinary viewers) appoint a convenient time, and place, to prove, and try, all such weights, and measures, and shal give publick, or due notice of it, and such weights or measures, as cannot be brought or conformed to the standard, shal be ordered or destroyed, that they be no more used in buying or selling.

Lastly, if any viewer, or officer, so chosen, and sworn, do neglect his duty and trust, in any part of the premises, he shal pay as a fine to the plantation, fourty shillings. If any person within this jurisdiction after such notice given, shal neglect to bring in his weights, and measures, at the time, and to the place appointed, he shal pay three shillings four pence for every such default, one halfe to the viewer, or officer, and the other half to the plantation. But if any person within this jurisdiction, shal at any time buy, or sel, by any false or unallowed weight, or measure, to the damage of his neighbour, he shal pay (besides restitution) such fine to the plantation, as the court considering the nature, and measure of the offence, shal judge meet.

Wills Inventories, and the estates of such as dye intestate.

It is ordered, That when any man dyeth possessed of an estate within this jurisdiction, whether it be greater, or lesse, the secretary of each plantation, or some officer thereunto appointed, shal enquire and call for the last wil and testament of every such person, together with a true inventory of all the goods and estate of the deceased, within this jurisdiction, which with the first conveniency shal be justly prized, and the estate disposed, or preserved, as the case shal require. But the will (if any be made and found) and the inventory, shal be duly and respectively proved by oath, the wil by witnesses, the inventory for the quantity of the goods, by executors, administrators, or such as have had the estate in custody. And for the valuation by the apprisers, who shal be approved and appointed thereunto, by the plantation court, or by some magistrate or authority there setled, and shal be recorded by the secretary or some other officer in all the particulars, and so kept among the plantation records, and after presented to the next court of magistrates, or at the furthest to the next court but one, after the party deceased, under such penalty as the court shal judge meet, and delivered to the secretary for the jurisdiction, who shal keep all original wils and inventories upon the file, and enter onely a brief abstract of them, among the jurisdiction records; namely, the date of the wil, the names of the witnesses, when proved, when the inventory was taken, the persons by whom the estate was prised, with the summe it amounts to, and writing upon the wil and inventory, in what folio the premises are entered in the book of record. And that six shillings be paid for every such wil and inventory. But in plantations where there is no court, the jurisdiction secretary shal at each generall court, call to the deputies for such wils, and inventories, which are to be brought in, and entered at large, in a book of records kept by the court of magistrates for that purpose, and the originals kept on the file, as before expressed. And in such cases the jurisdiction secretary to receive the fees due both to himselfe and the plantation secretary, and when either the wils, or inventories, or both, are large, and require much writing, the court of magistrates, or plantation court, may enlarge the secretaries fees. But if through the unskilfulnesse, or inadvertency of any person, any wil, or wils, made or left, want due form, or cannot be legally proved, in such case, the court following as neer as they rationally may, the scope, and aim of the testator, the executor, or administrator, before any of them intermeddle, or have any power of such an estate, shal (if the court see cause) put in sufficient security, which shall stand in force three years from the date, to deliver back the value of the whole estate, or such part of it, as the court shal finde just cause otherwise to dispose of.

But if no Wil be found, then the court of magistrates, or plantation court, shal consider, who hath the next right of administration and when any such doth administer, he, she, or they, shal give such bond, or security, as the court considering the value of the estate, with such questions as are like to arise, shal judge meet, to bring in a true inventory, within a convenient time limited, and to dispose of the whole estate, as the court according to the laws here setled, shall see cause to order. And concerning such as dye here intestate, It is ordered, That the true estate, all just debts being paid, and all necessary expences discharged; such as about the funeral of the deceased, prising the goods, bringing in the inventory, immediate and reasonable charges of housekeeping, til things (without unnecessary delay) may be setled, shal be divided and aloted as foloweth; Namely, one 3d part at least, to the widow of the deceased, if he leave a widow. And if there be children left, not or not duly provided for, two third parts at most to them, with due respect to the eldest son, who is to have a double child's portion, of the whole estate, real, and personal, unlesse the general court, upon just cause, and grounds, shal judge otherwise, either for dividing the estate, or for the portion of the first born. But in case the intestate leave his wife (who hath well deserved of him while he lived) and but one child, one third part of the estate, shal as before, go to the widow, and one third part to the child; but the other third part shal be divided by the plantation court, as they see cause, betwixt the widow and the child, reserving liberty for an appeal, either to the court of magistrates, or to the general court, as in other cases.

Wine, see *Impost.*

Witnesses.

That justice may have the more free passages, It is ordered, That any one magistrate, or other officer authorised by the general court, may upon oath, take the testimony of any person of fourteen yeares of age, or above, being of sound understanding, and of good reputation, in any case, civil, or criminal, out of court; and testifie the same, if it be desired, by his subscription, for evidence in another jurisdiction. But if it be for this jurisdiction, the magistrate, or officer is to keep the same in his own hands, or custody, til the court; or deliver it to the secretary, or other officer to be recorded, that nothing be altered in it. And yet where any such witnesse lives in the plantation where the court is held, or at furthest within sixteen miles of it, and is not disabled by sicknesse, or other infirmity; the said testimony so taken out of court (especially in capital causes) shal not be received, or made use of in court, except it were either at first, taken in the presence of the party testified against, or that the witnesse be after present in court, to be (if there be cause) further examined about it. And it is further ordered, That any person (by warrant from a magistrate, or other officer thereunto authorised) summoned to appeare as a witnesse, in any civil case betwixt party and party, shal not be compellable to travel to any court in another plantation, where he is to give his testimony, except he who procured the summons, shal first lay down, or give him satisfaction for his travel, and expences outward and homeward, after the rate of two shillings a day, in proportion to the length of the way, and for such time, as he shal necessarily spend in attendance about such case, at the court or place, due recompence shal be awarded by the court. And if any witnesse so summoned, and after such payment, or satisfaction, shal fail to appeare, to give his testimony, he shal (upon an action of the case) be liable to pay the parties dammages. And the like appearance (under such penalties as the nature and weight of the case may require) shal all witnesses (being so summoned) be bound to make, to give evidence in criminal causes, who shal also have due satisfaction from the treasurer, upon notice, and direction from the secretary of the court, where the cause was tried. And it is further ordered, that in all such causes, the charges of the witnesses shal be born by the delinquent, and shal be added to the fine or censure imposed. That what the treasurer upon such warrant from the court, shal disburse to the witnesses, may be duly repaid by the offender, that neither the jurisdiction nor plantation be unnecessarily burdened.

Wolves.

Upon experience of great hurt already done by wolves in these parts, and upon consideration how mischievous the increase of them may prove: It is (for the incouragement of all such as wil set themselves to kil, and destroy them) ordered; That whosoever shal kil an old wolf within this jurisdiction, and bring his head, shal have for the same 20*s.* and for each young wolf so kild, and brought 10*s.* And that the Indians have for each old wolfe's head so kild, five shillings; and for each young one 2*s.* & 6*d.* which several summs are to be paid by the plantation, within the limits wherof, any such wolfe is kild; The bounds whereof, are the lines betwixt each plantation; and to this purpose, so to be accounted 12 miles up into the country.

SOME PRESIDENTS AND FORMES OF THINGS FREQUENTLY USED.

Summons.

To (A. B.) husbandman of (B.) you are to appeare at the next Court, holden at (N.) on the day of the month next ensuing, to answer the complaint of (C. D.) for with holding a debt of due upon a bond or bill, &c. or for a horse &c. sould you by him, or for work, or for a trespass done him, in his corne, or hay, by your cattel, or for a defamation, or slander, you have raised, or brought upon his name, or for striking him, or the like. And hereof you may not fail at your peril. Dated the day of the month, 1655.

An Attachment.

To the Marshal or Constable of (N.) or to his deputy; you are required to attach (when the case requires it) the body, and goods, of (E. F.) and to take bond of him, to the value of with sufficient surety, or sureties, for his appearance, at the next Court holden at (N.) on the day of the month, then and there to answer the complaint of (G. H.) for &c. as before. And so make a true returne thereof under your hand. Dated the day, &c.

Bond for Appearance.

Know all by these presents, That we (E. F.) of (M.) husbandman; and (I. K.) of the same plantation carpenter, do bind ourselves, our heirs, and executors to (L. M.) marshal or (N. O.) constable of (N.) aforesaid, in pounds, upon condition, that the said (E. F.) shal personally appears at the next court at (N.) to answer (G. H.) in an action of And to abide the order of the court therein; And not to depart without license.

Replevin.

To the Marshal or Constable of ; you are required to replevi two heifers of (P. R.) now distreyned, or impounded by (S. T.) and to deliver them to the said (P. R.) provided he give bond to the value of with sufficient surety, or sureties, to prosecute his replevin, at the next court holden at (S.) and so from court to court, til the cause be ended; and to pay such costs, and damages as the said (S. T.) shal by law recover against him; and so make a true return thereof, under your hand. Dated, &c.

Oath of Fidelity.

You (S. T.) being by the providence of God, an inhabitant within Newhaven jurisdiction, do freely, and sincerely acknowledge yourself to be subject to the government thereof; and do here sweare by the great and dreadful name of the everlasting God, that you wil be true, and faithful to the same; and wil yeild due assistance thereunto, with your person, and estate, as in equity you are bound; and wil truly indeavour to to entertain and preserve all the liberties and priviledges thereof, submitting yourself to all the just and wholsome laws, and orders, which already are, or hereafter shal be by lawful authority there made, and established. And further that you will neither plot, nor practise any evil against it, nor consent to any that shal so do. But wil fully, and timely discover the same to lawful authority there setled, for the speedy preventing thereof. And that you wil as in duty you are bound, maintaine the honour of the same, and of all the lawful magistrates thereof, promoting the publick good whilst you shal continue an inhabitant there; and whensoever you shall be duly called as a free burgess, according to the fundamental order, and agreement for government in this jurisdiction, to give your vote, or suffrage touching any matter which concerneth this colony; you shall give it as in your conscience you shall judge may conduce to the best good of the same, without respect of person, or favour to, or from any man. So help you God in our Lord Jesus Christ.

Governor's Oath.

Whereas you (A. B.) are chosen to the place of Governor, within this jurisdiction for the insuing year; And til a new governor be chosen, and sworn, you do here swear by the great and dreadful name of the ever living God, to maintaine (according to your best ability) all the lawful priviledges of this common-wealth; according to the fundamental order and agreement made for government thereof, and that you wil carry and demean yourself for the said time of your government, according to the laws of God, and for the advancement of his gospel, the laws of this colony, and the good of the inhabitants thereof, you shal do justice to all without partiality, as much as in you lyeth. So help you God, &c.

Deputy Governor, and Magistrates.

Whereas you (C. D.) are chosen to the place of Deputy Governor &c., or you (E. F.) are chosen to the place of a Magistrate &c. as in the Governor's oath, *mutatis mutandis.*

Other Officers and Witnesses.

Several other oaths are to be administred to other officers, as Secretary, and Treasurer for the jurisdiction, Deputies for particular courts, Marshal, Constable, Witnesses, &c. But the substance of their oaths is to ingage them to a faithful discharge of the duty of their places, and trust, according to the best of their ability, to preserve the peace of the jurisdiction, and to give ful and true evidence, in the cases, wherein they give testimony.

VII.

LAWS, ORDERS, AND JUDGMENTS, OF THE NEW HAVEN COURTS, 1639-1660.

[From the Colonial Records, Vol. I.]

25th Feb., 1639-40.—Mrs. Higginson, late planter of Quillipieck dying without making her will, and leaving behind her eight children, an inventory of of her estate being taken, the court disposed of her estate and children as followeth, with the consent and approbation of Mr. John Higginson, her eldest son:

Charles Higginson is to have £40. to his portion, and to be with Thomas Fugill as his apprentice unto the full end and term of nine years from the first of March next ensuing the date hereof. And the said Tho: Fugill is to find him what is convenient for him as a servant, and to keep him at school one year, or else to advantage him as much in his education as a year's learning comes to,* and he is to have the ben-

*"Here is a proceeding which marks as distinctly as any measure could, the views entertained by the leaders of the colony, of the value of education, the protection which ought to be extended to the indigent, and their regard for popular rights. If any one hereafter shall wish to inspect the early colonial records of New Haven, to find subjects of reproach or merriment, let him be referred to the indentures of Charles Higginson........No suggestion for the adoption of a rule by which an elementary education was secured to apprentices could have been received *from any law of the parent country*."—Kingsley's *Hist. Discourse*, p. 39.

efit of the use of his portion till the said term be expired, and at the end thereof to pay it to the said Charles Higginson, if he live till the said nine years be expired, but if he die before, then the said Thomas Fugill is to pay the said portion to the rest of his brothers that are alive at the end of the said nine years. (pp. 29, 30.)

1639–40.—John Jenner, accused for being drunk with strong waters, was acquitted, it appearing to be of infirmity and occasioned by the extremity of the cold.

Mr. Moulenour, accused of being drunk, but not clearly proved, was respited. (p. 29.)

1640.—It was ordered that commodities well bought in England for ready money, shall not be sold here above three pence in the shilling for profit and adventure, above what they cost with charges, when sold by retail; when sold by the piece or vessel, by wholesale, less profit may suffice.

When bought from ships or other vessels here, not above 3*ob.* [half-pence] in the shilling by retail, nor above a penny in the shilling by wholesale. But commodities of a perishing nature, subject to waste and damage, fall not under the former rates, yet the rates to be so ordered that neither buyer nor seller suffer in the rates. (p. 35.)

It is ordered that every man that is appointed to watch, whether masters or servants, shall come every Lord's day to the meeting completely armed, and all others also are to bring their swords, no man exempted

---

* The references are to the first (printed) volume of the N. H. Colonial Records, edited by Mr. Hoadly. The spelling has been modernised, throughout.

save Mr. Eaton, our pastor, Mr. James, Mr. Samuell Eaton and the two deacons. (40.)

It is ordered that Mr. Gregson shall be truck master of this town for this year ensuing, to truck with the Indians for venison, so as he may afford to sell to the planters that have need at 3*ob.* [half-pence] a pound, all together, good and bad, one with another.

It is ordered that no English men that kills venison shall sell the fattest for above 3*d.* a pound, and the lean at 2*d. ob.* [2½ pence]. (43.)

1640.—Thomas Franckland for drinking strong liquors to excess and entertaining disorderly persons into his cellar to drinking meetings, together with his contempt of the court, was whipped, fined 20*s.* and deprived of his cellar and lot, his lot and liberty of staying in the plantation being only granted to him upon his good behavior.

Andrew Loe junior was whipped for breaking Richard Osborne his cellar and stealing, and that on the Sabbath day. (46.)

It was ordered that all that live in cellars, and have families, shall have liberty for three months to provide for themselves, but all single persons are to betake themselves forthwith to some families, except the magistrate see cause to respite them for a time.

1641.—It is ordered that seven hours shall be accounted a day's work for a team, if that whole time be diligently improved in work according to the nature of that employment, and the hire for a steer by the day 9*d.*, for a grown ox or bull 12*d.*, for a horse or mare 16*d.*, for cart furniture and man 6*d.*

For master carpenters, joiners, plasterers, bricklayers, mowers, coopers, thatchers, rivers of clapboards, pales, shingles, laths and the like callings which require skill and strength, not above 2*s.* in summer, and 20*d.* in winter.

But others of the same trades or callings, not allowed master workmen, not above 20*d.* in summer and 16*d.* in winter.

Plasterers, haymakers, fellers of timber, those that cross-cut timber, and all sorts of laborers experienced and diligent in their way, improving time as above, in summer not above 18*d.* in winter not above 14*d.*

Unskillful negligent laborers, and boys, both in summer and winter, in several employments, according to the service they do, which when any doubt ariseth shall be judged by able and indifferent. (52, 53.)

Diet for a laboring man with lodging and washing 4*s.* 6*d.* by the week. Venison sold by the English, if fat, not above 2*d.* *ob.* per pound, if leane 2*d.* per pound, fowl a proportionable abatement to what was set last year. (55.)

All commodities bought and sold among the planters, and all work wages and labor (henceforward, till some other course be settled by order), to be paid for either in corn, as the price goeth in the plantation, or in work as the rates settled by the court, or in cattel of any sort as they shall be indifferently prized, or in good merchantable beaver according to its goodness; and payment to be made at the times which shall be agreed upon. (55, 56.)

Feb., 1642.—It is ordered that a free school shall be set up in this town, and our pastor Mr. Davenport, together with the magistrates, shall consider what yearly allowance is meet to be given to it out of the common stock of the town, and also what rules and orders are meet to be observed in and about the same. (62.)

1642.—It is ordered that no young men shall live by themselves in cellars, but betake themselves to such families as the masters thereof may not only watch over them, but be able to give an account of or concerning them or their conversation when they shall be required. (70.)

Samuel H., and Elizabeth C., being desirous to join together in the state of marriage, and not being able to make proof of their parents' consent, but seeing they both affirm they have the consent of their parents, and with all having entered into contract, sinfully and wickedly . . . . . have both made themselves unfit for any other, and for which they have both received public correction, upon these considerations, granted them liberty to marry. (77, 78.)

1643.—Whereas goodman Osborne hath heretofore spoiled divers hides in the tanning which he allegeth was for want of skill or experience in the tan of this country, he promiseth for the time to come to make good what is spoiled in the tanning, for now he knows the nature of the tan, and therefore, if any hides be now spoiled it is through his default.

1643.—It is ordered that every family within this plantation shall have a coat of cotton wool, well and substantially made, so as it may be fit for service,* and that in convenient time the taylors see it be done. (121.)

April, 1644.—It was ordered that the judicial laws of God, as they were delivered by Moses, and as they are a fence to the moral law, being neither typical nor ceremonial, nor had any reference to Canaan, shall be accounted of moral equity, and generally bind all

*To be proof against Indian arrows.

offenders, and be a rule to all the courts in this jurisdiction in their proceeding against offenders, till they be branched out into particulars hereafter.

It was ordered that in case any of the magistrates in the smaller plantations see need of help in some weighty causes or difficult knotty cases, upon due notice and request to the Governor, provision shall be made accordingly, (130.)

1644.—The proposition for the relief of poor scholars at the college at Cambridge was fully approved of, and thereupon it was ordered, Joshua Attwater and William Davis shall receive of every one in this plantation whose heart s willing to contribute thereunto, a peck of wheat or the value of it. (149.)

1647.—The Governor propounded that the college corn might be forthwith paid, and that considering the work is a service to Christ, to bring up young plants for his service, and besides, it will be a reproach that it shall be said Newhaven is fallen off from this service. (311.)

1645.—Richard L., having been formerly convicted and censured for sundry miscarriages in ways of unrighteousness, now made an acknowledgment of his guilt in the court, thinking thereby to give satisfaction, who showed themselves willing to take satisfaction, but yet advised him to be careful to make his peace with God, and seek to get that bitter root, (whence such evil fruits did spring,) that a reformation of those evils may appear in his conversation. (153.)

1645.—James Russells, by reason of his lame thumb, was excused from bringing his musket on the Lord's days and other days of public solemn worships. (160.)

Joseph B. and Joseph C. were accused for drinking to excess; Joseph B. confessed that they had drunk sack in his father's cellar, out of the bung, with a tobacco pipe, and in the chamber out of a bottle, and that they went after that to the ordinary, and there drank a quart of beer. Sister Linge testified that she saw them as they came from the ordinary and Joseph B. did lead Joseph C. by the arm, and she speaking to them asked whether Joseph C. were drunk, whereupon Joseph B. let him go, and then she saw him stagger and reel and, as she conceived, being not able to go nor stand as a man, he sit him down upon a block or log by the pales, but could not sit as one sober, whereupon she again said he was drunk, because he could not go nor stand, and then Joseph B. called him to come to him which he did, but yet in a reeling manner. Mrs. Evance and her maid testified that when they first saw Joseph C. after this they could perceive nothing that he ailed.

The court being fully satisfied in the evidence given by sister Linge, and the Governor testifying that, upon [the] examination he had taken, they told abundance of lies, especially Joseph B., the premises considered, the court conceived they deserved to be severely whipped, but referred it to Mr. Evance and Mr. B. to give them correction in their families. (170, 171.)

Bamfeild Bell being reproved by Wm. Paine for singing profane songs, answered and said, "you are one of the holy brethren that will lie for advantage." It was testified by the said Wm. Paine and Joseph Brewster. Mr. Evance testified that it was his constant frame, to reproach those that walk in the ways of God. The premises considered, the sentence of the court was that he should be severely whipped.

Mrs. Brewster entreated the court that the execution of the sentence may be respited till her husband come home, because he is her husband's kinsman.

(173.)

1645.—Hannah M. complained that Mr. Brewster called [her] *Billingsgate slut*, and that she was sent for on shipboard to play the slut.

Mr. Brewster confessed he being much provoked and disquieted by her frowardness and brawling on shipboard, did call her slut, and Billingsgate slut, and said he hoped she would dance about the whipping post; and affirmed *&c.*

Mr. Brewster's maid and Mr. Lamberton's maid testified, that the said Hannah M. was very froward and contentious, and a cause of much contention and unquietness amongst them as they came from the Bay.

When the Govêrnor had shown what was the ordinary acceptation of "Billingsgate slut," namely, that some that were so called were convicted scolds, and punished at the cucking stool for it, and some of them charged with incontinency, Mr. Brewster said he had sufficiently proved the one true, and he would not acquit her in the other; being asked what ground he had to lay such an implicit charge upon her, he said he had nothing at all against her but what he gathered from Mrs. Norton's words. The court told [him] he ought to acknowledge his failing, and so repair her reputation, as much as he may. At length he did acknowledge he was to blame, and said he was sorry he had spoke so rashly, and that he intended no such charge against her. The court also according to the evidence reproved Hannah M. for her froward disposition, remembering her that meekness is a choice ornament for women, and wished her to take it as a rebuke from God, and to keep a better watch over her spirit hereafter, lest the Lord proceed to manifest his displeasure further against her.

Hannah M. did acknowledge it had been some trouble to her that she had been so froward and contentious to the disquieting of others, and hoped it should be a warning to her for time to come.

(180, 181.)

1645.—For the better training up of youth in this town, that through God's blessing they may be fitted for public service hereafter, either in church or commonweal, it is ordered, that a free school be set up, and the magistrates with the teaching elders are entreated to consider what rules and orders are meet to be observed and what allowance may be convenient for the schoolmaster's care and pains, which shall be paid out of the town's stock. According to which order, £20 a year was paid to Mr. Ezekiell Cheevers, the present schoolmaster, for two or three years at first, but that not proving a competent maintenance, in August, 1644, it was enlarged to £30 a year and so continueth.* (210.)

1646.—It was ordered, that whosoever fetcheth fire, or sends for it, and not in a covered vessel, though the fire be denied them, or upon any other occasions they come without it, they shall pay 6*d.* fine; but if they carry any fire away, they shall pay 12*d.*, because great damage may grow to the town by slightness and carelessness this way.

It was ordered, that whosoever shall be found taking

* This is from the revision, in 1644–45, of laws and orders then in force. The order for a free-school in New Haven, was made Feb., 1641–42. See, before, p. 278.

tobacco in an uncovered place, as in the street of the town, or in men's yards, shall pay 6*d.* fine each time, also if on training days, either in the company or the meeting house at any time. (241.)

Thomas Blatchley having formerly given the Court some offence, and neglecting the image of God in magistrates, and going away so irreverently, and saying he would have justice in another place if he had it not here; which now lying on his conscience, desires to clear himself; wherewith the court was satisfied. (271.)

1647.—It was propounded that those planters, householders and sojourners, would give in their names, who desire to have their seats in the soldiers' seats, engaging themselves to bring their arms constantly, to all public meetings for the worships of God. (291.)

1647.—George King charged with blaspheming the name of God by cursing; James Heywood said he heard him swear by the name of God, and told him the danger of such a course, and since, he hath heard him swear.

Thomas Morris affirmed he had been told of swearing aboard the ship, and since swore by the name of God, aboard a Dutchman, and he told him of it. The oath was a *by God.* George King confessed he spake the words.

The Governor told him, that when the son of an Egyptian blasphemed the name of God, it was not borne. It's the piercing through the name of God in passion, which is a high provocation of God, whereas the rule is, let your words be yea, yea, and nay, nay, and by a man's words he may lose his life.

It was hoped it was only a rash and sinful oath;

some have been bored through the tongue, others have been in the stocks, and their tongues in a cloven stick; but hoping this was not despitefully done, the sentence of the court was, that he should be whipped, and in the interim be kept in the marshal's hands. (293.)

Sergeant Nash propounded whether it was the court's mind that masters of watches should be freed from walking the rounds and standing sentinel on the Lord's days, but after some debate, the thing was respited till another court.

William Preston, who was intrusted to look to the shutting the meeting-house doors, was desired to keep them constantly shut, and that they be opened upon the Lord's days and lecture days before the first drum is beat, and William Andrewes was desired so to repair and order the doors that they may be opened on the outside when unlocked and unbarred, and at other times to shut fast and secure.

Robert Bassett was desired to beat both the first and second drum, upon Lord's days and lecture days, upon the meeting-house, that so those who live far off may hear them the more distinctly, and he promised so to do. (311.)

William Pert was warned to the court for taking water-melons one Lord's day out of Mr. Hooke's lot; and Mr. Hooke complaineth that he hath often been abused this way; and since that time, his orchard hath been robbed.

William Pert's answer was that his master sent him into the quarter and to see whether there were any hogs within the fence, and he was bid by his master to bring home a water-melon with him; he being bid to go that way through Mr. Hooke's lot, after the Sabbath, he took two water-melons; he said it was the first act of his in this kind and hoped it should be the last. For his unrighteousness and profaneness of his spirit and way, so soon thus to do after the Sabbath, he was to be publicly corrected, although moderately, because his repentance did appear. (325.)

It was propounded to the court to consider whether it were not meet to make a law for restraining of persons from their ordinary outward employments upon any part of the Sabbath, and the rather because some have of late taken too much liberty that way, and have been called to answer for it in the particular court. The court considering that it is their duty to do the best they can that the law of God may be strictly observed, did therefore order that whosoever shall, within this plantation, break the Sabbath by doing any of their ordinary outward occasions, from sunset to sunset, either upon the land or upon the water, extraordinary cases, works of mercy and necessity being excepted, he shall be counted an offender, and shall suffer such punishment as the particular court shall judge meet, according to the nature of his offence. (85.)

1648.—James T—— was warned to this court to answer for his contempt in not appearing the last court; he saith that he acknowledges he was served with a warrant to appear at the last court, but did not, but having a lighter-load of hay to empty, went about that, without asking leave of any magistrate.

Thomas Barnes informed the court that he served a warrant upon James T——, two or three months since, but he could not get him to appear, but hath always shifted him off one way or another, but this he hath to inform the court against him, that he, the said James, stole a scythe which he left in the field, taking it off from the snath and using it as his own, which charge James T—— owneth and acknowledgeth it to be true, and that he had slandered Thomas Barnes by reporting that he did but take his scythe as he, the said Barnes, had taken a grubbing axe of his, when as Thomas Barnes had borrowed the axe of James T—— as he now confesseth. Also Mr. Gibbard, the treasurer, informed the court that James T—— found a dead wolf in the woods, and cut off the head, and brought it to him to be paid for it, saying he had killed it by setting a gun, and got a note of him to receive 15*s* for it, and therein by lying deceived the town, whose order is that those that *kill* wolves, (and not *find* them dead,) should be paid for them; which lying and cheating James T—— could not deny.

The sentence of the court is, that for his contempt of the court in not obeying the warrants served, he pay 40*s* fine to the town; for the scythe that he make double restitution, the scythe being valued at 4*s*; for his lying, cheating and slandering, that he be severely whipped, and that he acknowledge the wrong he hath done to Thomas Barnes in slandering of him, and that he sit in the stocks as long as the weather will permit *with respect of mercy to him*, that all that pass by may see what manner of person he is. (418, 419.)

1649.—The Governor informed the court that he hath heard some complaints about the smallness of bread that is made and sold in the town, and therefore thinks that some course must be taken that it may be sized, that the baker may have a due profit and the buyer not wronged. It was enquired who had any book that might give any light concerning the sizing of bread. Jno. Brockett said he had one, and was desired to carry it to the governor who was desired to prepare this matter against the particular court. (466.)

[Colony Records, vol. ii.]

1653.—The deputies of Stamford acquainted the court that there is in their town some that do work great disturbance, professing they will pay no rates to these common charges, because nothing is done against the Dutch, and some saying they have been in bondage a great while, but now they will have their liberty, and being reproved for the same and told they must be bound over to answer it here, another answered, one and all. Wherefore the court doth advise the deputies to carry it as prudently and peaceably as they can and to gather up these rates due, but if by fair means (for the court is not willing to deal harshly in these times if it may be avoided) it cannot be attained, but some in a stubborn way refuse and grow boisterous in their spirits, working disturbance and giving ill example to others, that then they give notice thereof to the governor or deputy governor, who are ordered by this court to send a warrant from hence to bind such persons over to answer it at the court of magistrates in October next. (24.)

It is ordered that a serious view be made in every plantation in this jurisdiction, to see who have taken the oath of fidelity and who have not, and that all male persons from sixteen years old and upward, which have not already taken it, whether children, servants or sojourners, as well as planters, do take the said oath, and that at the general court in May next, a certificate be brought from each plantation and presented that they have so taken it, or if any refuse, their names are to be returned, but if the authority of the place find any unfitness in any person by their ignorance not understanding the nature of such an ordinance, they may dispense with them a convenient time for the better informing themselves, that the name of God may not be taken in vain. (57.)

1654.—It is ordered that upon the admittance of any man as a planter into any plantation in this jurisdiction, the fundamental laws and orders concerning votes, &c., shall be read to them, and if approved, the oath of fidelity shall be administered to them, the plantation which is to receive them being satisfied in other respects, by a satisfying certificate from sufficent credible persons, of their good behavior and conversation. (98.)

At a court of magistrates, Jan. 26, 1654-5:—Lawrance Corneliusson, a Dutchman, was called before the court and told that he is charged with several great miscarriages, in affronting the authority set up by this jurisdiction at Milford, in a very high degree and contemptuous manner, for when another Dutchman who had been scandalously, and for himself dangerously, drunk, and the complaint of it brought to the magistrate who sent the marshal for him, he, the said Lawrance, answered he should not come then, but when he listed; whereupon the marshal returned, but quickly after the man that was drunk came on shore, and the marshal seized him and was carrying of him before the magistrate, and the said Lawrance followed, crying aloud after the marshal, "Stay, you rogue, stay you rogue," and in the magistrate's house carried it with high contempt before all present, putting his hand to his mouth and pulling it back in a scornful manner, as if he would say, do your worst, I care not for you; and when the man should have answered for himself, he interposed, would not suffer him to speak, but bid the devil take him if he spake a word, and after put him out of the door and bid him begone; and that none might follow him, he shut the door and stood against it, and did utter several oaths with cursing before the magistrate; then the magistrate told him he must now stay and answer, both for the offender whom he had so rescued, and for his own miscarriages; he then went away, and being sent for in, would not come, but said he would be hanged and drawn first, and he would as soon come before the devil as before the magistrate; and the marshal being commanded to fetch him in, and, if he refused, to force him, he refused to submit, and took his knife in his hand and held it up and said, touch him who durst, and offering to take a stick to make resistance, one struck him and broke his head; so they brought him back to the magistrate, who, repeating his miscarriages to him, he told the magistrate he lied, though the marshal then present testified the truth of what the magistrate said to his face; then he demanded to see the law against drunkenness and swearing, which being read, he said, "This is the law of man, but not of God;" and when the magistrate commanded the marshal to take charge of him, he would not submit but said, kill him, hang him, he would not go with him; and when the next day the court at Milford (hearing of these miscarriages), sent for him, he contemptuously refused to come but said, kill him, hang him, draw him with horses, he would not come; wherefore they referred it to the court of magistrates, which thing he also desired; and when he was gone from the magistrate, he asked those that were about him, whether they knew the story of Samson's revenge upon the Philistines how he tied firebrands betwixt the tails of foxes and burnt their corn? and bade them remember it, as if he thought the English were Philistines and he purposed a revenge; and in further discourse, bidding them kill, hang him, &c., he added he would rather be cast into the sea then buried at Milford, his bones should not be in Milford, repeating the story of Joseph, who would have his bones carried out of Egypt, as if Milford were as Egypt to him; and to defend the Dutchman's drunkenness, he professed himself to be a drunkard, and asked the English about him if they were not so, "Have not you, and you, been drunk," adding that *at the Mannadoes* [New York] *they were not punished for drunkenness*, but used after they had been drunk to say, 'God forgive us,' or 'be merciful to us,' *and that was enough;* he asked also what witnesses they had against him, and when he was told they had many, he answered, "Many false witnesses came in against Christ."

His miscarriages being thus charged, he was told he had liberty to answer for himself, and if he objected against the truth of any of the particulars, proof was ready. . . . . . He said he submits to the charge, for he was in such a passion as he remembers not what he did or spake, and is ashamed of it.

The said Lawrance was asked, if he had any occasion given him that might cause him to carry it thus; he said, no, but God left him, and he is ashamed of it.

After which, the court considering how he had contemned and trampled upon authority, disturbed the peace of the jurisdiction (beside his slighting or censuring the English); that upon his earnest suit the magistrates were now called from several plantations at an unusual and inconvenient time to keep this court; that the marshal at Milford hath been put upon much attendance and upon two journeys from Milford hither, with other testimony, because he had here, (beside what passed at Milford,) more than once peremptorily denied some of his charges; and that the marshal at Newhaven, beside other attendance, had been charged with his diet, lodging, &c.; did by way of sentence order, that Lawrance Corneliusson pay as a fine to the jurisdiction, forty pounds, and that he make a due and public acknowledgment of his miscarriages, at Milford where they were committed, owning his sin and shame for it, which if not performed to satisfaction there, he is to be sent back to Newhaven and the court will further consider of it. (124-6.)

[On the petition of the offender, presented Jan. 30th, setting forth his inability to pay the fine, and professing penitence, the court mitigated the penalty to 30 £.]

1655.—It is ordered that no tobacco shall be taken in the streets, yards, or about the houses in any plantation or farm in this jurisdiction, or without doors near or about the town, or in the meeting-house, or body of the train soldiers, or any other place where they may do mischief thereby, under the penalty of six pence a pipe or a time, which is to go to him that informs and prosecutes; which, if refused, is to be recovered by distress; in which case, if there be difference, it may be issued without a court by any magistrate, or where there is no magistrate by any deputy or constable; but if he be a poor servant and hath not to pay, and his master will not pay for him, he shall then be punished by sitting in the stocks one hour. (148.)

1655.—To prevent much inconvenience which may grow by gaming, it is ordered that no person who, either as an innkeeper or seller of strong liquors, wine or beer, entertains strangers or others to lodge, or eat, or drink, shall permit or suffer any to use the game of shuffleboard, or any other gaming,within his house or limits, under the penalty of twenty shillings for time so offending, and whatever person or persons shall so play or game in any such house, or place, or in any other gaming house, where there is common resort to such play or gaming, shall forfeit for every such offence five shillings, and whosoever shall so play or game for money or money-worth, shall further forfeit double the value thereof, one half to the informer, and the rest to the plantation within the limits whereof he so played or gamed. (155-6.)

1656.—It is ordered that whosoever shall put or kindle any fire in woods, grounds, yards, orchards, or other place or places, lying in common or enclosed, so as the same shall burn fences, buildings, or cause any other damage in any season or manner not allowed by authority in that plantation, or on the last day of the week, or on the Lord's day, every such person shall pay all damages and half so much more for a fine to the plantation, and if not able to pay shall be corporally punished as the court shall judge meet.

But if any servant or servants, person or persons in relation, or any other whether male or female, shall wilfully, maliciously or by way of revenge, kindle or put any fire into any corn, hay, straw, hemp, flax, timber, hewed, sawn, or riven, heaps of wood, charcoal, other goods or combustible matter, especially in the night or on the Lord's day, by means whereof any dwelling house, barn, shed, or other buildings, hay, corn, cattle, household goods, or other estate of what kind soever may be endangered, burnt or destroyed, (much more if the life or lives of any person or persons shall be thereby lost or hazarded,) such mischievous person or persons shall be proceeded against, either by the court of magistrates, if the sin be heinous or capital, as a presumptuous or malicious offender or offenders against the fifth, sixth, or eighth commandments, to be punished by death or otherwise severely as the case may require, or by the plantation court, if the miscarriage be of a lower nature, by corporal punishment or paying double or treble damages, but if the damage be great and the offender or offenders not able to make such restitution, he or they shall by sentence or order of the court of magistrates be sold for a servant or servants, either into these English colonies or abroad, that due satisfaction (so far as may be attained) be made, as the court considering the offence with all the aggravating circumstances shall judge meet.* (175, 176.)

1657.—A complaint was brought from Stamford of the excessive price of shoes and boots there, and some instances were given, as six shillings for a pair of shoes of the tens, and thirty shillings for a pair of boots, as good as which may be bought here for twenty shillings, which the court thought was great oppression, and that some course should be taken about it; and therefore did now order, that those shoemakers be informed that if betwixt this and the

*This is the law which Peters caricatures, by: "Whosoever sets a fire in the woods, and it burns a house, shall suffer death." Compare the law concerning "Fire," in the code of 1655, (before, p. 222.)

court of magistrates in October next they do not give satisfaction for what they have done amiss the time past, and reform for time to come, that then they attend the said court, and come prepared to answer their miscarriages herein, and that those offended or wronged in the town, &c., come prepared to charge and prove. (215.)

It is ordered that no Quaker, Ranter, or other heretic of that nature, be suffered to come into, nor abide in this jurisdiction, and if any such rise up among ourselves that they be speedily suppressed and secured, for the better prevention of such dangerous errors. (217.)

It was propounded that the court would think of some way to further the setting up of schools, for the education of youth in each plantation, for though some do take care that way, yet some others neglect it, which the court took into consideration, and seeing that Newhaven hath provided that a schoolmaster be maintained at the town's charge, and Milford hath made provision in a comfortable way, they desire the other towns would follow their example, and therefore did now order, that in every plantation where a school is not already set up and maintained, forthwith endeavors shall be used that a schoolmaster be procured that may attend that work, and what salary shall be allowed unto such schoolmaster for his pains, one third part shall be paid by the town in general as other rates, the good education of children being of public concernment, and the other two thirds by them who have the benefit thereof, by the teaching of their children. (219, 220.)

Court of Magistrates, June, 1657.—William Meaker entered an action of defamation against

Thomas Mullenner, and declared that several pigs of Thomas Mullenner died, it seems in a strange way, and he thought them bewitched, and said if any more died he would use some means to make discovery, and he did cut off the tail and ears of one and threw into the fire; his maid said he knew who he meant, goodman Meaker; he said he had heard something of him.

George Smith informed that himself is wrapt up in the same case, and desires it may be considered, and that he hath also charged him with milking of the herd's cows, which is a great wrong to him.

Thomas Mullenner said he knew not of any pig's tail or ear burnt, yet said it was a means used in England by some honest people to find out witches, but if it was naught he desired to see it; wherein he seems to grant the thing he denied; and Mrs. Mullenner did own that it may be the tail or ear might be burned, but Robert Deny and Stephen Peirson, servants to Thomas Mullenner, both affimed, that after some of the pigs had died in this strange manner, their master said that he feared they were bewitched, and if it went on he would try what he could do to find it out, and when there was but one left, and that sick, he brought the pig to the fire and cut off the ear and tail and threw it into the fire, and after put the pig upon the fire till it was dead, and after he fell into discourse of this again, and said that he feared some of his neighbors are not very good, and the maid said, she knew who he meant, goodman Meaker; he said that he had heard something of him, and because he charged him with breaking open his fence, therefore he hath done this to his pigs.

Mrs. Mullenner said she heard her husband say so much as shows that he thought the pigs were bewitched, but she heard him not charge William Meaker nor any other man with it, and Thomas Mullener owned that it was so in his thoughts, and that he said if he lived among neighbors, or near neighbors, he should think they were bewitched.

* * * * * * *

Many other debates passed, but in the issue what had passed at Newhaven court before, about unrighteousness in marking and working other men's cattle, &c., were read, and upon a due consideration of all together, this court declared, that they agree with what Newhaven court then concluded, and therefore that he put in security for his good behavior for the future in these and the like cases, or remove himself to some other place. The taking of which security is referred to Newhaven court the third day of the next week, and also the issuing this matter betwixt William Meaker, George Smith, and him. They professed now, it is not his estate they seek, but a reformation and the clearing of their names, in which they have been much wronged by him.* (224-26.)

Oct. 1657.—William East was told there is a sad fame spread abroad of his excessive drinking and drunkenness, so that people as they go in the street do say, that Sergeant East was drunk yesterday before ten o'clock, and now he is drunk again to day already. He said he dares not say he is clear, but is sorry he hath given cause for such reports. He was told he hath now a black eye, and whether it came not by

*It is noticeable, that this action was brought, not for *witchcraft*, but for *defamation*. Conjuration by pigs' tails would have been accounted in England at this period "a most hideous witchery," and the delinquent would doubtless have fared harder than Thomas Mullenner did in New Haven; nor would Meaker, the suspected wizard, have escaped so easily.

some such course he best knows; of which he said nothing to clear himself, yet said he had some distemper which fell into his eye. Some of Milford being present, as Richard Baldwin, William Fowler and Steven Freman, were called to speak what they know or have heard in the case; but first Mr. Fenn, the magistrate, said that he thinks he hath been twice dealt with at Milford for drunkenness. (227.)

General Court, May, 1660.—The court being deeply sensible of the small progress or proficiency in learning that hath yet been accomplished, in the way of more particular town schools, of later years in this colony, and of the great difficulty and charge to make pay &c., for the maintaining children at the schools or college in the bay, and that notwithstanding what this court did order last year or formerly, nothing hath yet been done to attain the ends desired, upon which considerations and other like, this court for further encouragement of this work doth now order, that over and above the £40 per annum, granted the last year for the end then declared, that £100 stock shall be duly paid in from the jurisdiction treasury, according to the manner and times agreed and expressed in the court records, giving and granting that special respect to our brethren at Newhaven, to be first in imbracing or refusing the court's encouragement or provision for a school, whether to be settled at Newhaven town or not; but if they shall refuse, Milford is to have the next choice, then Guilford, and so in order every other town on the main within the jurisdiction have their liberty to accept or refuse the court's tender, yet it is most desired of all that Newhaven would accept the business, as being a place most probable to advantage the well carrying on of the school, for the ends sought after and endeavored after thereby; but the college (after spoken of) is affixed to Newhaven (if the Lord shall succeed that undertaking). It is further agreed that all and every plantation who have any mind to accept the propositions about the school, shall prepare and send in their answer unto the committee chosen (of all the magistrates and settled elders of this jurisdiction, to order, regulate and dispose, all matters concerning the school, as the providing instruments and well carrying on of the business, from time to time as they shall judge best,) before the 24th of June instant, that so if any plantation do accept, the committee may put forth their endeavors to settle the business; but if all refuse, then it must be suspended until another meeting of this General Court.

And for further encouragement of learning, and the good of posterity in that way, Mr. John Davenport, pastor of the church of Christ at Newhaven, presented a writing, (as before appears,) whereby and wherewith he delivered up all his power and interest, as a trustee by Mr. Hopkins, for recovering and bestowing of all that legacy given by him, for the end of furtherance to the settlement of a COLLEGE AT NEWHAVEN; he also propounded therewith, what he apprehends hath been granted and set apart by the town of Newhaven for the same end, with a request that matters thereabout might be ordered and carried on according to such propositions as are therein set down. All which the general court took thankfully, both from the donors and Mr. Davenport, and accepted the trust and shall endeavor by God's help to get in the said estate and improve it to the end it was given for.

By way of further answer to what was propounded

by Mr. Davenport in his writing presented, the court declared that it was their desire that the colony school may begin at the time propounded, and to that end desire that endeavors may be put forth by the committee of magistrates and settled elders formerly appointed for the providing a schoolmaster, &c., to whom also they leave it to appoint a steward or receiver, which steward or receiver they empower as is propounded, and to settle a committee from among themselves to issue emergent cases, and to take order that a chest be provided wherein the writings may be laid up that concern this business. The court further declared that they do invest Mr. Davenport with the power of a negative vote, for the reason and in the cases according to the terms in his writing specified, and that they shall be ready to confirm such orders as shall be presented which in the judgment of the court shall be conducible to the main end intended.

It is ordered for encouragement of such as shall diligently and constantly (to the satisfaction of the civil authority in each plantation) apply themselves to due use of means for the attainment of learning, which may fit them for public service, that they shall be freed from payment of rates with respect to their persons; provided, that if any such shall leave off or not constantly attend those studies, they shall then be liable to pay rates in all respects as other men are.

It is ordered that if the colony school shall begin any time within the first half year from this court of election, that £40 shall be paid by the treasurer for this year, and if it shall begin at any time before the election next, that £20 shall be paid by the treasurer upon that account. (374-76.)

VIII.

THE "BLUE LAW" FORGERIES OF PETERS.

Of the Rev. Sam. Peters and his veracious " General History of Connecticut," enough has been said in the Introduction to this volume (pages 41-46). After giving some account of the "Dominion of Hartford"—where the Rev. Thomas Hooker and his associates, by infecting bibles, had, "to the eternal infamy of the Christian policy," contrived to spread the small-pox among the Indians, and so "swept away the great Sachem *Connecticote* [an imaginary personage] and laid waste his ancient kingdom,"—Peters proceeds to sketch the history of the " Dominion of New Haven." "This Dominion, this tyrant of tyrants, adopted the Bible for its code of civil laws, till others should be made more suitable to its circumstances :" but afterwards, "they gave themselves up to *their own inventions* in making others, wherein, in some instances, they betrayed such an extreme degree of wanton cruelty and oppression, that even the rigid fanatics of Boston, and the mad zealots of Hartford, put to the blush, christened them the *Blue Laws*," etc. (p. 43). On page 63, he introduces his "sketch" of this code, as follows :—

"The laws made by this independent Dominion, and denominated *Blue-Laws* by the neighbouring Colonies, were never suffered to be printed ; but the following sketch of some of them will give a tolerable idea of the spirit which pervades the whole.

1. The Governor and Magistrates, convened in general Assembly, are the supreme power under God of this independent Dominion.*

* The General Court (which in New Haven Colony was never

2. From the determination of the Assembly no appeal shall be made.

3. The Governor is amenable to the voice of the people.

4. The Governor shall have only a single vote in determining any question; except a casting vote, when the Assembly may be equally divided.

5. The Assembly of the People shall not be dismissed by the Governor, but shall dismiss itself.

6. Conspiracy against this Dominion shall be punished with death.

7. Whoever says there is a power and jurisdiction above and over this Dominion, shall suffer death and loss of property.

8. Whoever attempts to change or overturn this Dominion shall suffer Death.

9. The judges shall determine controversies without a jury.

10. No one shall be a freeman, or give a vote, unless he be converted, and a member in full communion of one of the Churches allowed in this Dominion.*

11. No man shall hold any office, who is not sound

---

denominated the "General Assembly") consisted of the Governor, Deputy Governor, and Magistrates, "and two deputies for each plantation," chosen by the freemen: "and nothing shall be concluded, and pass as an act of the General Court (unless in cases expressly excepted,) but by the consent and vote of the major part of the magistrates, *together with the consent and vote of the greater part of the Deputies.*"—Fundamental Agreement; see, before, pages183, 186.

* The law only required membership "of some one or other of the approved churches of New England." See, before, page 180.

in the faith, and faithful to this Dominion; and whoever gives a vote to such a person, shall pay a fine of £1; for a second offence, he shall be disfranchised.

12. Each freeman shall swear by the blesssed God to bear true allegiance to this Dominion, and that Jesus is the only King.

13. No Quaker or Dissenter from the established worship of this Dominion shall be allowed to give a vote for the election of Magistrates, or any officer.

14. No food or lodging shall be afforded to a Quaker, Adamite, or other Heretic.*

15. If any person turns Quaker, he shall be banished, and not suffered to return but upon pain of death.

16. No Priest shall abide in the Dominion; he shall be banished, and suffer death on his return.† Priests may be seized by any one without a warrant.

17. No one to cross a river, but with an authorized ferryman.

18. No one shall run on the Sabbath-day, or walk in the garden or elsewhere, except reverently to and from meeting. ‡

---

* In another place (p. 198), Peters says that entertainment of Quakers, Anabaptists, or Adamites, was "punished for the first and second offence with fines, and *with death* for the third." He makes this statement in connection with what is perhaps the most atrocious lie in his whole book—which he professes to tell for the purpose of "shewing the danger of admitting a wife to give evidence against her husband, according to the Blue Laws."

† No Priest, &c. There was nothing like this in the code, but *New York* had such a law, and *Virginia* forbade any popish priest to remain in the province more than five days after notice, and subjected every popish "recusant" to a heavy fine, on conviction.

‡ "In 1750, an episcopal clergyman, born and educated in England, who had been in holy orders above twenty years, once broke

19. No one shall travel, cook victuals, make beds, sweep house, cut hair, or shave, on the Sabbath-day.

20. No woman shall kiss her child on the Sabbath or fasting-day.*

21. The Sabbath shall begin at sunset on Saturday.

22. To pick an ear of corn growing in a neighbour's garden, shall be deemed theft. †

---

their sabbatical law, by combing a discomposed lock of hair on the top of his wig; at another time, by making a humming noise, which they called a whistling; at a third time, by walking too fast from church; at a fourth by running into church when it rained; at a fifth by walking in his garden, and picking a bunch of grapes: for which several crimes he was complained of by the grand jury, had warrants against him, was seized, brought to trial, and paid a considerable sum of money."—Peters, p. 305. It is needless to add, that the "episcopal clergyman" and his trial, are as apocryphal as the "blue law" which he violated.

* No Woman shall kiss, etc. This reminds one of Josselyn's abstract of an (imaginary) law of Massachusetts, about 1673: "For kissing a woman in the street, though in way of civil salute,—whipping, or a fine."—*Two Voyages to N. England*, p. 179.

John Taylor ("the Water Poet") in his "Character of A Separatist," mentions one precaution for the strict observance of the Sabbath, which Peters forgot to add to his New Haven code:—

"Upon the Sabbath, they'l no Physick take,
Lest it should *worke*, and so the Sabbath breake."

† The penalty for robbing a garden or orchard, or stealing fruit, &c. was payment of double damages, and "such further fine and punishment as the Court shall judge meet." See the code of 1655, (before, p. 197,) title "Burglary, and Theft." With this compare the law of *Virginia*, 1610 - 12:—

"What man or woman soever shall rob any garden, public or private, being set to weed the same, or wilfully pluck up therein any root, herb, or *flower*, to spoil and waste or steal the same, or rob any vineyard, or gather up the grapes, or *steal any ears of the corn* growing, whether in the ground belonging to the same

23. A person accused of trespass in the night shall be judged guilty, unless he clear himself by his oath.

24. When it appears that an accused has confederates, and he refuses to discover them, he may be racked.*

25. No one shall buy or sell lands without permission of the selectmen.

26. A drunkard shall have a master appointed by the selectmen, who are to debar him from the liberty of buying and selling.

27. Whoever publishes a lye to the prejudice of his neighbour, shall sit in the stocks, or be whipped fifteen stripes.†

28. No Minister shall keep a school.

29. Every rateable person who refuses to pay his proportion to the support of the minister of the town or parish, shall be fined by the Court £2, and £4 every quarter, until he or she pay the rate to the Minister.

30. Men-stealers shall suffer death.

---

fort or town where he dwelleth, or in any other, *shall be punished with death.*"—Laws for the Colony of Virginea, (London, 1612,) reprinted in Force's Tracts (vol. iii.), p. 17.

* Torture was much employed by the Dutch at New Amsterdam, to extort confessions of crime and the betrayal of confederates; but it was never resorted to in New Haven or Connecticut.

†"The New Haven code [see, before, p. 239,] contained a law against lying; but it is not here correctly represented; though it is a little remarkable, that the author in this instance swerves less from the fact than perhaps in the case of any other law in his whole list. *He must have felt a peculiar horror of that ordinance;* which circumstance probably fixed the terms of it more exactly in his mind." Prof. Kingsley, *Hist. Discourse*, 107.

31. Whoever wears cloaths trimmed with gold, silver, or bone lace, above two shillings by the yard, shall be presented by the grand jurors, and the selectmen shall tax the offender at £300 estate.

32. A debtor in prison, swearing he has no estate, shall be let out, and sold, to make satisfaction.

33. Whoever sets a fire in the woods, and it burns a house, shall suffer death; and persons suspected of this crime shall be imprisoned, without benefit of bail.*

34. Whoever brings cards or dice into this Dominion shall pay a fine of £5.

35. No one shall read Common-Prayer, keep Christmas or Saints'-days, make minced pies, dance, play cards, or play on any instrument of music, except the drum, trumpet, and jews'-harp.

36. No Gospel Minister shall join people in marriage. The Magistrates only shall join in marrriage, as they may do it with less scandal to Christ's Church.

37. When parents refuse their children convenient marriages, the Magistrates shall determine the point.

38. The selectmen, on finding children ignorant, may take them away from their parents, and put them into better hands, at the expense of their parents.

39. Fornication shall be punished by compelling marriage, or as the Court may think proper.

40. Adultery shall be punished with death.

41. A man that strikes his wife shall pay a fine of

* "Whoever sets a fire," etc. See the law on this subject, in the code of 1655,—on page 222. The penalty was the payment of one and a half the damage, or in default of payment, corporal punishment at the discretion of the court.

£10; a woman that strikes her husband shall be punished as the Court directs.

42. A wife shall be deemed good evidence against her husband.

43. No man shall court a maid in person, or by letter, without first obtaining consent of her parents: £5 penalty for the first offence, £10 for the second; and for the third, imprisonment during the pleasure of the Court.

44. Married persons must live together, or be imprisoned.

45. Every male shall have his hair cut round, according to a cap."*

"Of such sort," remarks Peters, "were the laws made by the people of New Haven, previous to their incorporation with Saybrook and Hertford colonies by the charter. They consist of a vast multitude, and were very properly termed *Blue Laws*, i. e. *bloody Laws*; for they were all sanctified with excommunication, confiscation, fines, banishment, whippings, cutting off the ears, burning the tongue, and death."
(pp. 69, 70.)

In another place (pp. 40-42,) he gives "a specimen of the tenets established by Davenport" in the New Haven church:—

"That all other Kings, besides Christ and his elected People, are pestilent usurpers and enemies to God and man: that all Vicars, Rectors, Deans, Priests, and

---

*Every male, etc. "When caps were not to be found, they substituted the hard shell of a pumkin, which being put on the head every Saturday, the hair is cut, by the shell, all round the head." (Peters, p. 196.) "The pumpkin or pompion, is one of the greatest blessings, and held very sacred, in New England. . . . Its skin, or shell, serves for caps to cut the hair (as already mentioned), and for very useful lanthorns." Ibid, 246.

Bishops, are of the Devil; are Wolves, petty Popes, and antichristian Tyrants: . . . . that all things of human invention in the worship of God, such as are in the Mass-book and Common-Prayer, are unsavory in the sight of God: . . . . that all good people ought to pray always that God would raze the old Papal foundation of episcopal government, together with the filthy ceremonies of that anti-christian Church: that every particular who neglects this duty, may justly fear that curse pronounced against Meroz,—Judg. v. 23: . . . . that it is an heinous sin to be present when prayers are read out of a book by a Vicar or Bishop:" &c.

IX.

EARLY LAWS AND JUDGMENTS IN OTHER AMERICAN COLONIES.

NEW YORK.

(*UNDER THE DUTCH.*)

CRIMES AND PUNISHMENTS.

"Judge Daly, in his valuable and interesting paper on the Judicial organization of the State, says: 'Upon perusing the records of New Amsterdam tribunals it is impossible not to be struck with the comprehensive knowledge they display of the principles of jurisprudence, and with the directness and simplicity with which legal investigations were conducted. In fact, as a means of ascertaining truth and doing substantial justice, *their mode of proceeding was infinitely more effective than the technical and artificial system introduced by their English successors.*' The Dutch here were a humane as well as a just people."—*The Old Stadt Huys of New Amsterdam;* a paper read before the New York Historical Society, June 15th, 1875, by James W. Gerard; pp. 50, 51.

Most of the specimens here presented are taken from Dr. E. B. O'Callaghan's "Calendar of Dutch Manuscripts" in the Secretary's Office at Albany. To present these in their fairest possible light, they are unaccompanied by any comments, except such as are supplied by extracts from Mr. Gerard's historical monograph on "The Old Stadt Huys of New Amsterdam," and by Judge Daly's remarks on the *directness* and *simplicity* of Dutch legal proceedings. A note or two from Mr. Brodhead's History of New York, contrasting the Dutch with their bigoted neighbors of New England, will be introduced further on.

Torture, in Criminal Prosecutions.

Oct. 5, 1639: Hendrick Jansen, gunner's mate of

the ship Herring, from Bremen, charged with an assault on the deputy fiscal, was subjected to torture, "but he persisted in the lie."—*Calendar of Dutch Mss.*, p. 69.

Nov. 22, 1641: Jan Hobbesen, charged with theft (stealing a *sheet* from a tavern) "persisting in denying the charge, is *put to the torture*, after which he confessed his guilt;" is sentenced "to be whipped with rods," and banished. *Ibid.*, 77, 78.

May 31, 1646: Hans Tymonsen, a ship's gunner, "is asked to whom he sold the Company's powder, and remaining obstinate, is ordered to be imprisoned, and then *subjected to torture* if he do not confess." *Ibid.*, 101.

Sept. 30, 1647: Michel Picquet, a Frenchman, charged with slandering and threatening ex-director Kieft and director Stuyvesant. The opinion of Stuyvesant was, "that there being four witnesses in support of the above charge, it is *unnecessary to subject him to torture.*". *Ibid.*, 109, 113. [Picquet was sentenced to 18 years imprisonment at hard labor, and perpetual banishment.]

Aug. 24, 1654: A prisoner charged with burglary, subjected to torture, by order of the Council, "in order that he may discover his accomplices." *Ibid.*, 140.

Dec. 6, 1663: Frans Jansen, charged with theft: a motion that he be subjected to torture, to compel him to answer certain interrogatories, was denied by the council, because he "had already been *once tortured*, and *twice whipped*, without eliciting any additional information from him."—*Ibid.*, 256, 257. [He was sentenced "to be severely flogged in public, and then banished."]

Capital Offences.

1641. Jan, 17. Eight negroes who were accused of the murder of another negro, pleaded guilty. The Council sentenced the prisoners *to draw lots*, to determine who shall suffer death; whereupon, the lot "by God's providence" fell on Manuel Gerrit, "the giant" who was sentenced to be hanged. *Ibid.*, 74.

1644, July 7. Three soldiers tried by court martial, for having (accidentally) killed a man, by the discharge of a gun; sentenced to *be shot*,—but *pardoned*, "such sentence having been pronounced *only to make an impression* on them and others." *Ibid.*, 89.

1646, June 25. Jan Creoli, a negro, convicted of sodomy, the second offence; sentenced "to be conveyed to the place of public execution, and there choked to death and then burnt to ashes." The Court base their judgment on the ground that this crime is "condemned of God, Genesis, ch. 19; Levit., ch. 18, vv. 22, 29, as an abomination." *Ibid.*, 103.

1660, June 17. A soldier, found guilty of the same offence, sentenced to be stripped of his arms, his sword broken at his feet, and then "to be *tied in a sack and cast into the river* and drowned until dead." *Ibid.*, 213.

Peculiar Penalties.

1646.—A ship's chief-mate, for smuggling and theft, and for an assault on the commissary, sentenced by the Council, "*to jump three times from the yard-arm*, to be whipped by all the crew, and immediately afterwards turned out of the ship, with loss of three month's wages." *Ibid.*, 102.

1647, Nov. 15.—Jonas Jonassen, a soldier, for robbing hen-roosts and killing a pig, sentenced "to ride the wooden horse three days, from 2 P. M. till the conclusion of the parade, *with a fifty pound weight tied to each foot.*" *Ibid.*, 114.

1648, March 3. An Englishman, guilty of fornication, *pardoned* "on condition that he *saw firewood* one year for the West India Company." *Ibid.*, 115.

1642, Aug. 14. The defendant in an action for slander, is sentenced "*to throw something in the box for the poor.*" *Ibid.*, 81.

1644, Nov. 25. Thomas Cornel, an Englishman, in the service of the W. I. Company, tried for desertion, and pleading guilty, was sentenced by the Council, "to be conveyed to the place of execution, and there fastened to a stake, and a ball fired *over his head*, as an *example to other evil doers.*" *Ibid.*, 92.

1658, April 15. Nicholas Albertsen, for deserting his ship, and his betrothed, after publication of the banns, sentenced "to have his *head shaved*, then to be *flogged* and have his *ears bored*, and to work two years with the Company's negroes." *Ibid.*, 194, 195.

1664, May 12. Jan Willemsen van Iselstein, for abusive language and an insolent letter to the magistrates of Bushwyck, sentenced "to be fastened to a stake at the place of public execution, with a bridle in his mouth, rods under his arm, and a paper on his breast with an inscription, '*Lampoon Writer, False Accuser, and Defamer of Magistrates,*'—and afterwards banished, with costs." *Ibid.*, 265. [The bearer of the "insolent letter," for that offence and "for using very indecent language" received a like sentence.]

1664, July 29. Edward Wells, found guilty of having "asserted that Long Island was the King's territory, and that New Amsterdam would soon become so," was sentenced to be tied to a stake, at the place of execution," and a bridle put in his mouth, and to have a paper fastened to his breast, inscribed with the words '*Disturber of the Public Peace*,' and to pay costs." The sentence was afterwards commuted to a fine of 100 guilders. *Ibid.*, 268.

Treatment of Slaves.

"Although slaves were held in New Amsterdam, they were treated with great kindness, and allowed unusual license, and could not be beaten, *ad libitum*, by their owners."—Mr. J. W. Gerard's paper on the *The Old Stadt Huys*, (read before the N. Y. Hist. Society,) p. 51.

Nov. 17, 1639 :—"At the requisition of the Attorney General, it was declared by Gysbert Opdyck, Commissary in Fort Hope, that he gave his black boy, named Louis Barbese [Berbice ?] the pan to fry cakes, and whereas the fire was too hot for the boy, so Opdyck took the pan in his own hand, and placed his knife in the hands of the black, then he commanded the boy to fetch a dish, who brought one very unclean, on which Opdyck struck the black, who, to evade it, tried to take hold of Opdyck, who thrusted him away, so that the boy fell down on his left side, when he kicked him with his feet. The boy then went out of the door and fell down; when Opdyck discovered the knife, crooked as a hoop, and went to look at the boy, who was wounded in his body under the left arm, *and died very suddenly*."—Dutch Records (Translated), vol. ii. p. 72.

DEALINGS WITH DISSENTERS.

"When under the *insania* of religious sectarianism, the arm of the civil government in New England, as has been remarked by

Judge Story, 'was employed in support of the denunciations of the Church,' the Island of Manhattan was a refuge for the oppressed."—Gerard's *The Old Stadt Huys*, pp. 46-7.

"There were doubtless some who emigrated merely to enlarge their estates. But there were many others, whose only motive for the change was the religious intolerance of their own countrymen. They left New England to seek, in New Netherland, 'freedom to worship God.'—Brodhead's *History of New York*, i. 334.

"If the Fatherland gave an asylum to self-exiled Puritans of England, New Netherland as liberally sheltered refugees from the intolerant governments on her eastern frontier."—*Ibid.*, 749.

1654.—The *Lutherans* petitioned for permission to worship in a church of their own, and to call a clergyman. Director Stuyvesant refused, for the reason that he was bound by his oath to tolerate openly no other religion than the Reformed (Brodhead's Hist. of N. Y., i. 581). The Lutherans were "not allowed to call a minister, or to enjoy freedom of worship." (Calendar of Dutch Mss., p. 279.)

1656.—Proclamation against unauthorized Conventicles: "To promote the glory of God, the increase of the [Dutch] Reformed religion, and the peace and harmony of the country," all preachers not having been called thereto by lawful authority, are forbidden to hold conventicles not in harmony with the established religion as set forth by the Synod of Dort, "and here in this land and in the Fatherland, and in other Reformed churches observed and followed." Every unlicensed preacher who violated this ordinance, incurred a fine of 100 pounds Flemish, and every person who should *attend* such a prohibited meeting, became liable to a penalty of 25 pounds. Brodhead's *History*, i. 617.

1658, April 16.—The Rev. Johannes Ernestus

Gutwater, a Lutheran minister, was ordered by the council "to quit the province and return to Holland." —*Calendar of Dutch Mss.*, 195.

1659, Feb. 13.—The Directors order that Lutherans shall not be allowed the public exercise of their religion. *Ibid.*, 287.

Baptists.

1656, Nov. 8.—The sheriff of Flushing, Wm. Hallet, removed from office, fined 50*l.* Flemish, and *banished*, and to remain in prison till his fine and costs are paid,—for allowing Baptist conventicles in his house. *Ibid.*, 177.

William Wickendam, for officiating as a gospel minister, at Flushing, without authority, fined 100*l.* Flemish, and banished, and imprisoned until his fine and costs are paid.* *Ibid.*, 177.

Quakers.

1657, August.—Two English Quakers arrested and imprisoned at New Amsterdam, for public preaching. When discharged, they with other Quakers who had come in the same ship, left for Rhode Island, where (wrote Dominie Megapolensis) "all kinds of scum dwell, for it is nothing else than a sink for New England." Brodhead, i. 636.

1657.—Robert Hodgson, a Quaker, arrested at

*"Last year a fomenter of error came there. He was a cobbler from Rhode Island, in New England, and stated that he was commissioned by Christ. He began to preach at Flushing, and then went with the people into the river and dipped them. This becoming known here [at New Amsterdam], the Fiscal proceeded thither and brought him along." Letter of Aug. 5, 1657, from the Rev. Messrs. Megapolensis and Drisius to the classis of Amsterdam; in O'Callaghan's Doc. Hist. of New York, iii. 71.

Heemstede (L. I.) and committed to the dungeon of Fort Amsterdam. Sentenced by the Council to pay a fine of 600 guilders, or to labor two years at a wheelbarrow, in company with a negro. On his refusal to work, when chained to the barrow, he was beaten by a negro with a tarred rope, till he fell down. Finally, after frequent whippings, he was banished from the province. *Ibid.*, 636.

1657.—Proclamation against Quakers. Vessels bringing any Quaker into the province, were to be confiscated, and every person who should entertain a Quaker for a single night was to be fined 50 pounds. *Ibid.*, 637.

1658.—John Tilton, town clerk of Gravesend (L. I.), fined 12 pounds Flemish, for giving a lodging to a woman of "the abominable sect called Quakers." *Ibid.*, 188.

1658, Jan. 1.—The (English) magistrates and inhabitants of Flushing, L. I., arrested and tried, for having presented to the Council a remonstrance against the proclamation against Quakers. *Calendar of Dutch Mss.*, 187.

1661.—Henry Townsend, of Jamaica, fined 25 pounds for attending Quaker meetings. Samuel Spicer, a Quaker, fined 12*l.* John Tilton and John Townsend, Quakers, banished the province. *Ibid.*, 220, 224.

1662.—Another proclamation against the public exercise of any religion but the Dutch Reformed, "in houses, barns, ships, woods, or fields," under penalty of 50 guilders; double for the second offence; quadruple for the third, with other correction at the discretion of the court. *Brodhead*, i. 706.

1662, Sept.—John Browne, of Flushing, a Quaker, fined 25*l.* for lodging Quakers, and holding meetings of "that abominable sect." (Oct.) John and Mary Tilton for frequenting conventicles, and Michal Spicer and her son Samuel, for harboring Quakers and distributing Quaker pamphlets, were ordered to leave the province before Nov. 20th. *Calendar*, p. 240.

1663. Jan. 9th, John Bowne, refusing to pay his fine, after three months' imprisonment, was sentenced to be transported from the province, "in the first ship ready to sail." [Like Roger Williams, he was cast out "in the dead of winter."]—*Brodhead*, i. 706.

Support of the Ministry.

1662, May 25. Levy of execution granted against the inhabitants of Heemstede, L. I., who had refused to pay their tax for support of a minister.—*Calendar*, 237.

(*NEW YORK UNDER THE ENGLISH.*)

"The spirit of peace and good will that reigned in New Amsterdam still breathed benignly over the city changed in name, and stamped it then, as now, *imperial*, not only in commerce, but in humanity."—*The Old Stadt Huys*, p. 44.

Proclamation against Presbyterian Preachers.

1707. "Whereas I am informed that one Mackennan [Rev. Francis Makemie] and one Hampton [Rev. John Hampton], *two Presbyterian Preachers* who lately came to this City, have taken upon them to preach in a private house, without having obtained any license for so doing, which is directly contrary to the known laws of England; and being likewise informed, that they are gone into Long Island, with intent there to spread their *Pernicious Doctrine* and

Principles, to the great disturbance of the Church by law Established, and of the Government of this Province: You are therefore hereby required and commanded to take into your custody the bodies of the said Mackennan and Hampton, and them to bring with all convenient speed before me, at Fort Anne in New York. And for so doing, this shall be your sufficient Warrant. Given under my hand, at Fort Anne, this 21st day of January, 1706–07.

CORNBURY.

To Thomas Cardale Esqr. High Sheriff
of Queen's County," etc.

[The Rev. Messrs. Makemie and Hampton, who stopped a few days in New York, on their way to New England, had preached, the one in a private house in the city, the other at Newtown, L. I. Under the foregoing warrant from the Governor, both were arrested, and imprisoned nearly two months, before being admitted to bail. Mr. Makemie was tried, in June, 1707, and acquitted by the jury, but the Court compelled him to pay for the costs of prosecution and expenses, about 300 dollars. See "A Narrative *etc.*, of the Prosecution of Mr. Francis Makemie, for Preaching one Sermon at the City of New York," reprinted in Force's Tracts, vol. 4.]

Ministers paid and Churches built by Taxation.

1693.—Whereas Prophaneness and Licentiousness hath of late overspread this Province, for want of a settled ministry, whereby the Ordinances of God may be duly administered, *etc.*, Enacted, That in each of the cities and counties hereafter named, there be called, induced, and established one good and sufficient Protestant Minister, within one year after the date of this act.

And for the encouragement of the Ministers, there shall be paid to them, respectively, as follows: for the city and county of New York, 100 pounds per annum; for the two precincts of Westchester, 100 pounds; for the county of Richmond, 40 pounds, in country produce at money price; for the two precincts of Queen's county, 120 pounds to each, etc.

The Justices, Vestrymen, and Churchwardens, or a majority of them, shall lay a reasonable tax on the respective cities, counties, parishes, or precincts, for the maintenance of the Minister and Poor of their respective places.

A roll of the tax so made shall be delivered to the respective constables, with a warrant signed by any two Justices of the Peace, empowering them to levy the same, and on default of payment to distrain and sell by out-cry, and pay the same into the hands of the Churchwardens, *etc.*

1699. Enacted, that the Trustees of any Town, or any Persons chosen by a majority of the freeholders, shall have power once a year to make a yearly rate for the erecting a public edifice, or church for the worship of God, or for a town-house, or gaol, for the use of the respective town or place where the same is wanting.

The tax and rate to be laid and levied in the same manner as other public taxes are laid.

On the refusing or neglect of payment, the money to be levied by distress, by warrant from a Justice of the Peace.

Against Jesuits and Romish Priests.

1699. All Jesuits, Seminary Priests, Missionaries,

or ecclesiastical persons, made or ordained by any power or jurisdiction derived or pretended from the Pope, or See of Rome, now residing or being within this Province, must depart therefrom on or before the first day of November, 1700. If any such continue, remain, or come into the Province after the said first of November, he shall be deemed an incendiary, a disturber of the public peace, an enemy of the true Christian Religion, and *shall suffer perpetual imprisonment.*

If any such person being actually committed, shall break prison and escape, he shall be guilty of felony, and, if retaken, shall *die as a felon.*

Persons receiving, harbouring, succouring, or concealing any such person, and knowing him to be such, shall forfeit the sum of 200 pounds, half to the King and the other half to the prosecutor, shall be set in the Pillory three days, and find sureties for their good behavior, at the discretion of the Court.

Any Justice of the Peace may cause any person suspected to be of the Romish clergy, to be apprehended, and if he find cause may commit him or them, in order to a trial.

Any person without warrant may seize, apprehend, and bring before a magistrate any person suspected of the crimes above named, and the Governor with the Council may suitably reward such person as they shall think fit.

VIRGINIA.

The following are from the "Articles, Laws, and Orders, Divine, Politique, and Martial, for the Colony in Virginia: first established by Sir Thomas Gates, Knight, Lieutenant-General, the 24th of May, 1610. Again exemplified and enlarged by Sir Thomas Dale, Knight, Marshall, and Deputie Governour, the 22d of June, 1611."

3. That no man blaspheme God's holy name, upon pain of death; or use unlawfull oaths, taking the name of God in vain, curse, or ban, upon pain of severe punishment for the first offence so committed, and for the second, *to have a bodkin thrust through his tongue*; and if he continue the blaspheming of God's holy name, for the third time so offending he shall be brought to a martial court, and there receive censure of death for his offence.

6. Every man and woman duly twice a day, upon the first tolling of the bell, shall, upon the working days, repair unto the church, to hear divine service, upon pain of losing his or her day's allowance, for the first omission; for the second, to be whipt, and for the third, to be condemned to the galleys for six months. . . . . Every man and woman shall repair in the morning to the divine service and sermons preached, upon the Sabbath day, and in the afternoon to divine service, and Catechising, upon pain for the first fault to lose their provision and the allowance for the whole week following; for the second, to lose the said allowance and also to be whipt; and for the third *to suffer death.*

12. No manner of person whatsoever shall dare to detract, slander, calumniate, or utter unseemly and unfitting speeches against his Majesty's Honourable Council for this Colony, . . . or against the zealous

14*

endeavors and intentions of the whole body of Adventurers for this pious and Christian Plantation, ... upon pain, for the first time so offending, to be whipt three several times, and upon his knees to acknowledge his offence and to ask forgiveness upon the Sabbath day in the assembly of the congregation; [for the second offence, to be condemned to the galleys for three years, and for the third, to suffer death.]

22. There shall no man or woman, launderer, or launderess, dare to wash any unclean linen, drive bucks, or throw out the water or suds of foul clothes, in the open street, within the palisadoes, or within forty foot of the same, nor rench [rinse] and make clean any kettle, pot, or pan, or such like vessel, within twenty foot of the old well or new pump, ... upon pain of whipping and further punishment, as shall be thought meet, by the censure of a martial Court.

LAWS AND ACTS OF ASSEMBLY.

CRIMES AND PUNISHMENTS.

1643.—"*Be it also enacted and confirmed, etc.*, That what person or persons soever shall feloniously *kill a tame hogg*, being none of his owne, and being thereof lawfully convicted, shall suffer *as a felon*" [i. e. death]. Hening's *Statutes at Large*, i. 244.

[In November, 1647, this penalty was mitigated to a fine of 2000 lbs. of tobacco, or two years' penal servitude. *Ibid.*, 351.]

1662.—The Court, in every county, "shall cause to be sett up a pillory, a pair of stocks, and a whipping-post, neere the court-house, and a *ducking stoole* in such a place as they shall think convenient, that such offenders as by the laws are to suffer by any of them may be punished according to their demeritts."

Any court failing to execute this order, within six months, was to be fined 5000 lbs. of tobacco. *Ibid.*, ii. 75.

1662.—Whereas oftentimes many *brabbling women* often slander and scandalize their neighbours, for which their poore husbands are often brought into chargeable and vexatious suites, and cast in greate damages: *Be it therefore enacted, etc.*, That in actions of slander occasioned by the wife as aforesaid, after judgment passed for damages, *the woman shall be punished by ducking;* and if the slander be so enormous as to be adjudged at a greater damage than 500 lbs. of tobacco, then the *woman to suffer a ducking for each five hundred pounds* adjudged against the husband, if he refuse to pay the tobacco.—*Ibid.*, ii. 166-67.

1662.—Taking advantage of the law that "every woman servant having a bastard, shall serve two years" after the expiration of her original term, "some dissolute masters have gotten their maids with child," so as to retain them longer in service; whereupon, an act was passed, providing that

"Women servants got with child by their masters, shall, after their time expired, be sold by the Church-wardens for two years, *for the good of the parish.*"—*Ibid.*, 167.

AGAINST NONCONFORMISTS AND DISSENTERS.

[The Rev. Thomas W. Coit, D.D., remarks on the contrast the early legislation of Virginia presents to the exclusiveness and intolerance of Puritanism in New England. "How different," he writes, "the principle with which Episcopal Virginia commenced her career, viz, 'universal suffrage and equality'! . . . Well may Mr. Burk say of the noble State whose history he has undertaken. . . . Virginia, separated as it were from the whole world, heard the voice of liberty like sweet music in her wilds." —*Puritanism*, pp. 463-4.

With this glowing eulogy, compare the plainer prose of an illustrious son of Virginia,—Thomas Jefferson:—

"The first settlers of [Virginia] were emigrants from England, of the English church, just at a point of time when it was flushed with complete victory over the religions of all other persuasions. Possessed, as they became, of the powers of making, administering, and executing the laws, they shewed equal intolerance in this country with their Presbyterian brethren who had emigrated to the northern goverment . . . Several acts of the Virginia Assembly, of 1659, 1662, and 1693, had made it penal in parents to refuse to have their children baptized; had prohibited the unlawful assembling of Quakers; had made it penal for any master of a vessel to bring a Quaker into the State: had ordered those already here, and such as should come thereafter, to be imprisoned till they should abjure the country,—provided a milder penalty for the first and second return, but *death* for their third. If no capital executions took place here, as did in New England, it was not owing to the moderation of the church, or spirit of the legislature, as may be inferred from the law itself; but to historical circumstances which have not been handed down to us."—Jefferson's *Notes on Virginia*, 1788, p. 167.]

March, 1623-24.—"Whosoever shall absent himself from divine service any Sunday, without an allowable excuse, shall forfeit a pound of tobacco, and he that absenteth himself a month shall forfeit 50 lbs. of tobacco."—Hening's *Statutes at Large*, i. 123.

March, 1642-3.—"For the preservation of the puritie of doctrine and unitie of the church, *It is enacted*, that all ministers whatsoever that shall reside in this

Colony are to be conformable to the orders and constitutions of the *Church of England*, and the lawes therein established, and not otherwise to be admitted to teach or preach publickly or privately. And that the Governour and Counsel do take care that *all non-conformists*, upon notice of them, *shall be compelled to depart the Colony* with all conveniencie."—*Ibid.*, i. 277.

1645-46.—[By an act of June, 1641, continued by act of February, 1644, all ministers were required to "preach in the forenoon and catechize in the afternoon of every Sunday," under a forfeiture of 500 lbs of tobacco :] Be it now further enacted, that all masters of families upon warning given by the ministers, ... do cause their children and servants to repaire to the places appointed, to be instructed and catechized, upon the like penalty, . . . unless sufficient cause be shewn to the contrary."—*Ibid.*, i. 312.

1661.—No minister shall be allowed to officiate in this Country, but such as produce to the governor a testimonial, that he hath received his ordination from some Bishop in England, and shall then subscribe to be conformable to the Orders and Constitutions of the Church of England.—Mercer's Abridgment, (1737,) 177.

1652.—All persons inhabiting in this country, having no lawful excuse, shall every Sunday resort to their Parish Church or Chapel, and there abide orderly during the Common-Prayer, Preaching, and Divine Service, upon the penalty of being fined 50 lbs. of Tobacco by the county court.

This act shall not extend to *Quakers* or other recusants who totally absent themselves, but they shall be liable to the penalty imposed by the Statute, 23 Elizabeth, viz. £20 sterling for every month's absence.

1695.—Any person of full age, absent from divine service at his or her parish Church or Chapel, the space of one month, (except such protestant Dissenters as are excepted by the Act of Parliament of William and Mary,) to be fined five shillings, or 50 pounds of Tobacco; and on refusal to make present payment, or give sufficient caution for payment thereof, to receive, on the bare back, ten lashes, well laid on.—Mercer, p. 209.

Against Papists.

1641.—["Popish recusants" may not exercise the places of secret counsellors, register, commissioners, surveyor, or sheriff, under forfeiture of 1000 lbs. of Tobacco.]

1643.—[The assembly directs the above statute to be duly executed, and enacts:]

"That it should not be lawful, under the penalty aforesaid, for any *popish priest* that shall hereafter arrive, to remain above five days after warning given by the governor, or commander of the place where he or they shall be, if wind and weather hinder not his departure."—Hening, i. 268, 269.

1705.—Popish recusants convict, negroes, mulattoes, Indian servants, and others, not being Christians, shall not be received as witnesses, in any case whatsoever.—Mercer, 93.

Against Quakers.

March, 1660.—"An Act for the suppressing of the Quakers."—"Whereas there is an unreasonable and turbulent sort of people, commonly called Quakers, who contrary to law do dayly gather together unto them unlawful assemblies and congregations of people, teaching, and publishing lies, miracles, false visions, prophecies, and doctrines [etc.] . . . .To prevent and restrain which mischiefe,

"*It is enacted*, That no master or commander of any shipp or other vessell do bring into this Collonie any person or persons called Quakers, under the penalty of £100 sterling . . . . All such Quakers as have been questioned or shall hereafter arrive shall be apprehended wheresoever they shall be found and they be imprisoned without baile or mainprize till they do abjure this country or putt in security with all speed to depart the Collonie and not to return again. [If they "dare to presume to return," they are to be proceeded against and punished "as contemners of the laws," and caused to depart the country]. And if they should the third time be so audacious and impudent as to return hither, *to be proceeded against as felons*" [i. e. to be punished with death].—Hening, i. 532.

1662.—Quakers or other recusants who totally absent themselves from the Parish Church, shall be liable to a penalty of £20 sterling for every month's absence. And all Quakers assembling in unlawful Conventicles shall be fined, every man so taken, 200 pounds of Tobacco for every such time of meeting.

1663.—If Quakers, *or other Separatists whatsoever*, in this Colony assemble themselves together to the number of five or more, of the age of sixteen years or upwards, under the pretence of joining in a *religious worship not authorized in England or this country*, the parties so offending being thereof lawfully convict by verdict, confessions, or notorious evidence, shall for the first offence forfeit 200 lbs. of tobacco; for the second, 500 lbs of tobacco; and for the third offence, the offender being convict as aforesaid shall be banished the colony of Virginia.

Every master of a ship or vessel that shall bring in any Quakers to reside here, after July 1st next, shall be fined 5000 lbs. of tobacco.

Any person inhabiting this country, *entertaining any Quaker* in or near his house, to preach or teach, shall for every time of such entertainment be fined 5000 lbs. of tobacco.

Miscellaneous Enactments.

1662.—"An Act prohibiting the importation of unnecessary Commodities. Whereas the lowe prices of tobacco will hardly supply the urgeing and pressing necessities of the country, etc. . . . . *Be it enacted*, that no strong drink of what sort soever, nor silke stuffe in garments or in peeces (except for whoods and scarfes), nor silver or gold lace, nor bone lace of silk or thread, nor ribbands wrought with silver or gold in them, shall be brought into this country to sell, after the first of February next; under penalty of confiscation of the said goods by the seller to the governor, to be exported, and the value thereof by the buyer to that good commonwealth-man that shall discover it."—Hening, ii. 18.

[This law is crossed with a pen on the MS. record, and Mr. Jefferson "*conjectured* it was negatived by the governor."—*Ibid.*, note.]

1661.—Ordered, that the order of the quarter-court the 27th of March, 1661, prohibiting Roger Partridge and Elizabeth his wife, to *keep any maid servant*, for the tearme of three yeares, be by this Assembly confirmed and ratified.—*Ibid.*, 35.

1632, Sept.—"Mynisters shall not give themselves *to excess* in drinking or ryott, spending their tyme idelie by day or night, playinge at dice, cards, or any other unlawfull game, but at all tymes *convenient* they shall heare or reade *somewhat* of the holy scriptures, or shall occupie themselves with some other honest studies, or exercise, always doing the things which shall apperteyne to honestie, and endeavour to profitt the church of God, having always in mynd that they ought to excell all others in puritie of life, and should be examples to the people to live well and Christianlie."—Hening, i. 183.

1632, Sept.—"Because of the low price of Tobacco at present, it is further graunted and ordered, that there shall be likewise due to the Mynisters, from the first day of March last past, for and during the term of one whole year next ensueinge, the twentyeth calfe, the twentyeth kidd of goates, and the twentyeth pigge, throughout all the plantations is this Colony," etc.—*Ibid.*, 183.

1734.—When any Free Indian shall be tried for Murder or other Felony, any free Indian may be examined, without oath, upon the trial, for or against the criminal. "If it shall appear to the Court that such witness hath given false testimony, the Court, without further trial, shall order such witness to have one ear nailed to the Pillory, and there to stand an hour, then to have that ear cut off; and the other nailed to, and cut off, at the expiration of another hour."—Mercer's Abridgment, 1737, p. 30.

MARYLAND.

The charter of Maryland, granted to a Roman Catholic subject, by a protestant king moved by "a laudable zeal for extending the Christian religion," guaranteed the protection of Christianity as professed by the Church of England. It conferred the authority to enact, with the assent of the freemen, such laws as were "not repugnant, but agreeable, to the jurisprudence and rights of the realm of England," and expressly provided that no construction of it should be made whereby the Christian religion, or the allegiance due to the Crown, should suffer any diminution. The planters and their posterity were declared to be "entitled to the liberties of Englishmen, as if they had been born within the kingdom." Before the coming of Leonard Calvert in 1634, a protestant settlement had been established (at Kent Island) within the bounds of the Maryland patent, and of those who accompanied him in the first emigration "by far the larger number were Protestants" (Bancroft, cent. ed., i. 185). At the first assembly of the freemen, it was enacted "that offenders, in all murders and felonies, shall suffer the same pains and forfeitures as for the same crimes in England." The third assembly, in Feb. 1638–9, adopted a provisional code of laws, in which was incorporated the declaration (from Magna Charta) that "Holy church within this province shall have all her rights and liberties," but, as Chalmers observes, "what the franchizes of the church of Maryland were do not appear, and probably the wisest of her doctors would have been puzzled to tell." In 1676, this act was confirmed, as a perpetual law. So long as the proprietary was of a different religion from that professed by a great majority of the people, mutual toleration was a necessity. When puritanism was in the ascendant in England, and the abrogation of Lord Baltimore's charter was urged upon the Parliament, he appointed a protestant governor of Maryland and bound him, by his official oath, not "directly to trouble, molest or discountenance any person whatsoever in the said province, *professing to believe in Jesus Christ*; and, in particular, no Roman Catholic," etc.; and in April, 1649, the assembly, composed of Roman Catholics and Protestants, passed an act establishing the religious freedom of all *Christians*, but imposing the penalty of death for blasphemy, and the denial or reproach of the Holy Trinity, or any of the three persons thereof, and a fine of 5£ for speaking reproachfully against the Blessed Virgin or the apostles. Of the *earliest* laws of Maryland few have been preserved. The abstracts here given are from revisions of 1699 and 1700.

Blasphemy, Swearing, &c.

1649, 1699.—If any person whatsoever inhabiting this Province shall blaspheme, that is, curse God, deny our Saviour to be the Son of God, or deny the Holy Trinity, *or the Godhead of any of the three Persons*, or the Unity of the Godhead, or shall utter any reproachful words or language concerning the Holy Trinity, or any of the three Persons thereof, he or she shall for the first offence be bored through the tongue, and fined 20£ sterling, to the king, or if the party hath not an estate sufficient to answer the sum, then to suffer six months' imprisonment. For the second offence, he or she shall be stigmatized in the forehead, with the letter B, and fined 40£ sterling, (&c.) or be imprisoned for one year. And for the third offence, he or she so offending and thereof legally convicted, shall suffer death, with confiscation of all their goods and chattels to the king.

If any person prophanely swear or curse, in the hearing of any one justice of peace, or head officer of a town, or that shall be thereof convicted by the oath of one witness before any one justice or other head officer, or by confession of the party, he shall forfeit 5 *sh.* sterling to the king.

Ordinaries and Inns.

1699.—Every ordinary-keeper that shall demand or take above 10 lbs. of tobacco for a gallon of small beer, 20 lbs. of tobacco for a gallon of strong beer, 4 lbs. of tobacco for a night's lodging in a bed, 12 lbs. of tobacco for a peck of Indian corn or oats, 6 lbs. of tobacco for a night's grass for a horse, 10 lbs. of tobacco for a night's hay or straw, shall forfeit for every such offence 500 lbs. of tobacco.

No inhabitant of this Province shall sell without license any cider, quince drink, or other strong liquor, to be drunk in his or her house, upon penalty of 1000 lbs. of tobacco for every conviction.

No ordinary-keeper shall refuse to credit any person capable of giving a vote for election of delegates in any county, for any accommodations by him vended, to the value of 400 lbs. of tobacco, under the penalty of 400 lbs. of tobacco.

No ordinary-keeper within this Province, during the time of his keeping ordinary, shall be elected to serve as a deputy or representative in the General Assembly.

Religion.

1700.—The Book of Common Prayer and administration of the Sacraments, with other rites and ceremonies of the Church of England etc., shall be solemnly read by all ministers in the churches and other places of worship in this Province.

In every parish where any minister or incumbent shall reside, no justice or magistrate shall join any persons in marriage under the penalty of 5000 lbs. of tobacco, to the king.

For the encouragement of able ministers etc., instead of tithes, a tax or assessment of 40 lbs. of tobacco per poll shall be yearly levied *upon every taxable person* in every parish in this Province. Which said assessment shall always be paid to the ministers of every parish, etc.

MASSACHUSETTS.

The founders of Connecticut borrowed most of their laws and judicial proceedings from Massachusetts. Their legislation was certainly not more "blue" than that of the Bay Colony, their penalties were not more severe, nor more rigorously exacted. The following orders and sentences of the Massachusetts Court of Assistants and General Court (before the establishment of the "Body of Liberties" in 1640) are extracted from the printed Colony Records, Vol. I.

Sept. 1630.—It is ordered by this present Court, that Thomas Morton, of Mount Wolliston, shall presently be sett into the bilbowes, and after sent prisoner into England, by the shipp called the Gifte, nowe returning thither; that all his goods shalbe seazed upon to defray the charge of his transportation, payment of his debts, and to give satisfaction to the Indians for a cannoe hee unjustly tooke away from them; and that his howse, after the goods are taken out, shalbe burnt downe to the ground in the sight of the Indians, for their satisfaction, for many wrongs hee hath done them from tyme to tyme.

It is ordered, that noe person shall plant in any place within the lymitts of this Pattent, without leave from the Governor and Assistants, or the major parte of them.

It is ordered, that all Rich: Clougheʼs strong water shall presently be seazed upon, for his selling greate quantytie thereof to severall menʼs servants, which was the occasion of much disorder, drunckenes, and misdemeanour.

Nov. 1630.—It is ordered, that John Baker shalbe whipped for shooting att fowle on the Sabboth day, etc.

March, 1631.—Mr. Thomas Stoughton, constable of Dorchester, is fyned 5£ for takeing upon him to marry Clement Briggs and Joane Allen, and to be imprisoned till hee hath paid his fyne.

It is ordered, that if any person within the lymitts of this Pattent doe trade, trucke, or sell any money, either silver or golde, to any Indian, or any man that knowes of any that shall soe doe and conceales the same, shall forfeit twenty for one.

Nich. Knopp is fyned 5£ for takeing upon him to cure the scurvey, by a water of noe worth nor value, which he solde att a very deare rate, to be imprisoned till hee pay his fine or give securitye for it, or else to be whipped; and shalbe lyable to any man's action of whome he hath receaved money for the said water.

It is likewise ordered, that all persons whatsoever that have cards, dice, or tables in their howses, shall make away with them before the nexte Court, under paine of punishment.

June, 1631.—It is ordered, that noe man within the limitts of this jurisdiction shall hire any person for a servant for lesse time than a yeare, unles hee be a setled housekeeper; also, that noe person whatsoever shall travell out of this Pattent, either by sea or land, without leave from the Governor, Deputy Governor, or some other Assistant, under such penalty as the Court shall thinke meete to inflict.

It is ordered, that Phillip Ratliffe shalbe whipped, have his eares cutt off, fyned 40£, and banished out of the lymitts of this jurisdiction, for uttering mallitious and scandulous speeches against the government and the church of Salem, etc., as appeareth by a particular thereof, proved upon oath.

Sept. 1631.—It is ordered, that Henry Lynn shalbe whipped and banished the plantation before the 6th day of October nexte, for writeing into England falsely and mallitiously against the government and execution of justice here.

It is ordered, that Josias Plastowe shall (for stealeing 4 basketts of corne from the Indians) returne them 8 basketts againe, be fined 5£, and hereafter to be called by the name of Josias, and not Mr., as formerly hee used to be, * and that Willm. Buckland and Tho. Andrewe shalbe whipped for being accessary to the same offence.

April, 1632.—Tho. Knower was sett in the bilbov es for threatning the Court that, if hee should be punisht, hee would have itt tryed in England whither hee was lawfully punished or not.

August, 1632.—It is ordered, that the remainder of Mr. Allen's stronge water, being estimated about 2 gallands, shalbe delivered into the hands of the deacons of Dorchester, for the benefit of the poore there, for his selling of it dyvers tymes to such as were drunke with it, hee knowing thereof.

---

* This judgment has often been pointed to as a choice specimen of puritan jurisprudence. Hutchinson (Hist. of Mass., i. 384) cites it, amongst others, to show that the sentences of the early Massachusetts courts were "adapted to the circumstances of a large family of children and servants;" and he remarks, that the colonists were careful that no title or appellation should be given where it was not due, etc. The true explanation of the sentence passed on Plastowe is this: "Master" was the title of a *gentleman*, and gentlemen were *exempt from corporal punishment*. "Mr." Plastowe was *fined* for stealing, while his accomplices were *whipped*. The Court deprived him of his safeguard by reducing him to plain "Josias."

Sept. 1632.—It is ordered, that Robert Shawe shalbe severely whipt, for wicked curseing, sweareing, justifyeing the same, and gloryeing in it, as hath been proved by oath.

It is ordered, that Richard Hopkins shalbe severely whipt, and branded with a hott iron on one of his cheekes, for selling peeces and powder and shott to the Indeans. Hereupon it was propounded if this offence should not be punished hereafter by death.

Tobacco.

Oct. 1632.—It is ordered, that noe person shall take any tobacco publiquely, under paine of punishment; also that every one shall pay 1*d.* for every time hee is convicted for takeing tobacco in any place, and that any Assistant shall have power to receave evidence and give order for the levyeing of it, as also to give order for the levyeing of the officer's charge. This order to begin the 10th of November next.

Sept. 1634.—Victualers, or keepers of an Ordinary, shall not suffer any tobacco to be taken in their howses, under the penalty of 5*s.* for every offence. to be payde by the victuler, and 12*d.* by the party that takes it.

Further, it is ordered, that noe person shall take tobacco publiquely, under the penalty of 2*s.* 6*d.*, nor privately, in his owne house, or in the howse of another, before strangers, and that two or more shall not take it togeather, anywhere, under the aforesaid penalty for every offence.

March, 1635.—It is further ordered, that noe person whatsoever shall either buy or sell any tobacco within this jurisdiction after the last of September nexte, under the penalty of 10*s*. a pound, and soe proportionably for more or lesse, to be paide by buyer and seller, and that in the meane tyme noe person shall buy or sell any tobacco att a higher price then it shalbe valued att by the Governor for the tyme being, and two other, whome hee shall please to chuse, under the penalty aforesaid.

Nov. 1637.—All former laws against tobacco are repealed, and tobacco is sett at liberty.

Sept. 1638.—The [General] Court, finding that since the repealing of the former laws against tobacco, the same is more abused then before, it hath therefore ordered, that no man shall take any tobacco in the feilds, except in his journey, or at meale times, upon paine of 12*d*. for every offence; nor shall take any tobacco in (or so near) any dwelling house, barne, corne, or hay rick, as may likely indanger the fireing thereof, upon paine of 10*s*. for every offence; nor shall take any tobacco in any inne or common victualing house, except in a private roome there, so as neither the master of the same house nor any other guests there shall take offence thereat; which if they do, then such person is fourthwith to forbeare, upon paine of 2*s*. 6*d*. for every offence.

Noe man shall kindle fyre by gunpowder, for takeing tobacco, except in his journey, upon paine of 12*d*. for every offence.

April, 1633.—It is ordered, that if any swine shall, in fishing time, come within a quarter of a mile of the stadge att Marble Harbour, that they shalbe forfected to the owners of the said stadge, and soe for all other stadges within their lymitts.

Sept. 1633.—John Shotswell is fined 40*s*. for distempering himselfe with drinke att Aggawam.

Roberte Coles is fined 10£, and enjoyned to stand with a white sheete of paper on his back, wherein A DRUNKARD shalbe written in greate letters, and to stand therewith soe longe as the Court thinks meete, for abuseing himselfe shamefully with drinke, ... and other misdemeanour.

Capt. John Stone for his outrage committed in confronting aucthority, abuseing Mr. [Roger] Ludlowe both in words and behavour, assalting him, and calling him a Just as, &c., is fined 100£, and prohibited comeing within this pattent without leave from the goverment, under the penalty of death.

Pay of Mechanics and Labourers.

Oct. 1633.—It is ordered, that maister carpenters, sawers, masons, clapboard-ryvers, brickelayers, tylars, joyners, wheelewrights, mowers, &c., shall not take above 2*s*. a day, finding themselves dyett, and not above 14*d*. a day if they have dyett found them, under the penalty of 5*s*., both to giver and receaver, for every day that there is more given and receaved. Also, that all other inferior workemen of the said occupations shall have such wages as the constable of the said place, and two other inhabitants that hee shall chuse, shall appoynct.

Also, it is agreed, that the best sorte of labourers shall not take above 18*d*. a day if they dyett themselves, and not above 8*d*. a day if they have dyett found them, under the aforesaid penalty both to giver and receaver. Likewise, that the wages of inferior labourers shalbe referd to the constable and two others, as aforesaid.

Maister taylours shall not take above 12*d.* a day and the inferiour sorte not above 8*d.*, if they be dyeted, under the aforesaid penalty; and for all other worke they doe att home, proportionably, and soe for other worke that shalbe done by the greate, by any other artificer.

Further, it is ordered, that all workemen shall worke the whole day, allowing convenient tyme for food and rest. This order to take place the 12th of this present moneth.

It is further ordered, that noe person, howsehoulder or other, shall spend his time idly or unproffitably, under paine of such punishment as the Court shall thinke meete to inflicte; and for this end it is ordered, that the constable of every place shall use spetiall care and diligence to take knowledge of offenders in this kinde, espetially of common coasters,* unprofitable fowlers, and tobacco takers, and to present the same to the two nexte Assistants, whoe shall have power to heare and determine the cause, or, if the matter be of importance, to transferr it to the Court.

March, 1634.—John Chapman is fined 20*s.* for selling boards at 8*s.* per 100, contrary to an order of Court, and is remitted upon promise of 300 of 4 inch planke towards the Sea Fort.

Tymothy Hawkins and John Vauhan fined 20*s.* a peece for mispending their tyme in company keepeing, drinkeing stronge water, and selling other, contrary to an order of Court.

---

* "Coasters" or "cursetors" (i. e. "cursitors"); vagrants, vagabonds.

It is ordered, that Roberte Coles, for drunckenes by him committed att Rocksbury, shalbe disfranchized, weare aboute his necke, and soe [as] to hange upon his outward garment, a D, made of redd cloath, and sett upon white; to contynue this for a yeare, and not to leave it off att any tyme when hee comes amongst company, under the penalty of 40*s.* for the first offence, and 5£ the second, and after to be punished by the Court as they thinke meete: Also, hee is to weare the D outwards; and is enjoyned to appeare att the nexte Generall Court, and contynue there till the Court be ended. [In May, 1634, this sentence was remitted, upon the submission of the offender and testimony of his good behavior.]

Aug. 1634.—It was witnessed upon oath, that James Rawlens tooke 18*d.* a day, and meate and drinke, for ten dayes' worke, for one of his servants, for weeding corne, contrary to an order of Court, and therefore is to pay 5*s.* for every day hee hath soe transgressed.

Price of Meals.

Sept. 1634.—It is ordered, that noe person that keepes an Ordinary shall take above 6*d.* a meale for a person, and not above 1*d.* for an ale quarte of beare, out of meale tyme, under the penalty of 10*s.* for every offence, either of dyet or beare.

Fashions of Dress.

Sept. 1634.—The Court, takeing into consideration the greate, superfluous, and unnecessary expences occasioned by reason of some newe and immodest fashions, as also the ordinary weareing of silver, golde, and silke laces, girdles, hatbands, etc, hath therefore ordered that noe person, either man or woman, shall hereafter make or buy any apparell, either woollen, silke, or lynnen, with any lace on it, silver, golde, silke, or threed, under the penalty of forfecture of such cloathes, etc.

Also, that noe person, either man or woman, shall make or buy any slashed cloathes, other than one slashe in each sleeve and another in the backe; also, all cuttworks, imbroidered or needleworke capps, bands, and rayles, are forbidden hereafter to be made and worne, under the aforesaid penalty; also, all gold or silver girdles, hattbands, belts, ruffs, beaver hatts, are prohibited to be bought and worne hereafter, under the aforesaid penalty, etc.

Moreover, it is agreed, if any man shall judge the weareing of any the forenamed particulars, newe fashions, or long haire, or anything of the like nature, to be uncomely or prejudiciall to the common good, and the party offending reforme not the same upon notice given him, that then the nexte Assistant, being informed thereof, shall have power to bind the party soe offending to answer it at the nexte Courte, if the case soe requires:

Provided, and it is the meaneing of this Court, that men and women shall have liberty to weare out such apparell as they are nowe provided of (except the immoderate greate sleeves, slashed apparell, immoderate greate rayles, longe wings, etc.). This order to take place a fortnight after the publishing thereof.

Bullets, a Legal Tender.

March. 1635.—It is ordered, that muskett bulletts,

of a full bore, shall passe currantly for a farthing a peece; provided that noe man be compelled to take above 12*d.* att a tyme, in them.

Absence from Church.

Whereas complainte hath bene made to this Court that dyvers persons within this jurisdiction doe usually absent themselves from church meeteings upon the Lord's day, power is therefore given to any two Assistants to heare and sensure, either by fyne or imprisonment (att their discretion), all misdemeanours of that kinde committed by any inhabitant within this jurisdiction, provided they exceede not the fine of 5*s.* for one offence.

Wages and Prices.

Sept. 1635.—Whereas two former lawes, the one concerning the wages of workmen, the other concerning the prices of commodyties, were for dyvers good considerations repealed this present Court, nowe, for avoydeing such mischeifes as may followe thereupon by such ill-disposed persons as may take liberty to oppresse and wronge their neighbours, by takeing excessive wages for worke or unreasonable prizes for such necessary merchandizes or other commodyties as shall passe from man to man, it is therefore nowe ordered, that if any man shall offend in any of the said cases against the true intent of this lawe, hee shalbe punished by fyne or imprisonment, according to the quallity of the offence, as the Court upon lawfull tryall and conviction shall adjudge.

Excessive Profits censured.

Oct. 1635.—Josuah Huyes hath forfeit 5*s.* for

knyves, and 4*s*. 6*d*. for a sythe, which hee solde for above 4*d*. in the shilling proffitt.

Courts to observe the Laws of God.

May, 1636.—The Governor, Deputy Governor, Tho. Dudley, John Haynes, Richard Bellingham, Esqrs., Mr. Cotton, Mr. Peters, and Mr. Shepheard are intreated to make a draught of lawes agreeable to the word of God, which may be the Fundamentalls of this Commonwealth, and to present the same to the nexte Generall Court. And it is ordered, that in the meane tyme the magistrates and their assosiates shall proeeede in the Courts to heare and determine all causes according to the lawes now established, and where there is noe law, then as neere the lawe of God as they can; and for all busines out of Court for which there is noe certaine rule yett sett downe, those of the standing counsell, or some two of them, shall take order by their best discretion, that they may be ordered and ended according to the rule of God's word, and to take care for all military affaires till the nexte Generall Court.

Restraining the Tongue.

Sept. 1636.—Robert Shorthose, for swearing by the bloud of God, * was sentenced to have his tongue put into a cleft stick, and to stand so by the space of haulfe an houre.

Elisabeth, the wife of Thomas Aplegate, was censured to stand with her tongue in a cleft stick, for sweareing, raileing, and revileing.

* '*Odsblood*, or '*Sblood*, was an oath often heard in England, among the profane, at this period.

Against Lace.

Oct. 1636.—That no person, after one month, shall make or sell any bone lace, or other lace, to bee worne upon any garment or linnen, upon paine of 5*s*. the yard for every yard of such lace so made or sould, or set on; neither shall any taylor set any lace upon any garment, upon payne of 10*s*. for every offence; provided that binding or small edging laces may bee used upon garments or linnen.

The unmarried to be cared for.

Dec. 1636.—It is ordered, that all townes shall take care to order and dispose of all single persons and inmates with their towne, to service, or otherwise; and if any be greived at the order of a towne, the parties to have liberty to appeale to the Governor and Counsell or the Courte.

A Solemn Admonition.

June, 1637.—Benjamin Hubberd was solemly admonished of his failing, for being in company with James Browne and the rest, and often drinking of the strong-water bottle with them, and not reproving them.

Price of Liquors and of Meals at Inns, regulated.

Nov. 1637.—Whereas it hath appeared unto this Court, upon many sad complaints, that much drunkennes, *waste of the good creatures of God*, mispence of precious time, and other disorders have frequently fallen out in the inns and common victualing houses within this jurisdiction, whearby God is much dishonoured, the profession of religion reproached, and the welfare of this commonwelth greatly impaired, and the true use of such houses (being the necessary releefe of travellers) subverted; for redresse hearof it is now ordered, that after the last day of this present month, it shall not bee lawfull for any person that shall keepe any such inne or common victualing house, to sell or have in their houses any wine or strong waters, nor any beare, or other drinke, other than such as may and shall be sould for one penny the quart, at the most . . . . And it is further ordered-that no common brewer shall sell or utter to any inn or common victualing house, within this jurisdiction, any beare or other drinke of any stronger size than such as may and shalbe affoarded at the rate of 8 *sh.* the barrell, upon paine of 20£ for every offence against this order.

And whereas complaint hath been also made that diverse poore people, who would willingly content themselves with meane dyot, are forced to take such dyot as is tendered them at 12*d.* the meale or more, it is now ordered, that every keeper of such inn or common victualing house shall sell and alowe unto every of their guests such victuals as they shall call for, and not force them to take more or other than they desire, bee it never so meane and small in quantity, and shall affoard the same and all other dyot at reasonable prizes, upon paine of such fine as the Court shall inflict, according to the measure and quantity of the offence.

Against Cakes and Buns.

It is ordered, also, that no person shall sell any cakes or buns, either in the markets or victualing houses, or elsewhere, upon paine of 10*s*. fine; provided that this order shall not extend to such cakes as shalbee made for any buriall, or marriage, or such like spetiall occasion.

A Female Practitioner restrained.

March, 1638.—Jane Hawkins, the wife of Richard Hawkins, had liberty till the beginning of the third month, called May, and the magistrates (if shee did not depart before) to dispose of her; and in the meane time shee is not to meddle in surgery, or phisick, drinks, plaisters, or oyles, nor to question matters of religion, except with the Elders for satisfaction.

Swearing punished.

June, 1638.—Robert Bartlet, being presented for cursing and swearing, was censured to have his tongue put in a cleft stick.

John Smith of Meadford, for swearing, being penitent, was set in the bilboes.

March, 1639.—John Hogges for swearing [by] God's foote, and cursing his servant, wishing "a poxe of God take you," was fined 5£.

Extortion censured.

June, 1639.—Edward Palmer, for his extortion, taking 1£. 13*s*. 7*d*. for the plank and woodwork of Boston stocks, is fined 5£. and censured to bee set an houre in the stocks. This was remitted to 10 *sh*.

BLUE LAWS OF ENGLAND,

IN THE REIGN OF JAMES THE FIRST.

"In determining what kind of men our fathers were, we are to compare their laws, not with ours, but with the laws which they renounced." Something has been said in the Introduction to this volume, of English criminal law at the time of the colonization of New England. A few extracts from, and abstracts of, English statutes in force in the reign of James the First may be grouped here, to refresh the memory ot those who incline to believe that penalties for dissent, fines for absence from church and for non-observance of stated fasts, regulations of the hours of labor and wages of artisans, laws against tippling and card-playing, and against idleness and vagrancy,—above all, laws for the punishment of witchcraft and sorcery,—were peculiar to puritan legislation in New England.

PENALTIES OF NONCONFORMITY AND "RECUSANCY."

[By the Statute of 35 Elizabeth, c. 1; If any above the age of sixteen shall be convicted to have absented themselves above a month from Church, without any lawful cause, to have impugned the Queen's authority in causes ecclesiasticall, or to have persuaded others to be present at any unlawful assemblies, *conventicles, or meetings under color or pretence of any exercise of religion*, or to have themselves willingly joined in or been present at such conventicles or meetings, they shall be committed to prison, and there remain until they shall conform themselves, and make open submission. And if within three months after such conviction, they refuse to conform and make public confession and submission, they shall, being thereunto required by a Justice of the Peace, in open assise or sessions, *abjure the realm* forever, and shall thereupon depart the Realm, at such Port and at such time as the said Justices shall appoint. If any such offender shall refuse to make such abjuration, or to depart at the time appointed, or shall return into any part of the Realm, without special license, such offender shall be adjudged a *felon* and shall suffer as in case of felony, without benefit of clergy.]

No Recusant convict shall at anie time after the end of this session of Parliament (1605), practise the Common Law of this Realme, as a counsellor, clerke, attorney, or solicitor in the same, nor shall practise the Civil Law, as advocate, or proctor, nor practise Phisicke, nor exercise or use the trade or art of an Apothecarie, nor shall bee Judge, Minister, Clerke, or Steward, of or in any Court, or keepe anie Court, nor shall bee Register, or Town Clerke, or other minister or officer in anie court, nor shall beare anie office or charge, as Captaine, Lieutenant, Corporall, Serjeant, Ensigne-bearer, or other office in campe, troupe, band, or company of Souldiers, nor shall be Captaine, Master, Governour, or beare anie office or charge, of or in anie Shippe, Castle, or Fortresse of the King's majestie, his heyres and successors, but be utterly disabled for the same; and every person offending herein shall also forfeit for everie such offence, one hundred pounds.

No *Popish* recusant convict, nor any having a wife being a popish recusant convict, shall at any time after the end of this session of Parliament, exercise any publique office or charge in the Commonwealth, but shall be utterly disabled to exercise the same by himselfe, or by his deputie.

Everie Popish recusant, which is or shall be convicted of Popish recusancie, shall stand and be reputed to all intents and purposes disabled, as a person lawfully and duely excommunicated, and as if hee or shee had been so denounced and excommunicated, according to the lawes of this Realme, untill hee or shee so disabled shall conforme him or herselfe, and come to Church, and heare Divine Service, and receive the Sacrament of the Lorde's Supper, according to the laws of this Realme, and shall also take the oath preseribed, *etc.*—3 James I., c. 5.

PENALTIES FOR NOT GOING TO CHURCH.

All and everie person or persons inhabiting within this Realme, or any other the Queene's Majestie's dominions, shall diligently and faithfully, having noe lawfull or reasonable excuse to bee absent, endevour themselves to resort to the Parish Church or Chappell accustomed, or upon reasonable let thereof, to some usuall place where Common Prayer, and such Service of God shall bee used, in such time of let, upon everie Sunday, and other dayes ordayned and used to be kept as Holy dayes: and then and there to abide orderly and soberly, during the time of the Common Prayer, preachings, or other Service of God there to be used and ministred, upon payne of punishment by the censures of the Church; and also, upon payne that everie person so offending shall forfeit for everie such offence twelve pence, to be levyed by the Churchwardens of the Parish, where such offence shall be done, to the use of the pore of the same parish. —1 Eliz., c. 2. [Re-enacted, 3 James I., c. 4, with the addition that if the Churchwarden cannot levy the penalty by distress and sale of the goods of the offender, a Justice of the Peace shall commit such offender to prison, until payment be made.]

Everie person above the age of sixteene yeres, which shal not repaire to some Church, Chappell, or usuall place of Common Prayer, but forbeare the same, contrarie to the tenor of a Statute [above recited] made in the first yeare of her Majestie's raign for uniformitie of Common prayer, and being thereof lawfully convicted, shall forfeit to the Queene's Majestie, for every moneth after the end of this Session of Parliament, which he or she shall so forbeare, *twenty pounds* of lawfull English money. And that over and besides the said forfeitures, everie person so forbearing by the space of twelve moneths, as aforesaid, shal, for his or her obstinacie, after Certificat thereof in writing made into the Court commonly called the King's Bench, *etc.*, be bound with two sufficient suerties, in the summe of two hundred pounds at the least, to the good behaviour, and so to continue bound, untill such time as the persons so bound doe conforme themselves, and come to the Church, *etc.* . . . . And that everie person which shall forfeit any summes of money by vertue of this Act, and shall not be able, or shall faile to pay the same within three moneths after judgment thereof given, shall be committed to prison, there to remaine, untill he have paid the said summes, or conforme himselfe to go to church, and there doe as is aforesaid.—23 Eliz. c. 1.

Everie such offender in not repairing to Divine Service, but forbearing the same, contrarie to the said Estatute [above recited], as hath beene heretofore convicted for such offence, and hath not made submission, and been comformable, according to the true meaning of the said Estatute, shall without any other indictment or conviction, pay into the receipt of the said Exchequer, all such summes of money, as according to the rate of *twentie pounds for everie moneth*, sithence the same conviction, doe yet remaine unpayed. . . . And shall also for everie moneth after such conviction, without any other indictment or conviction, pay into the receipt of the Exchequer aforesaid, at two times in the yeare, that is to say, in everie Easter Terme and Michaelmas Terme, as much then as shal remain unpaid, after the rate of *twentie pounds for every month* after such conviction.

And if default shall be made in any part of paiment aforesaid, contrarie to the forme herein before limited: that then, and so often, the Queene's Majestie shall and may, by proces out of the said Exchequer, take, seise, and enjoy *all the goods*, and *two parts* as well of *all the lands*, tenements, and hereditaments, leases and farmes of such offendor, ... leaving the third part onely of the same lands, (*etc.*) to and for the maintenance and reliefe of the same offendor, his wife, children, and familie.—28 Eliz., c. 6. [Re-enacted, 3 James I., c. 4, with an additional provision, that the King may "refuse the penaltie of 20£. a month, though it be tendered readie to be payed according to the law," and may, instead, "seize and take to his owne use, and the uses, intents, and purposes hereafter limited, two parts in three parts of the lands *etc.* of the offendor, to be held to his own uses, till such offendor shall conform," &c.]

Everie person and persons which shall willingly

maintaine, retaine, *relieve*, *keepe*, or *harbour* in his or their house, any servant, sojourner, or stranger, who shall not goe to, or repayre to some Church, or Chappell, or usuall place of Common Prayer, to heare Divine Service, but shall so forbeare the same by the space of one moneth together, not having a reasonable excuse, *etc.*, shall forfeit *tenne pounds* for everie moneth that hee, shee, or they shall so relieve, *etc.*, such servant, sojourner, or estranger, in his or their house.—3 James I., c. 4.

If any person or persons, body politiqiue or corporate, shall keepe or maintaine any *Schoolemaster* which shall not repaire to Church, as is aforesaid, or be allowed by the Bishop or Ordinarie of the Diocesse where such Schoolemaster shall be so kept, shall forfeit and lose for everie moneth so keeping him, ten pounds . . . . And such Schoolemaster or Teacher presuming to teach, contrarie to this Act, and being thereof lawfully convict, shall bee disabled to bee a teacher of youth, and shall suffer imprisonment without baile or mainprise for one yeare.—23 Eliz., c. 1.

[By the act of 1 James I., c. 4, every person was forbidden to keep a school or be a Schoolmaster, out of the Universities or Colleges of this Realm, "except in some publique or free Grammar School, or in some such nobleman's or noblewoman's or gentleman's or gentlewoman's house, as are not Recusants," without a special license from the Archbishop, Bishop, or guardian of the Spiritualities of the diocese, under pain of forfeiture, by employer and teacher, of forty shillings for every day he shall so offend.

Against eating meat on Fish-days, and in Lent.

1564.—From and after the Feast of Pentecost next comming, it shall not be lawfull to any person or persons within this Realme, to eate any flesh upon any dayes now usually observed as Fish dayes, or upon any Wednesday now newly limited to be observed as fish-day, upon paine that everie person offending herein shall forfeit *three pound* for everie time he or they shall offend, or else suffer *three moneths close imprisonment* without baile or maineprise.—5 Eliz., c. 5. [In 1594, the penalty for eating meat on a fish day was abated to twenty shillings or one month's close imprisonment.—35 Eliz., c. 7.]

1603.—No butcher, or other person, whether he be licenced or not licenced to kill flesh, shall from henceforth at any time in the time of Lent, kill, or dress, to the intent to put to sale, any oxe or oxen, beeves, beevets, hogges, calves, ramme, eswes, orwethers, except oxen or beeves for victualling of shippes into forraine parts, and except all flesh to be killedthree days next before Easter yearely, upon paine to forfeit and lose the saip oxen, beeves, *etc.* so killed or dressed contrary to this statute, or the value of them.

And every taverner, innkeeper, keeper of everie common tabling house, common cooke, common tipler, or alehouse keeper, offending at any time hereafter in the dressing of anie flesh victuall, contrary to the statute of Anno 5 Elizabethæ, or contrary to this statute, shall not only forfeit all the said flesh so dressed, but also the penaltie imposed by the same Statute of Anno 5 Elizabethæ, for every offence to be committed, after the feast of Saint Michaell the Archangell next comming." 1 James I., ch. 29.

Drunkenness; Alehouses, &c.

[If any Inne-keeper, Victualler, or Alehouse-keeper

permit or suffer any person, dwelling in the same town, to sit tipling in his house, he shall forfeit ten shillings for every such offence.—1 James I., c. 9.]

If any Inne-keeper, Alehouse keeper, or Victualler, shall at anie time utter or sell lesse than one full ale quart of the best beere or ale for a penny, and of the small, two quarts for a penny, then everie such inne keeper *etc.* shall forfeit for every such offence, being duly prooved, twenty shillings [to the use of the poor of the Parish.]—Id.

[Any person who shall remain or continue drinking or tipling in any inne, victualing house, or alehouse, being in the same towne *etc.*, shall forfeit for every such offence three shillings fourpence, to the use of the poor; and if unable to pay, shall be set in the stocks four hours. For a second offence, he shall be bound with two sureties, in the sum of ten pounds, to good behavior.—4 James I., c. 5.

[Every person convicted of drunkenness shall forfeit, for every such offence, five shillings; and if unable to pay, shall be set in the stocks six hours.—Id.

Plays and Games.

Be it also enacted, etc.: That no manner of artificer or craftsman, of any handicraft or occupation, husbandman, apprentice, labourer, servant at husbandry, journeiman or servant of artificer, mariners, fishermen, watermen, or any serving-man, shall, from the feast of the Nativitie of St. John Baptist [now next comming], play at the Tables, Tennis, Dice, Cardes, Bowles, Closh, Coyting, Logating, or any other unlawfull game, *out of Christmasse*, under the pain of twenty shillings, to be forfeit for every time, and in Christmasse, to play at any of the said games in their masters' houses or in their masters' presence. And also, that no manner of person shall at anie time play at any bowle or bowles, in open places, out of his garden or orchard, under the paine of every time so offending, to forfeit five shillings eight pence. * * * Provided also, and be it enacted, *etc.*: That it shall be lawfull for every Master to licence his or theyr servant to play at cardes, dice, or tables, with their said master, or with any other gentleman repairing to their said master, openly in his or theyr house, or in his or theyr presence, according to his or theyr discretion.—33 Hen. VIII., c. 9.

Be it also enacted, etc.: That no manner of person or persons, of what degree, qualitie or condition soever hee or they be, by himselfe, factour, deputy, servant, or other person, shall for his or theyr gaine, lucre or living, keepe, have, holde, occupie, exercise, or maintaine any common house, alley, or place of bowling, coiting, closh, cailes, halfe bowle, tennis, dicing, tables, or carding, or any other manner of game prohibited by any statute heretofore made, or any unlawfull new game now invented or made, or any other new unlawfull game hereafter to be invented, etc., upon paine to forfeit and pay for every day keeping, having, or maintaining, or suffering any such game to be had, etc., contrary to the form and effect of this Statute, forty shillings.—Id.

Beggars and Vagrants.

All persons calling themselves Scholars, going about begging; all seafaring men, pretending losses of their ships or goods on the sea, going about the Countrie begging; all idle persons going about in any Countrey, either begging or using any subtill craft or unlawful games and playes, or fayning themselves to have knowledge in Physiognomie, Palmistrie, or other like craftie science, *etc.*; all persons that be, or utter themselves to be proctors, procurers, patent-gatherers, or collectors for gaoles, prisons, or hospitals; all fencers, beare-wards, common Players of Enterludes, and minstrels, wandering abroad (other than players of enterludes belonging to any Baron of this Realm or any other honorable person of greater degree, *etc.*); all jugglers, tinkers, pedlers, and petty chapmen, wandering abroad; . . . . . . all persons delivered out of gaoles, that begge for their fees, or otherwise travell begging; all such persons as shall wander abroad begging, pretending losses by fire, or otherwise, *etc.*, *etc.*, shall bee taken, adjudged, and deemed, Rogues, Vagabondes, and sturdie Beggers.

[If any such persons shall be taken begging, vagrant, wandering, or misordering him or herself, he *or she* shall by the appointment of any Justice of Peace, constable, head-borough or tithing man, "be stripped naked from the middle upwards and *shall be openly whipped until his or her body be bloody*, and shall be forthwith sent from parish to parish," the nearest way, to the place of their birth, or where they last dwelt. If the place of birth or last residence cannot be discovered, he or she is to be committed to the House of Correction or the common goal, and there set to work, and so to continue for one year or until placed in service.] —39 Eliz., c. 4.

[Such rogues as appear to be dangerous to the inferior sort of people or otherwise be such as will not be reformed of their rogueish course of life, shall be banished, and conveyed beyond the seas, or adjudged perpetually to the Gallies of the Realm. If a rogue so banished shall return, without license, he shall suffer death as a felon.—Id.]

For that the said rogues having no marke upon them to be knowne by, notwithstanding such judgement of banishment may returne *etc.* and so escape the due punishment, etc.; for remedie whereof bee it ordayned and enacted: That such rogues as shall bee adjudged [by two Justices of the Peace] as aforesaid incorrigible or dangerous, shall also by the judgement of the same Justices etc. be *branded in the left shoulder, with an hot burning yron*, of the breadth of an English shilling, with a great Roman R upon the yron, and the branding upon the shoulder to be *so thoroughly burned, and set on* upon the skinne and flesh, that the letter R be seene, and remayne for a perpetual marke upon such rogue during his *or her* life, etc.

If any rogue so punished shall offend againe, in begging or wandering contrary to the Statute, the party so offending shall be judged a *felon*, and shall suffer [death] as in cases of felonie, without benefit of clergie.—1 James I., c. 7.*

---

* This law continued in force till the reign of Queen Anne. "Every cruelty short of scalping," says Burn, "was practised on the English poor," even after the enactment of the Law of Settlement in 1662. "Whipping continued to be a favorite remedy for poverty. By an Act passed, not in the reign of Hengist or Canute, but of George the Second, 'a woman delivered of a child in a parish to which she does not belong, was liable to public whipping and six months' imprisonment.' In George the Third's time, an Act provides, 'that no justice of the peace shall order any vagrant to be conveyed by a pass [to the place of his settlement,] who has not been whipped, or imprisoned for at least seven days' (32 Geo. III., c. 45). Certificates of the whipping, produced as a title to relief, are still among the records of our parishes. Is there" asks

Laborers, Artisans, &c.

All Artificers and Laborers, being hired for wages by the day or weeke, shall, betwixt the midst of the months of March and September, be and continue at their worke, at or before five of the clocke in the morning, and continue at worke, and not to depart, untill betwixt seven and eight of the clocke at night except it be in the time of breakefast, dinner, or drinking, the which time at the most shall not exceede above two houres and a halfe in the day: that is to say, at every drinking one halfe houre, for his dinner one houre, and for his sleepe, when he is allowed to sleepe (the which is from the midst of May to the midst of August) halfe an houre at the most, and at everie breakefast one halfe houre:

And all the said labourers between the midst of September and the middest of March, shall be and continue at their worke from the spring of the day in the morning, untill night of the same day, except it be in time before appointed for breakefast and dinner, upon paine to lose and forfeit one penny for every houre's absence, to be deducted and defaulked out of his wages that should so offend.—5 Eliz., c. 4.

[The same act provides, that none that take work "in great, in task, or in gross" (by the job) shall leave the same before it be quite finished, except for non-payment of his wages, the Queen's service, or other lawful cause, under pain of a month's imprisonment and forfeiture of £5 to the party aggrieved, besides costs and damages.

---

an English historian—anything in Canciani [Laws of the Barbarians] more revolting to the instincts of freemen, or more surely proving the degradation of the people?"—Phillimore's History of the Reign of George the Third, p. 90.

And that Wages of laborers, artificers, and others, shall be yearly assessed, in each county, by the sheriff and justices of peace; and that none shall give greater wages than those so fixed, under penalty of £5 and ten days' imprisonment, and any laborer convicted of taking greater wages shall suffer twenty-one days' imprisonment.]

Conjurations, Enchantment, and Witchcraft.

1615.—Be it enacted, etc.: That if any person or persons, after the feast of S. Michael the Archangell next comming, shall use, practise, or exercise any Invocation or Conjuration of any evill and wicked Spirit, or shall consult, covenant with, entertaine, employ, feede or reward any evill and wicked Spirit, to, or for any intent or purpose, or take up any dead man, woman, or child, out of his, her, or their grave, or any other place, where the dead body resteth, or the skinne, bone, or any other part of any dead person, to be imployed or used in any manner of Witch-craft, Sorcerie, Charme, or Inchantment, or shall use, practise or exercise any Witch-craft, Inchantment, Charme, or Sorcerie, whereby any person shall be killed, destroyed, wasted, consumed, pined, or lamed, in his or her body, or any part thereof: That then every such offendor or offendors, their ayders, abbetors, and counsellors, being of any the said offences duly and lawfully convicted and attainted, shall suffer paines of death, as a felon, or felons, and shall lose the priviledge and benefit of clergie, and sanctuarie.

And further, to the intent that all manner of practise, use, or exercise of Witchcraft, Enchantment, Charme, or Sorcerie should be from henceforth utterly avoided, abolished, and taken away, Be it enacted etc.,

That if any person or persons shall from and after the said feast of St. Michael the Archangell next comming, take upon him or them by Witchcraft, Inchauntment, Charme, or Sorcerie, to tell or declare in what place any Treasure of Gold or Silver should or might bee found or had in the earth, or other secret places, or where goods or things lost or stolen should be found, or become, or to the intent to provoke any person to unlawfull Love, or whereby any Cattell or Goods of any person shall be destroyed, wasted, or impaired, or to hurt or destroy any person in his or her bodie, although the same be not effected and done: That then all and every such person or persons so offending, and being thereof lawfully convicted, shall for the said offence suffer imprisonment by the space of one whole yeare, without bayle or mainprise, and once in every quarter of the said yeare shall, in some market towne upon the market day, or at such time as any Fayre shall bee kept, there stand openly upon the Pillory by the space of sixe hours, and there shall openly confesse his or her error and offence.

And if any person or persons being once convicted of the same offences, as is aforesaid, doe eftsoones perpetrate and commit the like offence, that then everie such offendor being of any the sayde offences the second time lawfully and duely convicted and attainted, as is aforesaid, shall suffer paines of death as a felon, or felons, and shall lose the benefite and priviledge of Clergie and Sanctuarie.—1 James I., ch. 12.